Alter Orient und Altes Testament
Veröffentlichungen zur Kultur und Geschichte
des Alten Orients und des Alten Testaments

Band 234
Richard S. Hess
Studies in the Personal Names
of Genesis 1-11

Alter Orient und Altes Testament

Veröffentlichungen zur Kultur und Geschichte des Alten Orients
und des Alten Testaments

Herausgeber

Manfried Dietrich · Oswald Loretz

1993

Verlag Butzon & Bercker Kevelaer

Neukirchener Verlag Neukirchen-Vluyn

Studies in the Personal Names of Genesis 1-11

Richard S. Hess

1993

Verlag Butzon & Bercker Kevelaer

Neukirchener Verlag Neukirchen-Vluyn

Die Deutsche Bibliothek – CIP-Einheitsaufnahme

Hess, Richard S.:
Studies in the personal names of Genesis 1-11 / by Richard S. Hess. – Kevelaer : Butzon und Bercker ; Neukirchen-Vluyn : Neukirchener Verl., 1993
(Alter Orient und Altes Testament; Bd. 234)
ISBN 3-7666-9869-9 (Butzon und Bercker)
ISBN 3-7887-1478-6 (Neukirchener Verl.)
NE: GT

Herstellung: Weihert-Druck GmbH, Darmstadt
Printed in Germany
ISBN 3-7887-1478-6 Neukirchener Verlag
ISBN 3-7666-9869-9 Verlag Butzon & Bercker

For my aunts,
Helen, Luella, and Mary.

CONTENTS

Contents VII
Acknowledgements XIII
Abbreviations XV

Part I The Origins of the Personal Names in Genesis 1-11: The Onomastic Environment 1

Chapter 1 Introduction 3
1. 1. Problems concerning the Origins of Personal Names in Genesis 1-11 3
2. Identification of the Personal Names of Genesis 1-11 5
3. Methodological Considerations for the Study of Personal Names in Genesis 1-11 9

Chapter 2 The Narratives in Genesis 1-4, 6-9, and 11 13
1. Introduction 13
2. The Names in the Narratives of Genesis 1-4 14
a. Adam? 14
b. Eve 19
c. Cain 24
d. Abel 27
3. The Names in the Narratives of Genesis 6-9 28
a. Noah 28
b. Shem 29
c. Ham 30
d. Japheth 31
e. Canaan 32
4. Conclusions 33

Chapter 3 The Genealogy of Cain in Genesis 4 37
1. The Names 37
a. Cain 37
b. Enoch 39
c. Irad 40
d. Mehujael 41

e. Methushael 43
f. Lamech 46
g. Adah 46
h. Zillah 48
i. Jabal 49
j. Jubal 52
k. Tubal-Cain 52
l. Naamah 54
2. Conclusions 55

Chapter 4 The Genealogy of Seth 59
1. Genesis 4: 25-26 59
a. Adam 59
b. Seth 65
c. Enosh 66
d. Conclusions 67
2. Genesis 5: 1-32 67
a.-c. Adam, Seth, and Enosh 67
d. Kenan 67
e. Mahalalel 68
f. Jared 69
g. Enoch 70
h. Methuselah 70
i. Lamech 71
3. Conclusions 71

Chapter 5 The Table of Nations in Genesis 10 73
1. Introduction 73
2. The Names 73
a. Nimrod 73
b. Joktan 74

Chapter 6 The Genealogy of Shem in Genesis 11 77
1. The Names 77
a. Arpachshad 77
b. Shelah 79
c. Eber 80
d. Peleg 81
e. Reu 83
f. Serug 85

g. Nahor 86
h. Terah 88
i. Iscah 90
j. Milcah 90
k. Haran 92
2. Conclusions 94

Chapter 7 Conclusion 97
1. Summary 97
a. Mishqalim 97
b. Verbal Forms 97
c. Lexical Roots 98
d. Place Names 98
e. Divine Names or Epithets 99
f. Suffixes 99
g. Structures 99
2. Observations 99
a. Number of Names 99
b. Two Element Names 100
c. Single Element Names 100
d. Origins of the Names 103

Part II The Function of the Personal Names in Genesis 1-11: Wordplay 107

Chapter 8 Introduction 109

Chapter 9 The Narratives in Genesis 1-4, 6-9, and 11 111
1. The Names in the Narratives of Genesis 1-4 111
a. Eve 111
b. Cain 112
c. Abel 113
2. The Names in the Narratives of Genesis 6-9 115
a. Noah 115
b. Shem 118
c. Ham 119
d. Japheth 120
3. Conclusions 120

Chapter 10 The Genealogy of Cain in Genesis 4 125
1. Introduction 125
2. The Names 125
a. Jabal 125
b. Jubal 126
c. Tubal-Cain 127
d.-f. Adah, Zillah, and Naamah 127
3. Conclusions 128

Chapter 11 The Genealogy of Seth 130
1. Genesis 4: 25-26 130
a. Adam 130
b. Seth 130
c. Enosh 133
d. Conclusions 134
2. Genesis 5: 1-32 135
a. Introduction 135
b.-d. Adam, Seth, and Enosh 137
e. Kenan 137
f. Mahalalel 138
g. Jared 138
h. Enoch 138
h. Methuselah 139
i. Lamech 139
j Conclusions 140

Chapter 12 The Table of Nations in Genesis 10 141
1. Introduction 143
2. The Names 144
a. Nimrod 144
b. Joktan 144

Chapter 13 The Genealogy of Shem in Genesis 11 147
1. Introduction 147
2. The Names 151
a. Arpachshad 151
b. Shelah 151
c. Eber 151
d. Peleg 152
e. Reu 153

f. Serug 153
g. Nahor 153
h. Terah 154
i. Haran 154
3. Conclusions 154

Chapter 14 Conclusion 157

Bibliography 163

Indices 197

ACKNOWLEDGEMENTS

It is a privilege to express gratitude to those individuals whose co-operation made this work possible. The study was begun in the autumn of 1986 as a two-year research fellowship given by the Tyndale House Council. The fellowship was part of its Genesis 1-11 Project. The work was supervised by Professor Alan R. Millard, Professor Donald J. Wiseman, and Professor Kenneth A. Kitchen. All gave willingly of their time and expertise. Along with these, Dr. David Tsumura acted as a ready and interested partner in discussions and investigations into many of the issues touched upon in this volume. I should also like to thank the late Mr. Gösta Erikson for reading parts of this work and making helpful comments. His untimely death will leave a considerable gap in Nordic Old Testament studies.

My time at Tyndale House, Cambridge, was made altogether ideal for my research thanks to the efforts of the staff. I thank the acting warden, Professor Donald Carson, the present warden, Dr. Bruce Winter, and the librarian, Mr. David Deboys, who took every care to see that my research needs were met. I am grateful to Mr. Howel Jones and Mrs. Vera Waddleton who provided important help in the latter stages of the physical production of the manuscript. Finally, I wish to express gratitude to Professor M. Dietrich and Professor O. Loretz for their helpful comments and for their agreement to accept this work for publication.

Richard S. Hess
Glasgow Bible College
15 May 1993

ABBREVIATIONS

ABD - D. N. Freedman, ed., The Anchor Bible Dictionary. 6 volumes. Garden City, NY: Doubleday, 1992.
ADD - C. H. W. Johns, Assyrian Deeds and Documents. Second edition. Cambridge: Deighton, Bell and Co.; London: G. Bell and Sons, 1924.
AfO - Archiv für Orientforschung.
AHw - W. von Soden, Akkadisches Handwörterbuch, Bänd 1-3. Wisebaden: Otto Harrassowitz, 1965-1981.
AnOr - Analecta Orientalia.
ARM - Archives royales de Mari.
AT - D. J. Wiseman, The Alalakh Tablets. Occasional Publications of the British Institute as Ankara 2. London: British Institute of Archaeology at Ankara, 1953.
AUSS - Andrews University Seminary Studies.
BA - Biblical Archaeologist.
BASOR - Bulletin of the American Schools of Oriental Research.
BDB - F. Brown, S. R. Driver, and C. A. Briggs, A Hebrew and English Lexicon of the Old Testament. Oxford: Clarendon, 1906.
BE - Babylonian Expedition of the University of Pennsylvania, Series A: Cuneiform Texts.
Bib - Biblica.
BKAT - Biblischer Kommentar: Altes Testament.
BM - British Museum tablet.
CAD - I. J. Gelb et al., The Assyrian Dictionary of the University of Chicago. Chicago: Oriental Institute; Glückstadt: J.-J. Augustin.
CBQ - Catholic Biblical Quarterly.
CCENA - F. M. Fales, Censimenti e catasti di epoca neo-assira. Centro per le Antichità e la Storia dell'Arte del Vicino Oriente. Studi Economici e Tecnologici 2. Roma, 1973.
CIS - Corpus Inscriptionum Semiticarum pars prima: inscriptiones phoeniciae.
CIS II - Corpus Inscriptionum Semiticarum pars secunda: inscriptiones aramaicas continens.

col. - column.
CT - Cuneiform Texts from Babylonian Tablets &c. in the British Museum. London: British Museum, 1896-.
CTA - A. Herdner, Corpus des tablettes en cunéiformes alphabétiques découvertes à Ras Shamra-Ugarit de 1929 à 1939. Mission de Ras Shamra 10. Paris: Imprimerie Nationale; Paul Geuthner, 1963
D - I. J. Gelb, Sargonic Texts from the Diyala Region. Materials for the Assyrian Dictionary 1. Chicago: University Press, 1952.
Delaporte CCBN - L. Delaporte, Catalogue des cylindres orientaux et des cachets assyro-babyloniens, perses et syro-cappadociens de la Bibliothèque Nationale. Paris: Leroux, 1910.
DISO - C.-F. Jean and J. Hoftijzer, Dictionnaire des inscriptions sémitiques de l'ouest. Leiden: E. J. Brill, 1965.
DJD II - P. Benoit, J. T. Milik, R. de Vaux, et al., Les grottes de Murabbaʿât. Discoveries in the Judean Desert 2. Oxford: Clarendon Press, 1960.
DN - divine name.
E - Sargonic personal names in MDP 14.
EA - El Amarna.
fem. - feminine name.
FM - I. J. Gelb, Old Akkadian Inscriptions in Chicago Natural History Museum. Fieldiana: Anthropology Vol. 44 Number 2. Chicago: University Press, 1955.
Ges[18] - W. Gesenius, H. Donner, R. Meyer, and U. Rüterswörden, Hebräisches und Aramäisches Handwörterbuch über das Alte Testament. 1. Lieferung א-ג. 18th edition. Berlin: Springer, 1987.
GN - geographic name.
GTTOT - J. Simons, The Geographical and Topographical Texts of the Old Testament. Leiden: E. J. Brill, 1959.
HALAT - W. Baumgartner et al., Hebräisches und aramäisches Lexikon zum Alten Testament. Third edition. Leiden: E. J. Brill, 1967-1990.
HAR - Hebrew Annual Review.
HSS - Harvard Semitic Series.

HUCA - Hebrew Union College Annual.
IDB - G. A. Buttrick, ed., Interpreters Dictionary of the Bible. 4 volumes. Nashville: Abingdon, 1962.
inscr. - inscription.
IOS - Israel Oriental Studies
JAOS - Journal of the American Oriental Society.
JBL - Journal of Biblical Literature.
JCS - Journal of Cuneiform Studies.
JEN - E. Chiera, Joint Expedition with the Iraq Museum at Nuzi. American Schools of Oriental Research, Publications of the Baghdad School.
JOR - Jewish Quarterly Review.
JNES - Journal of Near Eastern Studies.
JSOT - Journal for the Study of the Old Testament.
JSS- Journal of Semitic Studies.
KAI - H. Donner and W. Röllig, Kanaanäische und aramäische Inschriften. 3 volumes. Wiesbaden: Otto Harrassowitz, 1962-1963.
KBo - Keilschrifttexte aus Boghazköi. Berlin.
Kish - Unpublished texts from Kish in the Ashmolean Museum in Oxford.
KTU - M. Dietrich, O. Loretz, and J. Sanmartín, Die keilalphabetischen Texte aus Ugarit. Einschließlich der keilalphabetischen Texte außerhalb Ugarits. Teil 1 Transkription. Alter Orient und Altes Testament 24/1. Kevelaer: Butzon & Bercker; Neukirchen-Vluyn: Neukirchener, 1976.
KUB - Keilschrifturkunden aus Boghazköi. Berlin 1921ff.
l. - line.
Levy SG - M. A. Levy, Siegel und Gemmen mit aramäischen, phönizischen, althebräischen, himjarischen, nabathäischen und altsyrischen Inschriften erklärt. Breslau: Schletter (H. Skutsch), 1869.
LXX - Septuagint.
MDP - Mémoires de la Délégation en Perse.
MT - Massoretic Text.
NS - new series.
NT - Unpublished texts excavated at Nippur after the Second World War, now in the Oriental Institute, University of Chicago.

NTS - New Testament Studies.
OA - Oriens Antiquus.
OIP - Oriental Institute Publications.
Oppenheim, CCTE - A. L. Oppenheim, A Catalogue of the Cuneiform Tablets of the Wilberforce Eames Collection in the New York Public Library. American Oriental Series 32. New Haven: American Oriental Society, 1948.
Or - Orientalia.
Orient. - Orientalia.
p. - page.
pp. - pages.
Pinches, AT - T. G. Pinches, The Amherst Tablets, Being an Account of the Babylonian Inscriptions in the Collection of the Right Hon. Lord Amherst of Hackney, F.S.A. at Didlington Hall, Norfolk. Part 1. Texts of the Period Extending to and Including the Reign of Bûr-Sin (about 2500 B.C.) London: Quaritch, 1908.
PN - personal name.
pp. - pages.
PRU - Le palais royal d'Ugarit. (Mission de Ras Shamra). Ed. F.-A. Schaeffer (Paris 1957-1970) Bd. II, III, IV, V, VI.
RA - Revue d'assyriologie et d'archéologie orientale.
RB - Revue biblique.
RES - Répertoire d'épigraphie sémitique.
RGG - K. Galling, ed., Die Religion in Geschichte und Gegenwart. 6 volumes. 3rd edition. Tübingen: J. C. B. Mohr (Paul Siebeck), 1957-1965.
RHA - Revue hittite et asianique.
RLA - Eds. E. Ebeling, B. Meissner, et al., Reallexikon der Assyriologie. Berlin und Leipzig: Walter de Gruyter.
RS - Ras Shamra.
RSO - Rivista degli studi orientali.
RTC - F. Thureau-Dangin, Recueil de tablettes chaldéennes. Paris: Leroux, 1903.
SEL - Studi epigrafici e linguistici sul Vicino Oriente antico.
TA - Unpublished texts from Tell Asmar in the Oriental Institute, University of Chicago.
TCL - Textes cunéiformes. Paris: Musée de Louvre.

TMH - TMHC
TMHC - J. Lewy et al., Texte und Materialen der Frau Professor Hilprecht Collection of Babylonian Antiquities im Eigentum der Universität Jena. Leipzig, 1932-.
TWAT - G. J. Botterweck and H. Ringgren (eds.), Theologisches Wörterbuch zum Alten Testament
U - Ur III personal name.
U 1ff. - Ur III personal name(s) in Orientalia 23-24 (Rome: Pontifical Bible Institute, 1927).
UCP - University of California Publications in Semitic Philology, vols. 9-10. Berkeley, 1927-1940.
UET - Publications of the Joint Expedition of the British Museum and of the Museum of the University of Pennsylvania to Mesopotamia. Ur Excavations. Texts. Oxford: University Press, 1928-.
UF - Ugarit Forschungen.
Ug V - J. Nougayrol, E. Laroche, C. Virolleaud, C. F. A. Schaeffer et al., Ugaritica V. Nouveaux textes accadiens, hourrites et ugaritiques des archives et bibliothèques privées d'Ugarit commentaires des textes historiques (première partie). Mission de Ras Shamra 16. Paris: Imprimerie Nationale; Paul Geuthner, 1968.
UM - Murašu - University of Pennsylvania, The Museum. Publications of the Babylonian Section, II.1.
UM - Ugarit - C. H. Gordon, Ugaritic Manual. Analecta Orientalia 35. Rome: Pontifical Bible Institute, 1955.
v. - verse.
VO - Vicino Oriente.
vol. - volume.
VS - Vorderasiatische Schriftdenkmäler der königlichen Museen zu Berlin. Leipzig, 1907-.
VT - Vetus Testamentum.
VTS - Vetus Testamentum Supplements.
vv. - verses.
WO - Welt des Orients.
WTJ - Westminster Theological Journal.
X - The Babylonian Expedition of the University of Pennsylvania, Series A, Vol. X.

ZA - Zeitschrift für Assyriologie und vorderasiatischen Wissenschaft.
ZAW - Zeitschrift für die alttestamentliche Wissenschaft.
ZDMG - Zeitschrift der deutschen morgenländischen Gesellschaft.
ZDPV - Zeitschrift des deutschen Palästina Vereins.

PART I

THE ORIGINS OF THE PERSONAL NAMES IN GENESIS 1-11

THE ONOMASTIC ENVIRONMENT

CHAPTER 1

INTRODUCTION

1. Problems concerning the Origins of Personal Names in Genesis 1-11

The personal names in Genesis have been the subject of controversy in scholarship. This has been especially true of those names found in Genesis 12-50, i.e. everyone from the generation of Abram and later. However, the issues have also affected the understanding of the names in Genesis 1-11. The questions raised concern the origin of these names. Recent literary studies as well as the tendency to emphasize the role of the Deuteronomist in the formation of the Pentateuch have led to a re-examination of the personal names.

For example, the personal names which form the lines of Cain and of Seth in Genesis 4 and 5 have evoked controversy as to their origins. Are they personal names which are the sort of names used in ancient Israel (or anywhere else) or are these names creations of the author(s) of Genesis 4 and 5 in order to serve their literary or theological/ideological purposes? J. Vermeylen (1991:181) writes, "Les noms propres des vv. 19-22 paraissent être des créations du rédacteur, qui joue avec les assonances." The redactor is of the Deuteronomist school. Again Vermeylen (1991:184) concludes concerning the list of names in Genesis 5:

> ...on peut imaginer une autre hypothèse: au point de départ se trouvait la double descendance de Caïn à Lamek et de Seth à Noé; pour des raisons qui relèvent de sa théologie autant que de l'influence de modèles mésopotamiens, P a voulu établir une liste de dix patriarches antérieurs au Déluge; il est donc parti de la

> liste des Séthites - les fils de Caïn représentant à ses yeux une branche à la fois latérale et disqualifiée par sa conduite - et il a intercalé entre Énosh et Noé sept personnages, pour lesquels il s'est tout simplement inspiré de la liste des Caïnites, mais en modifiant quelque peu les noms et leur ordre.

In addition to arguing a purely literary origin for the names in Genesis 4 and 5, Y. T. Radday represents the tendency to analyze the names which appear in the narratives of Genesis 1-11 as serving a purely literary purpose and therefore originating in such a context. After commenting on his understanding of the etymologies of the names Adam, Eve, Cain, and Noah, Radday (1990:75) continues:

> In short, four of the five principal protagonists of the Primordial Story bear names the meanings of which became appropriate only in their later lives and could, consequently, not have been given to them by their parents. At the same time it is noteworthy that the explanation of the name of the fifth is lacking. Why indeed is Abel called 'Abel'? The answer lies in what the word means (Heb. **hebel** = 'nothingness', 'transience', cf. Eccl. 1.1) and in what happened to him later on. He was murdered, and being murdered without any reason and vanishing from the scene is his only part in the plot. If Cain was to be a murderer, he had after all to have a victim. All this can only mean one thing which is given away by the plainly fictitious names: the tale is not a photographic report of factual events, but deals with Man's existential problems. It is indeed true, but in another and higher sense like all great fiction.

Are the personal names of Genesis 1-11 'fictitious'? Are they the creation of a priestly or deuteronomistic redactor? Or do they suggest traditions whose origins lie elsewhere? In this study I will attempt to identify the etymologies and origins of the personal names which appear in Genesis 1-11. I will take account of their present context in the Biblical literature, including the so-called 'folk etymologies' of the names. I will also consider previously proposed etymologies of the names. Using this information, as well as the published studies of Ancient Near Eastern onomastica, I will attempt to argue when and where these names would be most likely to appear in the Ancient Near East. The thesis which I will argue is that most of the personal names throughout Genesis 1-11 (in both the genealogies and the narratives) do have attestations among the proper names of the Amorite world as found attested in the early second millennium B.C. at sites such as Mari and those tels which are found throughout the region of the Upper Euphrates. In a final chapter I will consider the significance which this understanding of the personal names adds to the literary reading of the genealogies and narratives as they exist in the first eleven chapters of the book of Genesis.

2. Identification of Personal Names in Genesis 1-11

Proper names may be identified in a number of ways in a written text. The clearest method of identification occurs when the nature of the vocable as a proper name is specified within the context; e.g. "Her name is X," "This is the land of X," or "They are from the tribe of X." In the Biblical text these examples occur early and frequently:

וַיִּקְרָא הָאָדָם שֵׁם אִשְׁתּוֹ חַוָּה

"The man called the name of his wife, Eve " (Genesis 3:20);

הַסֹּבֵב אֵת כָּל־אֶרֶץ הַחֲוִילָה

"It surrounds the whole land of the **Ḥavilah** " (Genesis 2:11);

אֵלֶּה אַלּוּפֵי בְנֵי־עֵשָׂו

"These are the clans of the sons of Esau " (Genesis 36:15).

A second means of identification occurs when the type of literature or literary form indicates that what is to be found is a proper name. In English, examples of this may be found in the lists of personal names which occur in telephone directories and in the geographical names which appear on maps. Many similar illustrations exist in other cultures. In the Ancient Near East, personal names are often found on seals, in tax and tribute inventories, and in lists of kings, of witnesses, of royal enemies, and of captives. Geographic names may be observed in chronicles of war campaigns. In extrabiblical West Semitic materials, personal names are found on stamp seals and on ostraca. In the Biblical material, personal names may be found in lists of commanders (Numbers 13:3-16), of warriors (I Chronicles 11:26-47), of cultic functionaries (I Chronicles 24:7-18), of law violators (Ezra 10:18-44), of construction workers (Nehemiah 3:1-32), of witnesses (Nehemiah 10:1-27), of court officials (Nehemiah 36:12), and, of special interest for our study, in genealogies (Genesis 5:1-31). Geographic names may be found in genealogical descriptions of nations (Genesis 10:1-32), in travel itineraries (Numbers 33:1-49), and in lists of cities constructed (Numbers 32:34-7), allotted (Joshua 13-19), and conquered (II Kings 10:32-3).

A third means of determining proper names within written materials lies in clues found in the script and language. Sometimes the form of a proper name may be distinguished in writing style from its surrounding context. This occurs in English when the first letters of personal names are capitalized. On other occasions there may be some indication gained from markers preceding or following the name. In English markers such as Ms. or Mr. may precede personal names and be used to distinguish the sex of the name bearer. Markers may also appear which indicate profession or status. For academics, for example, titles such as doctor or professor may precede a personal name. Degrees and other honors also may be listed, usually in abbreviated form, after the name. Geographic names may also be capitalized. Sometimes the absence of markers may characterize a proper name. The determined nature of a proper name suggests that in some languages it will not be accompanied by an article. This is true for most contexts in which personal names appear in written English, and it is true for most geographic names. Indefinite articles, as well as definite articles, are missing. In the Ancient Near East, syllabic cuneiform scripts often, but not always, marked personal names with determinatives which preceded the names.[1] The markers tended to show a differentiation in gender among the name bearers. For males the DIŠ sign was used. For females the MÍ sign could be used. In Hebrew, there was no comparable marker (Zadok 1988:3), nor was there anything comparable to capitalization. The distinctive treatment given to the personal name included:(1) its number was always singular so that neither the masculine (ִים-, ֵי-) nor the feminine (וֹת-) plural morphemes ever occurred with it; and (2) it was always determined, and therefore did not take an article or pronominal suffixes. This is sometimes true of geographic names, but there are exceptions.[2] It is not true of personal names in Greek, specifically in the dialect(s) used in the Septuagint to translate the Hebrew text.[3] There, personal names may and do take articles. Titles or other appellations were not regularly attached to personal names although they could have gentilics and other descriptive words and phrases occurring alongside them.

Not all proper names can be identified by using these guidelines. Beyond these one is left with analysis of the texts themselves as well as an appreciation of the forms and constructions which proper names take in the language under study. This is all the more true when considering personal names in particular. In the Hebrew text of Genesis there are some points at which it is not clear as to whether what is written is to be understood as a personal name or as something else. Outstanding among these is the example of אדם, which, as I have discussed elsewhere,[4] occurs as a

---

[1]This is true for Hittite as well as Akkadian in all its dialects.
[2]E.g., in a designation such as הגלעד in Gen 31:21, 23, 25.
[3]Cf. e.g., *τὸν 'Αβιμέλεχ* (Gen 20:17) and *τοῦ 'Αβιμέλεχ* (Gen 20:18).
[4]See Hess 1990b.

common noun in Genesis 1, as a title (usually with an article) in chapters 2-3, and as a personal name in the genealogies of chapters 4 and 5.

A total of 42 different personal names may be identified in Genesis 1-11. They include the following:[5]

אַבְרָם	Ἀβράμ	11:26, 27, 29ab, 31ab, +
אָדָם	Ἀδάμ	4:25; 5:1, 3, 4, 5, -
אֱנוֹשׁ	Ἐνώς	4:26; 5:6, 7, 9, 10, 11
אַרְפַּכְשַׁד	Ἀρφαξάδ	10:22, 24; 11:10, 11, 12, 13
הֶבֶל	Ἅβελ	4:2ab, 4ab, 8ab, 9, 25
הָרָן	Ἁρράν	11:26, 27ab, 28, 29, 31
חַוָּה	Ζωή, Εὕαν	3:20; 4:1, -
חָם	Χάμ	5:32; 6:10; 7:13; 9:18ab, 22; 10:1, 6, 20, -
חֲנוֹךְ	Ἑνώχ	4:17ab, 18; 5:18, 19, 21, 22, 23, 24, +
יָבָל	Ἰωβέλ	4:20
יוּבָל	Ἰουβάλ	4:21, -
יִסְכָּה	Ἰεσχά	11:29
יֶפֶת	Ἰάφεθ	5:32; 6:10; 7:13; 9:18, 23, 27; 10:1, 2, 21
יָקְטָן	Ἰεκτάν	10:25, 26, 29 -
יֶרֶד	Ἰάρεδ	5:15, 16, 18, 19, 20, -
כְּנַעַן	Χανάαν	9:18, 22, 25, 26, 27; 10:6, 15, (GN in 11:31, +)
לוֹט	Λώτ	11:27, 31, +
לֶמֶךְ	Λάμεχ	4:18, 19, 23ab, 24; 5:25, 26, 28, 30, 31

[5]The names are listed in alphabetical order according to their Hebrew spelling (BHS text). Then follows the Septuagint (Göttingen ed.) spelling and a list of all occurrences of the Hebrew spelling as a personal name in the first eleven chapters of Genesis. Where the spelling appears as a geographic name (GN) in these chapters, this is noted. A plus (+) following the occurrences indicates that the name appears in later chapters of Genesis with the same spelling. A dash (-) indicates that proper names with similar spellings are to be found elsewhere in Genesis.

מַהֲלַלְאֵל	Μαλελεὴλ	5:12, 13, 15, 16, 17
מְחִיָּיאֵל, מְחוּיָאֵל	Μαιήλ	4:18ab
מִלְכָּה	Μελχά	11:29ab, +
מְתוּשָׁאֵל	Μαθουσαλὰ	4:18ab
מְתוּשֶׁלַח	Μαθουσάλα	5:21, 22, 25, 26, 27
נֹחַ	Νῶε	5:29, 30, 32ab; 6:8, 9abc, 10, 13, 22; 7:1, 5, 6, 7, 9ab, 11, 13abc, 15, 23; 8:1, 6, 11, 13, 15, 18, 20; 9:1, 8, 17, 18, 19, 20, 24, 28, 29; 10:1, 32
נָחוֹר	Ναχὼρ	11:22, 23, 24, 25, 26, 27, 29ab, +
נִמְרֹד	Νεβρώδ	10:8, 9
נַעֲמָה	Νοεμά	4:22, -
עֵבֶר	Ἔβερ	10:21, 24, 25; 11:14, 15, 16, 17, -
עָדָה	Ἀδὰ	4:19, 20, 23, +
עִירָד	Γαιδάδ	4:18ab, -
פֶּלֶג	Φάλεκ	10:25; 11:16, 17, 18, 19
צִלָּה	Σελλά	4:19, 22, 23
קַיִן	Κάιν	4:1, 2, 3, 5ab, 6, 8ab, 9, 13, 15ab, 16, 17, 24, 25, -
קֵינָן	Καινὰν	5:9, 10, 12, 13, 14, -
רְעוּ	Ῥαγοὺ	11:18, 19, 20, 21, -
שְׂרוּג	Σεροὺχ	11:20, 21, 22, 23
שָׂרַי	Σάρα	11:29, 30, 31, +
שֶׁלַח	Σάλα	10:24ab; 11:12, 13, 14, 15, -
שֵׁם	Σήμ	5:32; 6:10; 7:13; 9:18, 23, 26, 27; 10:1, 21, 22, 31; 11:10ab, 11, -
שֵׁת	Σὴθ	4:25, 26; 5:3, 4, 6, 7, 8
תּוּבַל קַיִן	Θοβὲλ	4:22ab, -
תֶּרַח	Θάρα	11:24, 25, 26, 27ab, 28, 31, 32ab

3. Methodological Considerations for the Study of Personal Names in Genesis 1-11

Unlike many of the personal names which occur elsewhere in the Bible, those in Genesis 1-11 cannot be attributed simply to one ethnic group, i.e. the Israelites. Nor have we evidence that the author(s) of Genesis 1-11 were concerned with this question. Sometimes the writer was aware of a root and the implication is there, as in the word play between the noun אָדָם, the personal name Adam, and the Hebrew word for ground, אֲדָמָה. But often this is not apparent.

The observation made above, that the Hebrew language, the related Canaanite dialects, and the West Semitic language family form the natural starting point in the study of the origin of these names, finds support in the text and in the names themselves. The author(s) of Genesis 1-11 always use(s) Hebrew roots when attempting an etymology. While the roots may not be correct etymologically, they do reflect a natural association with West Semitic. Further, as will be seen, many of the names have clearly identifiable Canaanite or West Semitic roots as part of their origin. We may compare the two other early West Semitic genealogical examples to which we have access, the king lists of the Hammurabi and Ugarit dynasties. West Semitic tribal and personal names appear in both cases.[6]

There is the possibility of finding other attestations of the same personal name in contexts outside those of Genesis 1-11. In those cases, we observe its linguistic environment (the language group which uses the name), the geographical regions in which the name is used, and the time periods when the name appears. These aid in isolating the onomastic environments.

There is also the possibility that the grammatical structure or the meaning of the name may have no comparison with any other names in West Semitic onomastica, but it may have close parallels in other linguistic environments. In such a case, we need to consider an origin for the personal name

---

[6]For the Hammurabi list, see the initial publication of Finkelstein 1966 and especially his comments on pp. 97-98, and the study by Malamat 1968a, with its Biblical comparisons. For the Ugarit king list, cf. KTU 1. 113 and the study of Kitchen 1977.

elsewhere. Here, however, we should exercise special caution to avoid etymological proposals from words in other languages which either (1) are not personal names or (2) require a complex series of steps to establish a linguistic relationship with the personal name in Genesis 1-11. The simplest solution is often the most likely.

We return to the proposal for the study of the origin of these names which was suggested at the beginning of this chapter. It includes two parts. The first part concerns the etymology of each personal name. Here we will study the name in its component parts, the vocables. We also observe the relation of these vocables to one another through the study of the structure of the name. The second part of the study of each name concerns its association with other names in the Bible and in the Ancient Near East. With the appearance of thousands of names in texts from the Ancient Near Eastern world we can now make comparisons with these names and observe the use of similar vocables or structures in names elsewhere.

Since we have no complete census of all names in any city or region of the Ancient Near East, it is always possible that names relevant to our comparative study may have been present but are now missing due to the vicissitudes of the preservation, discovery, and publication of the names. We therefore recognize the provisional nature of a study such as this. In terms of comparative Ancient Near Eastern research, its conclusions always remain open to adjustment by the identification of previously unrecognized data. However, sufficient publication of names and name studies has taken place to make a comparative study of this kind worthwhile in identifying where and when the vocables or grammatical structures occur in the Ancient Near Eastern onomastica. In this way the most suitable environment for the names may be found.

To summarize, the two aspects of study for each of the names are: (1) etymology or the semantic and grammatical elements which constitute the name; and (2) onomastic environment or the geographical and chronological location(s) in which the name has its closest associations with other names.

We will study the personal names in Genesis 1-11 according to the type of literature in which they occur. We will separate the names in the genealogies from those in the narratives and study each separately. Further, since several genealogies and at least two lengthy narrative sections occur in Genesis 1-11, it seems best to separate these literary divisions into their natural units, i.e. the narratives in Genesis 1 - 4:16 and in Genesis 6 - 9; and the genealogies in Genesis 4:17 - 24; 5:1-32; 10:1-32; and 11:10-32. Several factors must qualify such distinctions. First, the overall structure of Genesis 1-11 appears in terms of toledoth.[7] Second, genealogies and narratives blend throughout these chapters. Thus all such distinctions are to some extent artificial. Even so they represent the most convenient way in which to divide the material for consideration.

---

[7]For an argument which defines toledoth as "history," argues its position to be at the end of each section of Genesis, and compares it with the colophons of the cuneiform tablets, especially the Enuma Elish series, see Wiseman 1979:34-45, 143-152. For further comment on the meaning and usage of toledoth in Genesis 1-11, see the comment and bibliography in Hess 1989:249 n25.

CHAPTER 2

THE NARRATIVES IN GENESIS 1-4, 6-9, AND 11

1. Introduction

Aside from the genealogies in Genesis 4:17 - 5:32, and in chapters 10 and 11:10-32, chapters 1-11 include literature which is not primarily genealogical. In fact, there are a number of narratives which may be identified in the text as we now have it. These include the two creation stories in 1:1 - 2:3 and 2:4-25, the story of the serpent and the woman in 3, the tale of Cain and Abel in 4:1-16, the "sons of God" and "daughters of men" incident of 6:1-8, the Flood narrative of 6:9 - 9:17, the narrative of Noah and his sons in 9:18-29, and the tale of Babel's tower in 11:1-9. Among these narratives, the creation stories, "the sons of God" and "daughters of men" incident, and the narrative of chapter 11 contain no personal names.[8] The remaining narratives include personal names. Elsewhere some eight personal names appear: Eve, Abel, Cain, Noah, Shem, Ham, Japheth, and Canaan.[9] Each of these names will be examined in turn.

All of these names, with the exception of Eve, also appear in the genealogies. Cain is worthy of special mention. This name plays an important role in the genealogy of Cain in 4:17-24 as it does in the narrative of the first half of chapter 4. With the exception of Cain, these names do not play as significant a role in their genealogical slots as they do in the narrative sections.

The narratives with personal names fall into two sections in the present text of Genesis. There are the names in Genesis 1-4, i.e. Eve, Cain, and Abel. The second group of narratives,

---

[8] A name of a group, הַנְּפִלִים the Nephilim, appears in 6:4.
[9] On Canaan, see the discussion below and the doubts concerning this term's usage as a personal name.

Genesis 6-9, includes the names Noah, Shem, Ham, Japheth, and Canaan.

2. The Names in the Narratives of Genesis 1-4

a. Adam?

אדם appears as a common noun and title in the narrative materials of Genesis 1-4. It becomes a personal name in connection with the genealogy of Cain. Since it is used in word play throughout the narratives of chapters 1-4, the etymology of אדם will be examined here. For the onomastic environment of the personal name, we will wait until the section which studies the names in the genealogy of Cain.

In order to examine אדם within the Hebrew Bible, we shall make a comparative study of the root in its usage in other forms in Biblical Hebrew and in possible cognate forms in Semitic and in Sumerian. Thus the study is an investigation of historical lexicography.[10] It will form a model for the type of research which will be undertaken with each of the names. The study will not attempt to find the origin of the word, in the sense of a source and means by which the word came into being in the language. It often cannot do this because the evidence is not available. Further, even if it could do this, what it would find would be only one aspect of the history of the vocable under consideration and its usage at that point in its history. Even the study of the history of the usage of a vocable does not guarantee greater insight into its usage in a particular group of texts. However, this is not to discount such study. With a proper awareness of its limitations, a study which collects usages of a vocable in cognate languages and which locates the word in earlier sources may prove valuable. Even if the history of the vocable cannot be fully reconstructed, such a study provides a convenient source of information for creating semantic

---

[10]Cf. also Barr 1974.

ranges. Semantic ranges may be useful in understanding usages of a word in a newly identified environment or in already existing environments. With awareness of its limitations, a comparative and contextual lexicographical study may also help to identify the language environments in which a particular vocable is found. Such language environments have relevance for personal names insofar as they provide possible and even probable areas in which to search for appearances of personal names constructed with that particular vocable.

In what follows, consideration will be given to possible appearances and usages of ʾdm in other Semitic languages and in Sumerian. Semantic ranges will be noted. In so doing, primary consideration will be given to existing lexical studies, with an awareness that all such studies have their limitations.[11] An examination will then be made of the appearances of proper names similar to אדם which might be found in these languages. Thus semantic and language environments may be suggested for the history of both the common noun and the personal name.

We will begin our study of ʾdm with its appearance in the West Semitic languages. Within Classical Hebrew there are several additional meanings assigned to variations of אדם, which tend to cluster around the verbal root meaning "to be red:"[12] (1) אָדֹם - red(-brown), the color of blood; (2) אֹדֶם - a precious stone of red color; (3) אֲדַמְדָּם - bright red; (4) אֲדָמָה - earth, land, with geographical names; (5) אֲדָמָה - red blood; (6) אַדְמֹנִי - red; (7) אֲדֻמִּים - part of the geographic name אֲדֻמִּים מַעֲלֵה, literally "ascent of the red (stone)," referring to the road from Jericho up to Jerusalem; (8) אֱדֹם - the proper noun, Edom, with gentilic אֲדֹמִי.[13] From the Biblical period אדם also

---

[11]For further discussion of philological method in West Semitic languages, cf. especially Driver 1965, Barr 1968, Parker 1979-80.

[12]This root appears in the qal, pual, hiphil, and hithpael.

[13]HALAT 11-15. Cf. also BDB 9-11; Ges[18] 14-17. In addition, the Hebrew word for blood, דָּם, has been proposed as having some relationship with

occurs in Hebrew inscriptions with the meaning, "person."[14] Where it is not used as a proper name or as a gentilic, the root אדם continues to carry the associations of "red," "blood" and "earth" in later Hebrew.[15] The Phoenician and Punic occurrences carry the meaning, "person, individual."[16]

The evidence from Ugaritic is similar. The root 'dm occurs with the meanings, "to rouge oneself," "person," and possibly the name of a land.[17] There is also a geographic name, udm,[18] which may be a theophoric element related to an earth god who is identified by some as 'dm .[19] From the Akkadian texts at Ugarit, 'dm in the form of ad-ma-ni, "red soil," has been identified as West Semitic.[20]

The dialects of Aramaic present the following semantic range for the root אדם. In Aramaic, a Sefiré inscription preserves אדמה with the meanings, "land" and "field."[21] Jewish Palestinian Aramaic includes אֲדַם with the meaning, "blood," and אדמדמני with the meaning, "overripe grapes."[22] Other Rabbinic Aramaic occurrences, like those of Rabbinic Hebrew, exhibit a semantic range including "blood," "red," and "earth," "land."[23] In Syriac the roots are confined to 'dm,

---

the 'dm root described here. Cf. HALAT 215 for the appearance of dm "blood" in a wide range of Semitic languages.

14Cf. KAI inscriptions 191 B 2 (from a tomb at Silwan) and 194, 6 (a Lachish ostracon). Cf. also DISO 4.

15Ben Iehuda 1926 I:60-70; Jastrow 1950 I:15-7.

16KAI 14, 4; 26 A II 4-5; 69, 14; 79, 8-10; 119, 5. The אדם in KAI 43, 11, which KAI translates as "Blut," is uncertain in the reading of the original text. Cf. also DISO 4, 58; Tomback 1978:4.

17Cf. UM 233; Aistleitner 1963:7. Only Aistleitner includes the definition, "N(ame) e(ines) Landes."

18UM 32. It is found in the Keret epic. Cf. Astour 1973 and Ribichini 1982.

19Cf. Nougayrol 1957:82; M. Dahood 1963:58; Engnell 1967:163-5; Schoors 1972:29-30; Rummel 1981:299-302.

20The text is found in in PRU III 123, RS 15.145, lines 8 and 12. Cf. Kühne 1974:162-163; Sivan 1984:195; Huehnergard 1987b:104. Sivan also cites the GN, URU ad-mu from Alalakh [Wiseman 1953:154], text 341, line 11.

21KAI 222 A 10.

22Kutscher 1967:53.

23Jastrow 1950 I:17.

"Adam," "person" (and an Aphel form of **dm**, "blood," meaning "to fetch blood") and various forms of **'dmt'**, "earth" and "soil."[24] Mandaic includes the form **adma**, related to **dma**, "blood."[25]

Of the South Semitic languages, Arabic provides the largest range of meanings for the **'dm** root. These include verbal forms related to "mixing," words for "seasoning," "colors mixed with whiteness or blackness," "skin," "level ground," and "human."[26] In Ethiopic, meanings for **'adama** include "to be red," "leather (skin) tinted red" (**'adim**), "red," "to be pleasant," and "to enjoy."[27] The appearance of **'dm** in the Sabaean dialect of Old South Arabic includes a semantic range in two areas of meaning; that containing the verbal form "to resist" and nouns such as "military mission," "rebellion;" and that containing nouns such as "servants," "serfs," "subject tribes," and "worshippers."[28]

The Akkadian dialects provide a range of meanings for **adam**-related words: **adamatu** - ("a plant"); "black blood;" **adamātu** - "dark red earth (used as a dye);" **adammû** - "battle," "onslaught (personified);" **adammumu**- "wasp," "wasp-shaped ornament;" **adamu**- "blood," ("red garment"), ("important, noble person"); **adāmu** - "to own a share in a common fund;" **ammatu** "earth."[29] The root **'dm** is attested in Old Akkadian in the form **adammum**, apparently a reference to a garment.[30]

From this survey of **'dm** in the Semitic languages, three semantic areas emerge:"red," "person," and "land." Corresponding to each of these three, is another group: "blood," "skin," and "soil." It is reasonable to expect אָדָם in

---

[24]Brockelmann 1895:3; Smith 1903:3.
[25]Drower and Macuch 1963:8.
[26]Lane 1968:35-37.
[27]Dillmann 1865:799-801; Grébaut 1952:250-251; Ullendorff 1956:191-192; Leslau 1969:22; Gispen 1966:68.
[28]Beeston, Ghul, Müller, and Ryckmans 1982:2; Biella 1982:4-5.
[29]CAD 1/1 94-96, 128, 75; AHw 10.
[30]Gelb 1957:19.

Hebrew to possess one or more of these meanings. However, it is not necessary for it to possess them all. That it appears primarily to possess one of these meanings, that of "person," is not surprising in light of other vocables with the same root (ʾdm or dm) which appear for "blood,"[31] "red," and "land," "soil."[32]

One additional source suggested for the noun is the Sumerian language. Although Sumerian is not a Semitic language, it does provide loanwords in the early Semitic vocabulary. The Sumerian form, á-dam, occurs. The term corresponds to the Akkadian nammaššû and namû. In Akkadian these carry the meanings:"herds of (wild) animals;" "settlement," "people;" "pasture land," "steppe."[33] The relationship of Sumerian á-dam and Hebrew אדם was noticed by S. Landersdorfer.[34] Its usage with the meaning of "humans" and "humanity" is found in Sumerian literary texts.[35] Thus it is not surprising that the connection continues to be noted, most recently by Å. W. Sjöberg.[36] He observes that á-dam has no Sumerian etymology (á means "arm" or "side;" dam means "spouse") and suggests that it is a "Canaanite, West-Semitic loanword in Sumerian." If

---

[31]See the connection which Strus 1978:99 has observed between דָּם "blood" and אָדָם in Genesis 9:6.

[32]Cf. above. For problems with attempts to identify meanings of "skin" and "leather" for אָדָם in Biblical Hebrew, see Hess 1987.

[33]CAD 11/1 233-234, 249-51; AHw 726, 729, 771. Cf. Heider 1985:96-100, 409.

[34]Landersdorfer 1916:59-60.

[35]Cf. Falkenstein 1959:40-41, with examples cited there. A second approach is that attempted by Walker 1962. He argues for a compound name, AD or ADDA "father" followed by MU "man," "humanity." This yields "father of man," "father of humanity." This interpretation moves us farther away from the sort of meaning associated with the term in Semitic languages. For a phonological objection to this interpretation, which argues that this form of the Sumerian m appears in Akkadian as g rather than m, see Moran 1958:99.

[36]Sjöberg 1984:223. However, Sjöberg's argument for an exclusive meaning, "human(s)," "humanity," is challenged by the uru and á-dam word pair, to be understood as "town" and "pasture." Cf. Hallo 1970:58; Gispen 1966:73-74.

Sjöberg is correct, then the Sumerian evidence does more to demonstrate the importance and influence of the Semitic term on languages such as Sumerian than it does to argue for an influence from Sumerian to Semitic.

The following conclusions may be drawn. First, as a common noun, אדם is at home throughout the Semitic world of the third to first millennia B.C. Given its semantic range in the Biblical text, it is most like the 'dm of West Semitic in the second millennium B.C. (and possibly the third millennium B.C.) and the Sumerian á-dam (if this indeed is to be identified with the 'dm of Semitic) of the same period. Second, as will be seen in the discussion of Adam, the personal name appears to be more at home the earlier one goes. It is quite rare in the late second and in the first millennia B.C. However, it is found earlier in Amorite, in Old Akkadian, and possibly at Ebla. These attestations of personal names with spellings related to 'dm add weight to the argument that a common noun formed from this root was in use in the third millennium B.C. Third, there is a close correspondence between the semantic range of 'dm in its Sumerian(?) and later West Semitic usage, and the semantic range of Classical Hebrew אָדָם. This supports the hypothesis of a common linguistic environment for this term, one which extends from at least as early as the second half of the third millennium.

Does this argue a third millennium environment for the emergence of 'dm as a personal name? Any such conclusion must await the study of the onomastic environment of Adam. That study will be undertaken in the chapter on the genealogy of Seth, where Adam first appears as a personal name.

b. Eve

The most exhaustive study to date, exploring the various suggestions for the etymology of the name Eve, was written by Heller (1958). This work attempts to argue the plausibility of an association with the major Hurrian female deity, Ḥebat. It is not clear that Heller is successful in overturning the phonological objections to this equation made by Speiser. However, too little is known about the Hurrian culture of c. 2000 B.C., when Heller would place the emergence of this deity. Indeed, evidence for the argument remains too scanty to prove convincing.[37]

In Hebrew, Eve (ḥawwāh חַוָּה) suggests a word related to the root חיה "live." However, several other hypotheses have been advanced concerning its etymology. For example, the verb "to enliven" is designated by the logogram TI in Sumerian. This reading is also a homonym of the word for "rib." Although this interpretation provokes an interesting pun which is followed by many scholars,[38] it remains unlikely as a derivation for the Hebrew word in a text whose author would have been unfamiliar with Sumerian and in a language family (Semitic) where the Sumerian word play does not occur.[39]

Zimmermann (1966:318) has suggested the Arabic root ḥawwah with the meaning "to be empty" and "to fail." He bases this observation on the context and the problem with the proposed etymology. As Cassuto (1961:170-171) observed, the context suggests that the explanation is misplaced. If the original meaning of the name was a reference to Eve's

---

[37]This criticism also calls into question Heller's 1967:264 analysis of the name association in 3:20 as "ein verklungener Widerhall des in Palästina früher einheimischen Kultes der 'großen Mutter'." Although one may quibble with various attempts of Heller to explain words similar in spelling to Eve in the Hebrew Bible as of Hurrian extraction, there does seem to be validity for some of his conclusions. See, for example, the continued recognition of a northern (Anatolian?) provenance for the Hivites in Mazar 1986:39-42.

[38]Kramer 1963; Kapelrud 1977:cols. 796-797; Koenig 1982:395. An alternate Sumerian derivation from EME "mother" has been suggested by Walker 1962:66-67, however this involves both consonantal and vocalic shifts, and has not been followed. Alternatively, an Egyptian pun has been suggested recently. Goedicke 1985 observes that the Egyptian imw forms a homonym for both "clay" and "rib."

[39]Lambert 1980:72-73; Wenham 1987:69.

motherhood, we would expect it to come at the point of her giving birth to one of her offspring. Instead, the name and an explanation appear after the curse. Therefore, Zimmermann suggests the original meaning for the name as sharing with the Arabic root the meanings "hunger, deprivation, ruin." However, this root does not appear elsewhere in Hebrew and there is no onomastic environment for such a root in the West Semitic world of the Ancient Near East.

Cassuto himself favors a long observed homonym to Eve which is found in Aramaic . There a word **ḥwh** appears as early as the first millennium B.C. in a treaty curse (KAI 222A:30-31) with the meaning "snake" (Brauner 1974:183). The suggestion has arisen over the last century that an earlier narrative lay behind the present one in Genesis 3. In the proto-narrative, there was no Eve, only God, man, and a serpent deity.[40] An identification of precisely these figures in two incantation texts from Ugarit has been made by de Moor (1988). The texts are the much discussed KTU 1.100 and the lesser studied and more fragmentary KTU 1.107.[41] If they are to be connected and understood as de Moor proposes, then we may find here another West Semitic version of a story about a forbidden tree, a threatening serpent, and the hope of salvation from the divine. This could imply that the original text had no woman involved and that the addition of such a figure only occurred later, when Aramaic/Hebrew homonyms for "serpent" and "Eve" created the existence of a woman in the narrative.

However, the cogency of such an opinion remains dubious. First, the key Ugaritic text, KTU 1.107, is fragmentary and considerable reconstruction is required. Second, the connection of the two Ugaritic texts cannot be proven. Third, the word for "serpent" in the Ugaritic evidence is always **nḥš**,

---

[40]For the history and literature of this theory see Kapelrud 1977:cols. 794-795 and Heller 1958.

[41]See the discussion of these texts and bibliographies of previous literature in Pardee 1989:193-256.

equivalent to the Hebrew term in Genesis. There is no trace of the Aramaic ḥwh. Fourth, this sort of word play between two languages (Aramaic and Hebrew) requires caution, even where they are closely related linguistically, geographically, and chronologically. ḥwh does not carry the meaning in Hebrew which it has in Aramaic. Such a crossover may have been more apparent to later Targumists and Rabbinic scholars, who worked in both languages, than it was to the original authors, for whom we lack the evidence of such comparative knowledge or interest in comparative word play between two languages. Fifth, the original etymology has itself been challenged (Williams 1977). Finally, this root is not productive of personal names in Aramaic.

However, the root suggested by the clause which follows the name's first appearance is productive of personal names. The Hebrew expression in Genesis 3:20 is: כִּי הִוא הָיְתָה אֵם כָּל־חָי "for she was the mother of all living." Although this expression may find parallels in honorary titles of deities elsewhere in Ancient Near Eastern myths,[42] its presence in the context of Genesis invites comparison with the cultural innovators of Cain's line, Jabal, "the father of those who dwell in tents..." and Jubal, "the father of all who play the pipe and lyre." Whether mother or father, the implications of the title suggest that the figure is the first in humanity to undertake a task and thus becomes remembered as its originator. Eve begins the line of those who live and who are concerned with life.

This has particular interest for our purposes as it provides an association with the word חָי, understood as "living," "alive" and as deriving from the root related to "live," חיה. Thus the root is associated with the name of Eve in the text. It is also most likely to be understood as associated with the name from a philological perspective. There are three aspects to this etymology: (1) The consonantal form, ḥwt, though not

[42]Kikawada 1972:33-35 compares it with the title of the creatress in the Atra-ḫasīs epic (Lambert and Millard 1969), Mami, bēlet kala ilī, "mistress of all the gods."

found in Hebrew, does appear in Ugaritic as the common means of designating "life."[43] This suggests that the word was in use in West Semitic with this meaning in the second millennium B.C. (2) The actual form as vocalized in Masoretic Hebrew (**ḥawwāh**) may reflect a factitive expression of the root, i.e. "make alive ."[44] (3) The form as it appears in the name is best understood as a nominal form, possessing a Hebrew noun formation often used to designate role, occupation, or profession. One of the best known examples of this mishqal is גַּנָּב "thief."[45] In the case of Eve it denotes the role of giving and nurturing life. This parallels the explanation which follows it in Genesis 3:20 and provides a basis for our conclusion that the name Eve contains the root חיה "live."

Examples of personal names possessing a **ḥwy** or **ḫay-**, **ḫayy-** root with the meaning "live, living" appear in West Semitic of the second millennium B.C., in Amorite texts[46] and in those from Ugarit.[47] It may also be found in third millennium names from Ebla.[48] The root occurs in West Semitic names of the first millennium B.C. in Hebrew,[49]

---

[43]Kapelrud 1977:col. 796.
[44]Greenfield in Kikawada 1977:34 n9; see also Zimmermann 1966:317 for the comparative arguments adducing the similar expression, "the one who gives birth." Zimmermann notes similar conclusions reached in earlier studies by Halévy and Eitan.
[45]For others see Sagarin 1987:21-22.
[46]This includes names from the Mari texts as well as other Amorite sources:**ya₈-aḫ-wi-AN**, **ya₈-aḫ-wi-AN**, **[ḫ]a-a-a-ia-tum** (ARM XIII 1 xiv 13), **mil-ki-ḫa-a-ia** (Iraq 16. 40); in Bauer 1926:26; Huffmon 1965:192; Gelb 1980:19, 248.
[47]**ḫa-wa /ya-il** (Syria 18, RS 8.213.32), **abdi-ḫa-ya** (Syria 28, RS 14.16.25), **ḥyil** (PRU II 10 3, V 131 3), **ḥyl** (PRU II 35 A 6), **abdḥy** (UM 301 r. iv 10), **ʿbdḥy** (UM 301 iv 10), **ḥyn** (PRU II 35 A 8, II 46 35), **adnḥwt** (PRU II 140-8), **yḥṣdq** (PRU V 84 r. 14); in Kinlaw 1967:289; Gröndahl 1967:137, 333. Of interest is Kinlaw's note on Virolleaud's 1951:178 interpretation of **Ḫawa** as a DN based on Thureau-Dangin's 1937:253 reading of PI as wa. However, Sivan 1984:225 mentions no DN reading PI as wa.
[48]Krebernik 1988:34, 83.
[49]Biblical Hebrew **yᵉḥîʾēl**, **yᵉḥîyāh**, and inscriptional Hebrew **ḥwyhw** (Seal in Bordreuil and Lemaire 1976:48 no. 7), **yḥwʾly** (Samaria ostracon 55. 2); in

Phoenician,[50] and Assyrian[51] texts. In addition, in a Punic oath from Carthage, the goddess addressed is defined as rbt ḥwt ʾlt, a divine name (KAI 89, 1) or possibly an epithet of Tannit/Asherah (Wallace 1985:152-154; Olyan 1988:71). Thus there is an onomastic environment for the root behind the name Eve, an environment whose attestations span the history of at least two millennia.

The etymology of the name Eve in the root חיה "live" is supported both by the Bible's own explanation and by the linguistic existence of such a root in various forms in West Semitic. For the former, it is used in a word play in the Biblical text which includes (1) the explicit explanation of the name in 3:16 and (2) the usage of the name in a context exemplifying that role in 4:1-2.[52] For the latter, it is confirmed by an onomastic environment reflecting the common use of this element in personal names.[53]

c. Cain

Cain (qayin קַיִן) seems related to the Semitic root qyn. This root does not occur in Hebrew of the Biblical period. It appears in Arabic of a later period with the meaning "smith." If Cain does come from the root meaning "smith," we have a play on the name with the occupation of Tubal-Cain, a forger of metals. The modern scholarly interest in connecting Cain and his line with the Kenites and with metal working, particularly in the desert, often assumes the name's association with metal forging.[54] An advantage of this would be the function of the name as a description, role, or

Fowler 1988:344. See also Ryckmans 1934-35 I 228 for Epigraphic South Arabic.

[50]ʿštrtḥwt (RB 13:1), and Punic pmyḥwyʾ (CIS 5981, 1); in Benz 1972:308.

[51]gír-ḫa-a (ADD 197.4); in Zadok 1978a:67.

[52]For this meaning as part of the larger context of Eve's role in the narrative of Genesis 2-3, see Clines 1990:36-40.

[53]Wallace 1985:150-152 adduces the comparative evidence for both "serpent" and "to live." He suggests a common origin for both etymologies in the verb "to live," arguing that the serpent was the beast par excellence.

[54]See the discussion under Cain in the chapter on the line of Cain.

occupation, as we have seen with Adam and Eve. However, the lack of a sufficient context in the Hebrew text to establish this meaning for the name has meant that this interpretation is not certain.[55]

Another suggestion for a derivation of the root may be q̂înāh "song," which does appear in Biblical Hebrew. If so, we may have a connection with Cain's later descendants, both Jubal who produces musical instruments, and Naamah, whose name may imply a relationship to music, as will be seen. In such a case, the root could refer to an occupation or to the shortened form of a name of praise to a deity, i.e. "song of DN." However, no examples occur of q̂înāh in a QATIL form. Thus we have the absence of attestations of the former option ("smith") in Classical Hebrew, and uncertainty about the form if the latter option ("song") is preferred. Does this mean that the root has not been identified or that both roots played a role in the understanding of the name in Genesis?[56]

A third suggestion derives from the lexica of Old South Arabic. This is the qyn root used for the title of an administrator. The term appears both in Sabaean and in Qatabanian.[57]

A root qyn has been found in personal names in Old South Arabian inscriptions,[58] including a qynw who appears as a Qedarite ruler in a 5th century B.C. Aramaic inscription from Tell el-Maskuṭeh at the entrance to Wadi Tumīlāt (Eph'al 1982:194, 211, 212, 226, 227). However, these appearances of the root do not occur in any contexts useful for determining

---

[55]So also Westermann 1974:394. However, this does not demonstrate that the Cain of 4:1-16 cannot be identified with the Cain of 4:17-24.

[56]This interpretation refers to the possible understanding of the name by the early readers of this text. It is not intended to set forth some sort of double etymology for the name itself. On the other hand, the author could have chosen such a name, recognizing the possibility of wordplay with both roots.

[57]Beeston et al. 1982:112; Biella 1982:454; Ricks 1989:146.

[58]E.g. qyn (masculine) and qynt (feminine); in Ryckmans 1934 I 190; Müller 1963:314; HALAT 3:1025. Cf. Nabatean attestations in Negev 1991:58.

its meaning in Old South Arabic. It appears in titles, clan names, and personal names (Beeston et al. 1982:112; Biella 1982:454). Biblical scholars who seek etymological support for Cain's association with the Kenites and with metalworking traditions, have sought a derivation from Classical Arabic of a later period, rather than from the contemporary Old South Arabic. Certainty of identification in the derivations of this name is not possible, but it is more likely to be found in this earlier usage than in the later reference to a metal smith.

The root's association with metal working has received support from the discovery of Hittite-Hurrian bilingual inscriptions from Boghazköy and the identification of the Hittite logogram for (metal) smith (lú SIMUG) with the Hurrian, ta-ba-li-iš (Dietrich and Loretz 1990a). If the first element of Tubal-Cain can be identified with this Hurrian reference (see below), then "Cain" possesses clear association with metal working from an early period. The later identifications in Arabic would have an earlier antecedent associated with the same usage. The South Arabic titles could be interpreted in a similar context, and would testify to the importance of metal working among groups possessing this name. This would suggest the possibility that the name be understood as an occupation related to that of the smith.

Nevertheless, the author(s) of Genesis 4 chose to associate Cain with the grammatically and semantically distinct, but similar sounding root qnh; a root which itself is productive of personal names at Ugarit[59] and Alalakh[60] in the second

[59]qnmlk (UM 321 [CTA 119, KTU 4.63] i. 21); il-táq-nu, ìl-táq-ni:(Syria 15:133. 14, 15); ia-aq-ni (Ug V no. 9. 5); in Gröndahl 1967:176; Kinlaw 1967:65, 313; Sivan 1984:262. However, Gröndahl 1967:201 associates il-táq-nu with the root tqn

[60]qa-ni (149. 38; in Dietrich and Loretz 1969-1970:77); qa-ni-ia (154, 30 [not 19]; in Wiseman 1953:145); in Sivan 1984:262.

millennium B.C., and in Hebrew,[61] Phoenician, and Punic[62] texts of the first millennium B.C.

d. Abel

Landersdorfer (1916:67-68) related the Sumerian ibila "heir" to the name Abel. The suggestion of the Akkadian synonym **aplu** brings us within the Semitic family of languages (van Beek 1916:67-68). Certainly, **aplu** is a word with a well known usage. There are many examples of its usage in name formation in Akkadian personal names. However, the appearance of an initial ה in the Hebrew name would be unexpected. Another suggestion is that of Zimmermann (1966:324) who compares the Arabic root **habala**, which in the IV conjugation means "bereave a mother of her son." Although fitting the context such an otherwise unattested meaning remains doubtful in Hebrew.

A word known to the West Semitic reader and listener to this story is the common (100+ occurrences) Hebrew lexeme הֶבֶל, with its meaning, "breath, nothingness." This term, with a spelling and vocalization identical to Abel, is so obvious that it may explain why Abel is the only member of Eve's offspring not to have a note appended to his name in chapter 4 (Wenham 1987:102). This may be a shortened form of a theophoric construction, e.g. "breath of DN." On the other hand, it may have served as a name describing a characteristic of the infant, e.g. a small or frail infant. In any case, the narrative context does not inform us and we have no onomastic environment for this Hebrew name in any of our West Semitic textual sources. There is no clear evidence for the supposition that the name should be related to Jabal and Jubal (Skinner 1930:103) who appear in the genealogy of Cain. As will be seen, these names have etymologies

---

[61]**miqnēyāhû** and **'elqānāh** in biblical Hebrew; **mqnyhw** (Vattioni 1969 nos. 162 and 272; Aharoni, Naveh, et al. 1981 no. 60. 4); **qnyhw** (Vattioni 1969 no. 13); in Fowler 1988:359.

[62]**mqnmlk** (Phoenician Levy SG 24.4 [not 3]); **qn'l** (Punic CIS 135.5); **qny** (Punic CIS 4026. 4); in Benz 1972:404-405.

unrelated to Abel. Though lacking an onomastic environment, Abel has an obvious etymology.

3. The Names in the Narratives of Genesis 6-9

a. Noah

The name invites comparison with the verbal root נוח "to rest" in the Qal.[63] While there are no examples of this root with the sort of vocalization which appears in the name Noah, it does occur in West Semitic personal names of the earliest and latest periods; from Eblaite of the third millennium B.C.[64] and Amorite of the late third / early second millennium B.C.[65] to Jewish names of the Chaldean and later periods in the mid-first millennium B.C.[66] Of interest is the Nabatean name **Nwḥ** (CIS 2/1, 274). We also note the Israelite place name **Yānōaḥ**. The root occurs in two possible personal names of the Biblical period, Nohah (נוֹחָה),

---

[63]On the basis of Sumerian, Babylonian, and Greek parallels to Noah, all having different names, Zimmermann 1966:318-319, who accepts this etymology, argues that "Noah may not have been the real name in the Hebrew account at all, but that the name was suited to his character and action, supplanting the previous name." For the role of name and character, see our discussion in the conclusion to this chapter. For the similar sounding Hurrian "Noah," see below.

[64]**ni-ḫ̮i-li-im, i-nu-ḫ̮i-li-im, a-nu-ḫ̮u**; in Krebernik 1988:58.

[65] Imperfect verb forms include **ya-nu-uḫ̮-sa-mar, ta-nu-uḫ̮-na-wu-um** (fem.), **t[a]-nu-ḫ̮a** (fem.), **^{d}a-mi-ta-nu-uḫ̮**, also passive participle **ni-ḫ̮a-tum** (fem.), **su-mu-ni-ḫ̮u-um**; in Bauer 1926:39; Stamm 1939:79, 85, 168-9; Huffmon 1965:237. For earlier Amorite, see also Gelb 1980:28, 329-330, of which the closest is **nu-ḫ̮i-DINGIR** (Babylonian Inscriptions in the Collection of J. B. Nies, New Haven IX 408, 34); in Buccellati 1966:176-177.

[66]**Nu-ḫ̮a-a** (BE 9, 4.12); in Zadok 1978a:143.

in I Chronicles 8:2,[67] and Manoah (מָנוֹחַ), the father of Samson in Judges 13.[68]

In the Hurrian version of the Gilgamesh epic, the personal name ᵈna-aḫ-ma-zu-le-el occurs.[69] Although there has been no analysis of this name or its initial element, the form of the first syllable invites comparison with the Biblical Noah.[70] Further comparison requires better understanding of the name and the Hurrian background of the narrative.

b. Shem

The name of Noah's first son, Shem (šēm שֵׁם), corresponds to that of the Hebrew word for "name," whose spelling and vocalization are identical. Such an etymology is assured by the broad geographic and lengthy chronological witness which this element finds in personal names.[71] Limiting ourselves to the West Semitic environment, we find examples of this element in texts from early second millennium Mari and Amorite sources (Huffmon 1965:247; Gelb 1980:351-355), from later Ugarit (Gröndahl 1967:193-194; Kinlaw 1967:327-328; Sivan 1984:276) and Amarna (Hess 1984:333), and from Hebrew (Fowler 1988:362; Zadok 1988:316, 319), Aramaic (Kornfield 1978:74; Zadok 1978a:65-66; Maraqten 1988:220), Phoenician, and Punic (Benz 1972:419) sources of the first millennium. Most frequently the

---

[67]The name is given as one of Benjamin's sons. However, as it does not occur in the names of Benjamin's sons mentioned in Numbers 26:38-40 and Genesis 46:21 (Zadok 1988:208), it may reflect a variant spelling, perhaps identified with נעמן Naaman (Curtis and Madsen 1910:157-158).

[68]For morphological problems with the identification of this root in Nahat (Genesis 36:13), cf. Layton 1990:225-227. Layton associates the PN with the root nḥt.

[69]KUB VIII 61 + KBo VIII 144 verso 22; in Laroche 1966:125. Laroche 1966:131 also lists the name nu-u-ḫa-ti-iš. See H. Otten RLA 3:372.

[70]See already Burrows 1925:281-282; also cited by Cassuto 1961:288.

[71]Thus atttempts to identify the "name" of 11:4 as a deity (Lubetski 1987) are unlikely in the present context of Genesis 1-11. The wordplay with Shem, son of Noah, and the appearance of the term in the promise to Abram in Genesis 12, seem to be the primary concerns.

element appears in construct with a divine name or theophoric element which follows it. For example, we find šu-um-ad-da "name of DN (H)ad(d)u" as a plunderer of caravans in the Galilee (EA 8. 18, 35). Of the use of this element in Semitic personal names, Cross (1974:243) writes, "The element sum- refers to the name of the god of the family or clan (that is, the personal god) on whom he can call or by whom he swears."

c. Ham

Ham (ḥām חָם) is a name with three possible etymologies. First, Ham may be related to the Egyptian word for "servant," ḥm. In personal names, this element appears by itself as well as with divine and other elements following it, e.g. "servant of DN."[72] This element occurs in the name of an Egyptian commissioner in Canaan during the Amarna period, pa-ḫa-am-na-ta, with the meaning "the servant of god."[73] A second possibility for this name occurs in the West Semitic word for "paternal kinsman, uncle" which appears in Hebrew with the same spelling as Ham. This term is found throughout the West Semitic world in personal names. It occurs at Mari,[74] Amarna,[75] and Ugarit,[76] as well as in Aramaic[77] and Punic.[78] A third possibility, Hebrew חָם "hot," from the root ḥmm, is less likely as it does not occur in personal names.

---

[72]Ranke 1935:239-240. Ranke also cites examples of feminine forms, with ḥmt.

[73]EA 60. 10, 20, 32; 62. 1; 68. 22; 131. 35; in Hess 1984:202. The name also appears as pa-ḫa-na-te.

[74]ḫa-am-ma-an, ḫa-mu-AN, ḫa-am-mu-^{d}da-gan; in Huffmon 1965:196-198; Gelb 1980:19, 81;

[75]am-mu-ni-ra, ḫa-mu-ni-ra (EA 136, 137, 138, etc.); in Hess 1984:57, 355; Sivan 1984:203-204.

[76]am-mu-ra-pí (PRU III 13.7-B, PRU IV RS 17.226, RS 17.335, Ug V), ʿmṯtmr (PRU II 8-2, PRUII 9-2 etc.); in Gröndahl 1967:109.

[77]ḥmḥlt (CIS II 149, D3.G2); in Kornfield 1978:250.

[78]ḥmy (CIS 3179, 3); ḥmbʿl (CIS 4734, 3); bʿlḥmʾ (CIS 2773, 2); in Benz 1972:311-312. See also Zadok 1978a:55-56.

We may accept either of the first two etymologies. The Egyptian root could have come into the Canaanite world during a period such as the Amarna Age. If the Egyptian etymology is accepted as the original one for the Ham of Genesis 9 and 10, the West Semitic etymology could be understood as a reinterpretation in a different linguistic context.

d. Japheth

Japheth (*yepet* יֶ֫פֶת) is the one name among those found in the narratives of Genesis 6-9 which has neither a West Semitic etymology nor an onomastic environment. Unlike Ham's son, Canaan, it has no comparison with place names, either. Thus we must look elsewhere for a source for this name. Neiman (1973) observes the origin of the descendants of Japheth in the Table of Nations as located in the "region of Hellas and the islands of the Aegean Sea" (p. 122). Whether every group mentioned can be so located is beside the point. We have sufficient evidence in the preponderance of place names and gentilics to seek Japheth among the Greeks and their ancestors. It is there where Neiman finds a comparable name; in Ἰαπετός, the Titan father of Prometheus and the progenitor of humanity. This figure already appears in Homer's Iliad (VIII, 479) and in Hesiod's Theogony.

There is an obvious word play with Japheth which occurs in Noah's blessing on his son in 9:27: יַפְתְּ אֱלֹהִים לְיֶפֶת "May God enlarge Japheth." The verb in this wish is the second root פתה "to be wide, open." The form is a third person masculine jussive (and so shortened by the loss of the final ה) of the hiphil stem. The causative meaning of the root is "to enlarge," although this is the only occurrence of the hiphil stem of this root in Biblical Hebrew. The only Hebrew name bearing any similarity to this root is פְּתוּאֵל. However, its initial element is best related to a different, though homonymic, root with the meaning, "to be youthful."[79] None of the פתה roots provide an etymology for Japheth, since they do not explain the difference in vocalization.

e. Canaan

Canaan (**kĕna'an** כְּנַעַן) seems to be a personal name in the narrative concerning Noah's drunkenness and subsequent curse. The name appears five times, the first two times in a gloss noting Ham's paternity (vv. 18, 22) and three times in the curse (vv. 26-27). In these three occurrences the fact of Canaan's servanthood is repeatedly stressed. The name is always associated with the Hebrew "servant" עֶבֶד. Since the name bearer never appears in the text to speak or to act it remains a moot point whether this name is to be understood as a gentilic rather than a personal name. If the latter is true, it would conform to the description of Canaan's descendants in 10:15-19, a description which incorporates many of the cities and population groups mentioned elsewhere in the Bible as members of the land of Canaan.

However, if Canaan is understood as a personal name, it has no easily identifiable West Semitic or Egyptian etymology. Despite earlier attempts, there is no accepted interpretation of the name.[80] As a place name in the second millennium B.C. (especially in the Amarna texts of the fourteenth century),[81] it identifies the land which Israel would occupy. It seems best, therefore, to regard the figure of Canaan as portrayed in the latter part of Genesis 9 as a land and a people, rather than as an individual. It is unlikely that the name was intended as a personal name either here or in any of its many other occurrences in the Bible and in extraBiblical sources. For this reason Canaan belongs among the place names and gentilics of the Table of Nations. It is different from the other

---

[79]So also Layton 1990:90, with comparisons of South Arabic PNs which contain the same root.
[80]So Weippert RLA V 352-355; Millard 1973:34; Aharoni 1979:67-68.
[81]See de Vaux 1978:127-128. Hess 1984:460 cites some thirteen occurrences in eleven letters.

personal names studied here which, although they may originate in place names, are attached to name bearers who function as persons in Genesis 1-11. For example, Irad appears in a line which includes figures who are clearly persons who perform actions and make statements at the beginning, in the middle, and at the end of the genealogy.[82]

4. Conclusions

1. Five names have identifiable etymologies in West Semitic and particularly in Hebrew; Eve, Abel, Noah, Shem, and Ham. The two names which do not share this characteristic, Cain and Japheth, represent two lines of descendants which do not continue the main part of our story; i.e. neither stand in the line which leads from Adam to Abram.

2. The structure of all the names is that of a single element. There are no hypocoristic suffixes present. Where identifiable, they are nouns. Although some of the names have word plays with verbs, e.g. Cain, Noah, and Japheth, it is not clear that any of these names itself is to be understood as a verb.[83]

3. Among the five names with identifiable etymologies, only Abel has an element with no onomastic environment in the West Semitic world.

4. All seven names share two characteristics . First, they are single element names without any hypocoristic suffixes. Second, they would all possess some relationship to the

---

[82] A. Guillaume (1964:283) has argued for a word play on the name of Canaan and the verbal root כנע "to be humble." He suggests that the son, Canaan, appears in the curse rather than Ham because the son's name carried a verbal root which better fit the subservient status to which the offender was degraded. However, the failure of this root to appear in the curse as well as the unexplained final nun in the proper name, leaves this conjecture without a confident basis. Note that a כְּנַעֲנָה appears in the line of Benjamin and as an Israelite in the 9th century (Zadok 1988:214, 247).

[83] The form of נֹחַ remains unclear.

reader of the Hebrew text of Genesis, either through a root in the name which is also found in the West Semitic world or through word play in the narrative which attaches the name to a Hebrew root which sounds similar.

5. The names of Eve, Noah, Shem, and Ham provide an interesting contrast to Cain, Abel, and Japheth. The first four have an identifiable Hebrew etymology in the name (apart from any assonance or other wordplay in an explanation in the text) which also has a clear onomastic environment. Of these four, Ham represents the only figure who has a plausible non-West Semitic etymology (Egyptian) as well as one which is in the West Semitic language family. If the Egyptian etymology is accepted as the original with a later supplement of the similar sounding West Semitic term for "paternal kinsman," then only Eve, Noah, and Shem remain as sharing the features of an original Hebrew etymology in their names and having an onomastic environment for that element in the world of Israelite and other West Semitic names.

These three are the only names in the narrative sections which have as their name bearers figures who are in the direct line from Adam to Abram. Such is perhaps more than coincidence. It suggests that the narrator did not borrow these names from outside the West Semitic world. These names represent the type found at all periods in that cultural and linguistic sphere. The etymologies of Ham and Japheth have already been related to their origins in the respective areas of the world associated with them in the Table of Nations, i.e. Hamitic and Greek. This reinforces the view that all these names have elements with onomastic associations with the peoples and language groups which the text of Genesis 1-11 suggests; whether Semitic, Hamitic, or Indo-European. It remains to identify the origins of Cain and Abel. Cain has an onomastic environment only in the in the South Semitic onomastica of the first millennium B.C. However, it also has associations with a Hurrian word for "smith." See further considerations in the following chapter.

Abel has a ready etymology but it has no witness in West Semitic onomastica.

6. The onomastic environment of these names is varied. The names Ham and Japheth probably originate from outside the West Semitic world. Both of these names have attestations which may be attributed to the second half of the second millennium B.C., though they should not be limited to that period. Of the other names with West Semitic derivations, Eve, Noah, and Shem contain elements which occur in names from a variety of periods. Adam occurs as a personal name only in the period before 1200 B.C. Cain is not certain. If it is attributed to the later **qyn** of the South Semitic languages, then it could be dated to the latter part of the first millennium. This will be considered further in the next chapter. The number of the names in the narratives of Genesis 1-11 is small. Therefore, we will consider the names found in the associated genealogies before drawing conclusions concerning the onomastic environment.

CHAPTER 3

THE GENEALOGY OF CAIN IN GENESIS 4

1. The Names

a. Cain

Cain (qayin קַיִן) is the first name mentioned in Genesis 4:17-24. The name appears at the end of this section in 4:24. The name also occurs as part of Tubal-Cain. As we have already considered the etymology of this name in the section on names in the narratives of Genesis 1-4, we will consider these implications for its onomastic environment.

Studies have placed Cain in particular geographical and chronological contexts in the Ancient Near East. The figure of Cain has been associated with the region south of ancient Israel, i.e. the modern Negev and the Arabian peninsula. In part, this is because (as noted above) the קין root occurs in names of persons in South Arabian tribes of the first millennium. It does not occur in the second millennium. Both the geographical and chronological parameters on this name should allow us to locate it specifically in first millennium South Arabia. The presence of names with this element at the beginning and end of the genealogy of Cain might suggest such a location and date for the whole line, a conclusion reached by others who have studied this line (cf. Sawyer 1986). The **qyn** root has been related to the South Arabian **qyn** '(metal) smith'. A clinching argument has been the identity of Cain as eponymous ancestor of the Biblical Kenites (קֵינִי), a tribe associated with Jethro and the Midianites. The names seem to be explicitly associated in Numbers 24:21-22 (Rouillard 1985:451-456).

However, there are problems with this view. First, as already noted, the meaning of the root in Biblical Hebrew is dependent upon cognate usages. In the early South Arabian materials, its appearance as the title of an administrator provides a referent but not much in the way of significance or meaning. Since it only appears as a proper name or a title and not as a common noun in all contexts where it can be discerned, we must rely on later usages of the word. Qatabanian and Sabean attestations of the root carry the meaning "administrator" (Ricks 1989:146). Further, the association of Cain with Tubal in the name Tubal-Cain, and the possible meaning of Tubal as "(metal) smith," is based upon a Hittite-Hurrian bilingual inscription (see under Cain, chapter 2). This may suggest a northern origin or at least northern influence in the associations of the name with metal working. If so, it would remove the name from the desert to the south.

Second, all attempts to relate these roots through groups such as the Kenites suffer from the same difficulties. On the one hand, the existence of such a tribe in the Biblical material may appear to move the relationship between the Biblical figure of Cain and the South Semitic name bearers closer. On the other hand, like the association with Tubal any relationship to the Kenites also serves to trace the origins of this tribal element to the beginning of Israel's history.[84] Such a period predates the attestations of this root in personal names in South Arabian and Egyptian inscriptions. This means that the Kenites can only be related to the later inscriptional material by assuming a history for the people bearing these names which extends as early as the history of Israel. Such connections vitiate the assumption of first millennium restrictions for the קין element. However, they do not argue for a southern provenance for this name, and perhaps for the line of Cain as a whole. All such conclusions

---

[84]For a summary of the discussion regarding Balaam's setting and origin, see Moore 1990:1-11. Moore chooses not to address the issue in his own study. The assumptions regarding the early origin of these oracles are not universally held. The Kenites appear throughout Biblical narratives associated with Israel's earliest history. They virtually disappear in narratives associated with Israel's later history. Thus an early date seems preferable.

remain provisional until the remaining names in the line are examined.

b. Enoch

Enoch is a QTÔL form of the West Semitic root ḥnk, "to introduce, initiate" (Rankin 1930:27-38; Reif 1972; TWAT III/1:20-22).[85] Attempts to compare the word ḥanîkîm, "armed retainers," which appears in Genesis 14:14 and in a text from the fifteenth century B.C. (in Taanach No. 6; cf. Albright 1944:24 n87)[86] must reckon with its probable Egyptian origin.[87] We also may compare the Sumerian UNUG which is used to designate the city Uruk. Phonologically, this logogram could be related to the Hebrew Enoch.[88] If this is the case, it may suggest independent origins for the two Enochs of Genesis 4 and 5. However, the identity of the consonantal spelling of Enoch with the proposed West Semitic root justifies a preference for a West Semitic etymology. If Genesis 4:17 intended Enoch as the founder of the city, then the meaning "founder" may lie behind the use of the name here (Westermann 1974:444). The Enoch of chapter 5 may reflect a different nuance of the root. A Hanoch, spelled the same as Enoch (i.e. ḥănôk חֲנוֹךְ), appears in Pentateuchal and I Chronicles genealogies as the eldest son of Reuben, the first born of Jacob.[89] Thus the context of the Hebrew Bible associates the name Enoch, like Cain, with the onomastic environment of the Patriarchal period. Also like Cain, Enoch lacks attestations outside of the Bible during the period of the Hebrew Bible. However, attestations of a ḥnk

---

[85]Cf. Hannukkah, which shares the same root.

[86]Taanach No. 6, lines 6b-8a: (6) ša-ni-tam la-a-mi (7) i-na ma-an-ṣa-ar-ti i-ba-aš-š[u] (8) ḫa-na-ku-u-ka; "Further, in the garrison there are none of thy retainers" Albright 1944:24; "Furthermore, your ḫanakū-men are not among the guardsmen ..." Rainey 1977:59.

[87]The verb, ḥnk, "to send a gift," already appears in the Pyramid texts. See Albright 1931:22; Lambdin 1953:150.

[88]I thank Prof. K. A. Kitchen for this suggestion.

[89]Genesis 46:9; Exodus 6:14; Numbers 26:5; I Chronicles 5:3; Zadok 1988:198.

root in personal names are found in later South Arabian inscriptions.[90]

c. Irad

Irad (ʿîrād עִירָד) is the son of Enoch. Irad occurs only as part of the genealogical information found in v. 18.[91] Attempts to identify Irad with the city of Eridu (Cassuto 1961:229-231; Hallo 1970:64; Sasson 1978:174; Miller 1985:241-242 n. 9; Wenham 1987:111) often replace the second occurrence of "Enoch" in v. 17 with "Irad." If Enoch founded the city, then its name (the name of his son) would be Irad. This would correspond with the Mesopotamian tradition of the antiquity of Eridu as the earliest city. Jared of Genesis 5 has been identified with Irad by scholars attempting to find correspondences between the two genealogies. However, a difference exists between the initial yodh of Jared and the initial ʿayin of Irad.

Although the initial ʿîr in Irad forms the Hebrew word for "city" (cf. Jacob 1934:148), this does not account for the final daleth. Cassuto's attempt to identify the root with the Arabic "cane huts"[92] has not been followed. ʿrd appears as a root meaning "wild ass, onager" in a number of Semitic languages.[93] It is productive of personal names in Amorite,[94] and in first millennium B.C. Akkadian.[95]

The best option for the etymology of Irad remains the place name Eridu.[96] The phonological objection that no ʿayin

---

[90]Knauf 1988:81-82.
[91]LXX's Gaidad (possibly reflecting the similarity of rēš and dālet in later Heb orthography), is not followed by the other versions.
[92]Where the initial ʿayin is read as a ghayin; Cassuto 1961:231-232.
[93]This occurs in Arabic, Akkadian, Hebrew and Ugaritic. Cf. CAD, vol. 9, p. 88; DISO 221; Gabriel 1959:412-413; Huffmon 1965:204; Dahood 1975.
[94]ḫa-ar-du-um (ARM II 12. 9; IX 289. 3); ḫa-ar-da-tum (feminine) (ARM IX 291.iii 30′, 43′); ḫa-ar-da-nu-um (ARM I 118.4); ar-du-um (TCL I 168. 4); in Huffmon 1965:204; Gelb et al. 1980:15, 96-97.
[95]a-ra-di; in Zadok 1977b:120.
[96]As suggested by Wiseman 1955:20. See also Hallo 1970:64.

phoneme exists in Sumerian has no cogency. It assumes an original Sumerian name for the city. Eridu may be a pre-Sumerian name. Furthermore, Akkadian word plays on the name of Eridu, which use an initial URU (= eri_4) "city" logogram to explain the name (RLA II 464-470), may correspond to a Hebrew word play on Irad which makes use of the initial ʿîr "city." Thus Eridu remains a phonologically feasible explanation and one that agrees with the Mesopotamian tradition concerning the earliest of cities. Our knowledge of the onomastic environment of the name Eridu is limited. It may appear in an Assyrian personal name, but not spelled syllabically.[97] Irad remains unattested in the Ancient Near Eastern environment of personal names.

d. Mehujael

Mehujael (mĕḥûyāʾēl מְחוּיָאֵל, mĕḥîyyāʾēl מְחִיּיָאֵל)[98] is the son of Irad. Scholars have compared Mehujael with Mahalalel in Genesis 5 (Wilson 1977:161-162). However, a difference exists between the initial mḥw/y of Mehujael, and the mhl of Mahalalel.

The name Mehujael comprises two elements, the second of which is ʾl, either "god" or the divine name "El." Three suggestions have been made concerning the meaning of the first element:(1) Akkadian, maḫḫu, "an ecstatic" (Cassuto 1961:232; for the word see CAD vol. 10/1 90-91); (2) West

---

[97]URU ḪI-a-a (ADD 618. 4); in Tallqvist 1914:76. Cf. also Huber 1907:31-32. For the reading of the first two signs as eri-du_{10}, see also Postgate 1976:215; Roth 1987:352 n5.

[98]The two appearances of the name in Genesis 4:18 are spelled with a slight difference in the consonantal Hebrew text (mḥwyʾl in the first occurrence; mḥyyʾl in the second). The targums tend to follow the MT. The Peshitta and the Vulgate follow the first spelling (cf. also targum Neofiti). The best attestations of the LXX seem to follow the second spelling. The Samaritan Pentateuch avoids the issue by omitting the disputed syllable. It is an attestation to the care taken in preserving such differences, even when they exist side by side, that the Hebrew text was not harmonized (Cassuto 1961:232-233).

Semitic mḥʾ, "to smite;"[99] and (3) a participial form of ḥyh, "to live" (Skinner 1930:117, who also notes Philo and Jerome; Gabriel 1959:414), active or passive in voice. The name could then mean: "ecstatic of God," "god/El has smitten," "god/El gives life," or "given life by god/El."

The first two forms do not produce personal names, while the root ḥyh generates names at all periods in West Semitic:in Amorite;[100] at Ugarit;[101] in Hebrew;[102] and in Phoenician/Punic.[103] However, none of the examples found elsewhere have a mem preformative. Cf. also Eve. The second element, ʾl, "god/El" has frequent attestation, including occurrences in a number of names with ḥyh.[104]

Thus the name includes two elements, the first with a root meaning "to live," and the second one as the noun/name "god/El." If the initial element functions as a verb, the name may mean something like, "god/El enlivens" (HALAT 538; Fowler 1988:127), or in a passive form, "enlivened by god/El." Such a verbal sentence name may express thanksgiving for the birth of the child. On the other hand, if the initial element functions in a nominal sense, the name may reflect a construct relationship and mean something like, "life of god/El," i.e. divine life. Although either

---

[99]Phoenician/Hebrew מחה may suggest an original mḥy. Note Aramaic "to strike," perhaps related to מחץ. See DISO.

[100]ya-aḫ-wi-AN (CT VIII 20a 3; ARM VII 215. 5); e-ki-la-aḫ-wi (ARM VII 185 ii 3′); la-[aḫ-]wi-AN (Birot 1955:I 57); ḫa-yú-um-ra-pí (ARM VIII 24. 12); in Bauer 1926:74; Huffmon 1965:191-192; Gelb 1980:19, 248.

[101]ḫa-ya-il (Syria 18, RS 8.213. 32); abdi-ḫa-ya (Syria 18, RS 14.16. 25); ḥyil (PRU II 10. 3; PRU V 131. 3); ḥyl (PRU II 35 a 6); abdḥy (UM 301 r. iv 10); ʿbdḥy (UM 301 iv 10); in Gröndahl 1967:137; Sivan 1984:225.

[102]יְחִיאֵל (Ezra 7:9) and יְחִיָּה (I Chronicles 15:24); in Noth 1928:206, 246. For examples from Hebrew seals and inscriptions, see Fowler 1988:344.

[103]ʿštrtḥwt (RB 13, 1); pmyḥwy' (CIS 5981. 1); yḥw'ln (CIS 981. 1; et al.); yḥw' (CIS 515. 3; et al.); in Benz 1972:308-309.

[104]Cf. the initial examples listed above for Ugaritic and Hebrew. The high frequency of the appearance of this element as Il in Old Akkadian personal names led Gelb 1962:6 to conclude that Il was "the chief deity of the Mesopotamian Semites in the Pre-Sargonic Period." See Cross 1974:243.

possibility exists, the initial element appears most frequently in personal names in a verbal form.[105] Thus the former alternative seems more probable.

The etymology places Mehujael within the West Semitic world. The most suitable period for the name is difficult to determine as examples of the name elements occur in personal names in all periods of the Ancient Near East.

e. Methushael

Methushael (mětûšāʾēl מְתוּשָׁאֵל) is the son of Mehujael (Gen 4:18). Although Methushael and Methuselah (in the genealogy of Seth) appear to be similar (Wilson 1977:161-162), there is a difference in the spellings of the two names. The final two consonants, ʾl for Methushael, contrast with the lḥ for Methuselah.

The name Methushael comprises two elements which form a genitive relationship. The initial element relates to the West Semitic mutu, "man, warrior, hero."[106] Three possibilities have been suggested to explain the second half of the name (Gabriel 1959:414-415). First, it could comprise two elements; the relative š followed by ʾl, "god/El." In such a case, the name Methushael would mean "man of god/El." The other two possibilities involve a single element, šʾl. If this root means "to ask," the name could mean "man of the request (i.e. prayer)." However, if the proper name "Sheol" occurs, then Methushael would mean "man of Sheol."

If the name is West Semitic, we must reject the first option due to the absence of such relatives in personal names.[107]

[105] Cf. e.g. Huffmon's analysis 1965:71-72, 79-80.

[106] For attestations of mt with these meanings in the mythological and epistolary literature from Ugarit, cf. Dietrich and Loretz 1990b: 57-64.

[107] Gray 1896:164-165. As to Gray's reference to Müller's identification of bt šir as a Phoenician town in a list of Seti I; the town should be identified with Bethshan, not with a hypothetical bytšʾl (Simons 1937:204; Aharoni 1979:178).

This absence includes names in Amorite, despite one uncertain example, zu-ul-ša-a-bi.[108] As for the second option, the use of the root š'l "to ask" in a nominative form has few parallels in personal names.[109] On the other hand, a term such as "man" in construct with a proper name has a parallel in Methuselah. Sheol might here function as a deity.[110] The name would then mean "man (i.e. devotee) of the god Sheol."

Examples of mutu followed by a place name appear in Amorite personal names.[111] Examples of mutu followed by a divine name also occur in West Semitic personal names of the second millennium B.C.[112] The onomastic structure, mt plus divine name, occurs frequently. mt, "man," lacks attestation in the Canaanite onomastica of the first

---

[108]Cf. Birot 1955:ii. 51. Cf. Moran 1961:61, 70 n76; Huffmon 1965:265; Gelb 1980:33. Although BDB 607 and Fowler 1988:123 follow this option, citing a Babylonian name mutu-ša-ili in support, the evidence lacks West Semitic examples. Fowler's creation of a category of names with the pattern qeṭû'ēl, in which all names have a similar vocalization of the first element with אֵל as the second element, does not consider Methushelah. This name agrees in vocalization with the initial element of this form but has a different second element, just as Methushael. The Babylonian mutu-ša-ili does not seem to exist (Layton 1990:70-71).

[109]There are two examples in Hebrew: šĕ'alfî'ēl and šalfî'ēl (Fowler 1988:90, 134, 175, 361). However, both of these names have the element in an initial position in the name.

[110]On the presence of underworld deities in Semitic culture and onomastica, cf. Tsevat 1954a:45; Aḥituv 1968:643-644; Parker 1976:224; Gelb 1980:26, 158-160.

[111]Cf. Durand 1991.

[112]For Amorite at Mari, cf. mu-tu-d IM (ARM IV 39. 10); mu-tu-d da-gan (ARM VI 21. 7; ARM VII 155. 5; ARM VIII 42. 6'); in Huffmon 1965:234; Birot 1979:156-159. For Ugarit, cf. mu-ut-d IM (PRU III RS 16.155. 6; PRU IV RS 17.112. 6); mtb'l (UM 322 v 11; PRU II 65. 10; 137. 4); in Gröndahl 1967:161-162; Kinlaw 1967:305-306. From the Amarna texts, cf. mu-ut-d IM, prince of Pella (EA 255. 3; EA 256. 2, 5); in Hess 1984:190. This element should not be confused with the first millennium mtʿ/mty element which appears in Aramaic and later South Arabian personal names. See KAI II 242; DISO 172; Gibson 1975:34; Biella 1982:285-286; Kaufman 1989:101.

millennium B.C.[113] As a common noun meaning "man" in first millennium B.C. West Semitic, mt appears only in Biblical Hebrew and there only in the plural.[114] Although no other examples of personal names containing a divine name, š'l, exist, we do find underworld deities appearing in West Semitic personal names. These include Nergal, Reshef, and Mot.[115] Pertinent is the observation of Fowler (1988:281) that, among West Semitic onomastica, "Only Hebrew names portray the deity as 'death' (mwt)."[116] This would suggest another related semantic item appearing only in Hebrew names, similar to our element which describes the place of the dead and seems to appear only in this name. The problem of the difference in vocalization between Sheol and Methushael does not require a loss of the original vocalization of Methushael (Layton 1990:72). Since the etymology of the root is not known (KB^3 1274) it is possible that there were two separate vocalic developments before the root appeared in Biblical Hebrew; one in the direction of the "place name" Sheol and the other as the divine name Shael, which appears in the personal name Methushael.

We see the second example of a personal name in Genesis 4:17-24 which has no literary context to allow for explicit wordplay but does have an apparently West Semitic etymology and an onomastic environment. This latter seems to fit well in the second millennium B.C.

---

[113]Maraqten 1988:89, 182 identifies a 7th century Aramaic name from Tell Halaf, mty. He notes Palmyrene parallels. He is uncertain about the etymology but notes mutu, "man." More likely is Stark 1971:98 who identifies both mty and mt' as hypocoristica, in which mt is a root meaning "gift." This root does not explain the etymology of Methushael as well as mutu.

[114]The plural absolute מְתִים may appear in Deuteronomy 2:34; 3:6 and possibly in Judges 20:48. The plural construct מְתֵי appears in Genesis 34:30; Deuteronomy 26:5; 28:62; Psalms 26:4; Job 11:11; 22:15; Sirach 7:16; and 15:7; and possibly elsewhere. Cf. HALAT 617-618.

[115]Cf. Huffmon 1965:263; Gröndahl 1967:162, 181-182; Kinlaw 1967:309, 318-319; Benz 1972:411-412; Gelb 1980:30, 347; Sivan 1984:265; Tigay 1986:66-67 n. 12

[116]She cites the example, אֲחִימוֹת.

f. Lamech

The tri-radical nature of the name, lmk, suggests a Semitic etymology. However, no such root is known in West Semitic. The Arabic, ylmk, "strong man," has found support in the etymological search (HALAT 505). Outside the Semitic language family, the Sumerian lumga serves as the title of the god Ea as patron of music (Landersdorfer 1916:19; Gabriel 1959:415; Westermann 1974:446). This has had special interest due to Jubal, son of Lamech and "father of those who play the lyre and pipe." We also find compared the obscure Akkadian, lumakku, the title of a priest of lower rank which appears in lexical texts.[117]

As to the onomastic environment of Lamech, earlier attempts found it in third millennium B.C. personal names,[118] or in names from Mari of the early second millennium B.C.[119] These names remain tentative as to their value, and at best lie at the periphery of the West Semitic world. In addition, they can now be read differently.[120] The discovery of the tribal names Beni Lamk and Lamki in Oman suggest the presence of a possible Semitic root but nothing about the origins or the environment.[121] As neither the etymology of Lamech nor possible parallels have received certain identification, all such comparisons remain tentative and precarious. Further, evidence remains lacking for the lmk root in West Semitic.

g. Adah

---

[117]Cassuto 1961:233; CAD vol. 9 244-245; the Sumerian equivalent is gudu$_4$.tur.ra.

[118]See lam-kí-um and lam-gi$_4$-ma-rí in the Man-ištušu obelisk with index in MDP 2 pp. 41-52; RA 31:140; in Gelb 1957:162. Cf. also Gevirtz 1963:26.

[119]See the šakkanakku texts, which include two occurrences of the personal name, lam-ki, ARM XIX (Limet 1976) 311. 5; 332. 4.

[120]LAM is to be read as iš$_{11}$; Archi, Biga, and Milano 1988:228 [Archi]; Krebernik 1988a:62; 1988b:68 accept this reading for the personal names at Ebla. See also Biggs 1988:96 for additional evidence from Abu Salabikh.

[121]Cf. Vollers 1895:514. I thank T. Schneider for this reference.

Adah (ʿādāh עָדָה) is the first wife of Lamech, mother of Jabal and Jubal, and an addressee of Lamech's song (Gen 4:19-20, 23). In terms of etymology, Adah may be compared with the Hebrew ʿădî (עֲדִי) "ornament" (Gabriel 1959:416; Sawyer 1986:159), perhaps based on a verbal root עדה "to ornament, deck oneself" (Fowler 1988:354). If so, the use of the name in the context of Genesis 4:17-24 may suggest a word parallel with Zillah, as noted below.

The onomastic environment of Adah occurs quite broadly in the Ancient Near East. The name Adah appears five times in Genesis 36, as wife of Esau and daughter of Elon the Hittite (v. 2), and mother of Eliphaz (v. 4). Noth (1928:182) observes forms of this root in the Biblical names אֶלְעָדָה (I Chronicles 7:20), עֲדָיָה(וּ) (II Kings 22:1; Ezra 10:29; I Chronicles 11:12; II Chronicles 23:1; et al.), and probably shortened forms in עִדֹּא (I Kings 4:14) and עִדּוֹ(א) (Zechariah 1:1; I Chronicles 6:6; et al.). Stamm (1967:334) observes this name as a shortened form with a theophoric element missing. Thus the meaning would be "Er (Gott) hat geschmückt."

In other first millennium souces the ʿdy / ʿdh root may occur in names in Aramaic,[122] in Hebrew,[123] and perhaps in the name of a-di-ia[-a], an Arabian queen who lived during the time of Ashurbanipal (Moritz 1926:84; Eph'al 1982:151-153, 224). Personal names with the root may appear at Ugarit.[124] The nature of syllabic cuneiform orthography renders difficult a distinction between the root ʿdy/h and the divine name [H]addu in West Semitic personal names of the second millennium B.C. Thus the many personal names listed

---

[122] ʿdyh:CIS II 122, 1; in Vinnikov 1964:224.

[123] Yʿdh (DJD II 17 B 2; ʿdyhw (Aharoni et al. 1981:no. 58. 1; Vattioni 1959:no. 148. 2; 154. 1); ʾyʿdh:Vattioni 1959:no. 151); in Israel 1987a:84. See also the examples from Hebrew seal inscriptions, collected by Fowler 1988:354:עדיהו (Vattioni 1969:Nos. 148, 154, 1978:417; Bordreuil and Lemaire1976:50-51 no. 14; Aharoni, Naveh, et al. 1981:no. 58 l. 1), עדאל (Vattioni 1969:No. 146), איעדה (Vattioni 1969:No. 151) and אלעדה.(Gibson 1971:32 Murabaat Inscr. B l. 3).

[124] [y]a-a-du-na:PRU VI no. 72, 4′; in Sivan 1984:205.

under the divine name element (in Amorite cf. Gelb et al. 1980:243-47) may include some with the same element as that found in Adah (Huffmon 1965:190). A suggestion of Gevirtz to find a similarity with the Ur III personal names a-ti-ma-tum and [a]-ti-ma-at, contrasts with Gelb's decision to list them under the element ʿd "up to," "until," "as long as."[125] The onomastic environment may extend through a variety of periods in the West Semitic world of the Ancient Near East.

h. Zillah

Zillah (ṣillāh צִלָּה) is the second wife of Lamech and the mother of Tubal-Cain and of Naamah (Gen 4:19-22). The etymology of Zillah relates either to the Hebrew noun ṣēl "shadow, shade; protection;" or to the verb ṣll "to shrill."[126] If we accept the former meaning, then it may carry the sense of refreshment, of darkness, or of protection. On the other hand, acceptance of the latter meaning suggests the identification of Zillah's etymology with "a shrill war cry" or of "a cymbal," the latter with possible reference to the beauty of the voice (Gabriel 1959:416). Cassuto (1961:234) has observed a word parallel in Canticles 2:14 which relates the roots behind the names of Adah as "ornament" and Zillah as "cymbal" (ṣilṣûl).[127]

Forms of personal names with the same root may occur in the Hebrew Bible in haṣṣĕlelpōnî[128] and in bĕṣalʾēl.[129] In the Arad inscriptions, the name bṣl occurs.[130] We may understand the bĕṣalʾēl as "in the shadow/protection of El."[131]

---

[125] U 203; Analecta Orientalia VII p. 19; and TMH n.F. I/II 338; in Gelb 1957:16. Cf. Gevirtz 1963:25-26.
[126] Cf., however, Stamm 1967:337, who regards the name as of unclear meaning.
[127] Cf. Garsiel 1987:25.
[128] A feminine name in I Chronicles 4:3; Sawyer 1986:159; but cf. Noth 1928:241.
[129] Exodus 31:2 et al.; Noth 1928:152; Cassuto et al. 1971:733.
[130] Aharoni, Naveh, et al. 1981:no. 49 l. 1; in Fowler 1988:358. Fowler also lists bēṣay and bṣy as examples of forms with the final lamedh omitted.
[131] Fowler 1988:127, 358.

The root ṣll "shade, protection" appears in personal names in Old Akkadian[132] and in Amorite.[133] A ṣll root occurs in the name of a profession at Ugarit where it means "cymbalist."[134] It occurs in Nuzi personal names (MacRae 1943:312). There we may suggest an Akkadian element in light of the absence of this element from elsewhere in the West Semitic onomastica of the latter second millennium B.C. Those putative West Semitic names in Babylonia during later periods may have the same explanation.[135] A single occurrence of a ṣl in a Punic name may appear as a shortened form of the deity ṣlm.[136] Occurences of ṣillu "shade, protection" commonly appear in West Semitic names of various periods, as well as in Akkadian (Tallqvist 1914:303).

If we understand the name Zillah as meaning "cymbal" then an implicit wordplay with the name of Lamech's other wife, Adah, may have been intended. Both have names referring to the development of the arts. However, if Zillah reflects the meaning "shadow, protection" then it fits well in the onomastic environment of the Semitic world. Either option is possible.

i. Jabal

Jabal (yābāl יָבָל) is a son of Adah and Lamech, and the brother of Jubal (Gen 4:20). Jabal's etymology appears as a QĀTĀL noun form of the root ybl "to bring." Hoffner (1980) observes

---

[132] i-lí-zi-lí (UET III 11; U); zi-la-šu (OIP 37:50; U); as well as personal names with ṣillu written logographically as MI, a-ḫi-MI-lum (Pinches, AT 77; U); a-ḫu-MI-lum (AnOr I 97; U); in Gelb 1957:243-244. Cf. also Gevirtz 1963:25-26.

[133] za-li-lum (Bauer 1926:41); ka-ma-zi-lum (feminine) (Bauer 1926:33); ku-mu-zi-li (feminine) (Bauer 1926:33); ṭà-ab-ṣi-lu-ú (TCL X 38. 7); as well as personal names ṣillu written logographically as MI, MI-lí-ak-ka (ARM VIII 1. 49); MI-lí-dḫa-na-at (ARM XIII 83. 8); in Huffmon 1965:257; Birot 1979:187-188; Gelb 1980:34, 365.

[134] LÚma-ṣi-lu (PRU VI 93. 25); in Huehnergard 1987b:171.

[135] ŠEŠ-ṭal-li (ADD 317. 5); a-da-di-ṭa-al-li (feminine) (CCENA 23. 28); in Zadok 1977b:47, 55, 98.

[136] yrbṣl (CIS 1312. 3); in Benz 1972:399.

its attestation in Akkadian,[137] Amarna Canaanite,[138] Ugaritic, and Aramaic.[139] All verbal uses in Hebrew occur either as hiphil or hophal stems. The passive participle, yĕbûl, appears in Hebrew as a noun with the meaning, "(agricultural, non-arboreal) produce." Hoffner suggests that, in the absence of a G stem verbal form in Hebrew, that language borrowed the noun from a Canaanite dialect in which the G stem does appear, such as Ugaritic. Attestations of ybl in West Semitic occur throughout the second and the first millennia B.C. The root lacks attestation as a verb in Phoenician or Punic.[140]

Its attestation in personal names is a different matter. In Hebrew (outside Genesis 1-11), Phoenician, Punic,[141] and Aramaic we find no evidence for personal names with this root during the Biblical period (cf. Benz 1972; Noth 1928; Tigay 1987; Vinnikov 1962:228; and the dictionaries).[142] However, the root does appear in Akkadian personal names (Stamm 1939:140, 182). In names of the early Babylonian and Kassite periods it appears in constructions such as ì-lí-ub-lam, "my god has brought (to me)."[143] Here it is found in a name expressing thanksgiving for the god's aid in bringing forth

---

[137] For the Akkadian root wbl, cf. abālu, CAD vol. 1/I pp. 10-29.

[138] Sivan 1984:256 records its use as the participles, ú-bi-li-ma and ú-bi-il, "porter," in EA 287 and 288, both from Jerusalem; as well as possibly in the Canaanite GN, ya/yu-bi-lì-ma, in EA 256, line 28.

[139] With a causative use of the pael form; cf. Brauner 1974:238.

[140] Tomback 1978:123 identifies a ybl vocable in a Punic inscription. There, however, he understands it as "ram." Cf. below under Jubal.

[141] Cf. however, Punic nbl in KAI no. 105. 3.

[142] Barr 1969-1970:25-28 suggests a possible derivation for the name of Nabal in I Samuel 25 from the root ybl. He notes a South Arabic and an Ethiopic parallel and would translate the name as a shortened theophoric name, "God has sent (this child)." However, Stamm 1980 disputes this argument, observing that the testimony in South Semitic is not clear or compelling. Stamm presents an alternative derivation. Nor is the suggestion of Albright 1921-22:24 to associate Balaam with this root likely, especially given the presence of an ʿayin in the name. Cf. Layton 1990:171-172.

[143] Ranke 1905:102. Cf. also $^{(d)}$Sin-ub-lam (CT IV 7. 10; CT VI 31. 28; CT VI 44. 16; et al. in Ranke 1905:165) and ^{d}Addu-ub-la (BE XIV 150. 6; BE XV 200 v. 5; in Clay 1912:49); in Stamm 1939:140.

the child. This form of the abālu root, with a divine name, also appears in examples from Nuzi.[144] In Old Akkadian, a name expressing prayer for a god's support, ì-lí-bi-la-nì, "my god, support me," occurs, using the abālu root.[145] In names from the Sargonic and Ur III periods, these forms occur as well as the D participle form, muttabbilum, all in conjunction with divine names.[146] Perhaps we may also compare the name wa-ba-lum from Ebla (Pettinato 1979:220 no. 4920; Krebernik 1988:38). Note that these examples come from before the second millennium B.C.

In West Semitic, personal names from the early second millennium include this root. The form i-ba-al followed by a divine name serves to create many Amorite names.[147] As for the later second millennium, we note no similar examples of this root in personal names from Alalakh or the Amarna archives. However, Kinlaw (1967:120, 253) finds the ybl root in the personal name tub-ba-li-ni, which appears in two texts, both from Ugarit.[148] Gröndahl (1967:265) had identified this name as Hurrian, composed of Hurrian, tb, "strong." Laroche (1976-1977:272) lists this word under the lemma tuppi. However, he cites no example of a nominal or verbal form such as tuppal (tubbal). Thus it seems preferable to regard this name as Semitic, composed of the ybl root.

If so, West Semitic onomastica use this root only during the period of time preceding the first millennium B.C. In fact, in its G stem form it occurs most frequently in the period of the Amorite names, in the first half of the second millennium

---

[144] E.g. zi-nu-ub-la (JEN 503. 9); dUTU-ub-la (JEN 503. 16; HSS XIII 250. 13; 287. 10; 292. 2; 406. 23; HSS XIV 170. 7, 9; 503. 19); in MacRae 1943:295; Cassin and Glassner 1977:118.

[145] D; RTC 245; U 1623; in Gelb 1957:13.

[146] be-lí-mu-da-bíl (2 NT 618); AN-mu-da-bíl (Delaporte, CCBN No. 91; OIP XLIII 142); AN-mu-ta-bíl (CT XXI 1c); AN-mu-tab-bíl (TCL II 5498 ii); in Gelb 1957:14.

[147] i-ba-al-dIM (ARM II 33. 11'; 37. 4; 62. 12'; ARM VIII 9. 27; et al.); i-ba-al-da-mu-um (Dossin 1971:x. 43); i-ba-al-IŠDAR (Birot 1955:i. 2); in Bauer 1926:20-21; Birot 1979:110-111; Huffmon 1965:155; Gelb 1980:21, 270-271.

[148] PRU III p. 144, RS 16.138. 13; and PRU III p. 119, RS 16.204. 3.

B.C. It regularly appears in compounds with divine names, where we can best understand it as a prayer or thanksgiving name, often associated with the role of the god in assisting in the birth of a child. Examples of the verbal form shortened by omission of the divine name occur in Amorite personal names as well as in the personal name from Ugarit noted above. It seems best to see this shortened construction as closest to those Biblical names containing the ybl root, Jabal and Jubal. Jabal could then mean, "DN leads (in procession)" (North 1964:380).

Jabal, as well as Jubal and Tubal-Cain, may contain identical roots whose West Semitic onomastic environment is associated with the early second millennium B.C.

j. Jubal

Jubal (yûbāl יוּבָל) is the second son of Lamech and Adah, and the brother of Jabal (Genesis 4:21). As a QŪTĀL form derived from the root ybl, the name implies a passive meaning such as "brought in procession."[149] For further consideration of the root and its onomastic environment, cf. above under Jabal.

k. Tubal-Cain

Tubal-Cain (tûbal qayin תּוּבַל קַיִן) is the son of Lamech by Zillah, and the brother of Naamah (Gen 4:22). Tubal-Cain's name is the first compound form in the Bible. The Septuagint omits the second part of the name, which has led some scholars to regard it as a gloss.

Some have identified Tubal with the geographic name of Tabal, mentioned in Assyrian texts and located in eastern Anatolia (Barnett 1975:420-428; Yamauchi 1982:25).[150] If so, this etymology recalls that of Irad, which also may have its

---

[149] Cf. the possible relationship with the yôbēl, the Jubilee Year (North 1964:380).

[150] Cf. also the Tubal (tūbāl), son of Japheth in Genesis 10:2.

origin in a geographic name. The name appears in Ezekiel 27:13. There its association with metal trade resembles the association of Tubal-Cain with metalworking. The differences in context may provide grounds for some objection to this identification (Cassuto 1961:237; Westermann 1974:451). This provenance is also suggested by the publication of the Hittite-Hurrian bilingual inscription from Boghazköy. Dietrich and Loretz (1990a) have identified in this text the logogram for "(metal) smith," lú SIMUG, which is associated with the Hurrian ta-ba-li-iš. This word may be related to the geographic name, Tabal, which lies in or close to presumably Hurrian-speaking regions. It also could be applied to Tubal-Cain, as the first element of that name. In such a case, it could be that Tubal-Cain is a two element name in which either (1) one element serves as a gloss of the other, so that the two are synonyms; or (2) Cain is a root related Tubal in some other way, perhaps describing a particular type of (metal) smith.

Another etymology of Tubal occurs as a form of the root ybl which is the basis of the names Jabal and Jubal. For further discussion concerning the etymology and the onomastic environment of this root, see above under Jabal. A Hophal or a Qal passive of ybl, "to be brought" seems to appear in Tubal-Cain. The contextual relation of Tubal-Cain to his half brothers, all of whom might then possess names derived from a common root, would suggest that the author of Genesis 4:17-24 understood this latter etymology of Tubal as the most useful for the genealogical context.[151]

---

[151] In the light of the discussion under Jabal, which observes the frequent connection of the ybl root with divine names in onomastica, there may be some question as to whether Cain is to be understood as a divine name in Tubal-Cain. This seems unlikely for several reasons: (1) there is no evidence elsewhere for a divine name Cain; (2) such sentence names most often occur where the ybl element appears as i-ba-al. There are no examples of this type of name with a t-prefixed verb; (3) there are examples of the ybl root appearing in names without a divine element, so the latter should not be presumed as necessary.

For the etymology and onomastic environment of Cain, see under that name.

l. Naamah

Naamah (naʿămāh נַעֲמָה) is a sister of Tubal-Cain and the daughter of Zillah and Lamech (Gen 4:22). The name also appears:(1) as the mother of Rehoboam (I Kings 14:21); (2) as a town in the southwestern district of Judah (Joshua 15:41; Rainey 1983:7-10); and (3) as the home of Zophar, one of Job's comforters.[152]

The nʿm root means "to be pleasant;" "lovely" in Hebrew[153] and possibly Phoenician. A form of this root serves as a title of David in II Samuel 23:1.[154] A root, nʿm, which is related to singing, occurs in Ugaritic, later Hebrew, Syriac and Arabic (Gabriel 1959:418). The context provides no clear direction as to the preferred option (Wallis 1966:135).

Stamm (1967:323) finds semantic parallels in Akkadian and Egyptian, but rejects the Ugaritic parallel to a masculine name.[155] Noth (1928:166) finds the root as a predicate element in the biblical names אֲבִינֹעַם, אֲחִינֹעַם, אֶלְנַעַם, נַעַם, and נַעֲמִי. אֲחִינֹעַם and נַעֲמִי are feminine names. Noth also records א[ח]נעם,which appears in the Samaria ostraca.[156] To these Fowler (1988:351) adds the name נעמאל which occurs on a seal.[157] The root appears in personal names in Phoenician

---

[152] Sawyer 1986:159 locates this in Midian or Edom, along with the homes of Bildad (Shuah) and of Eliphaz (Teman).

[153] North 1964:379 suggests "Gorgeous." The association of the name with prostitution (Vermeylen 1991:176, 182) is unnecessary as the meaning is not limited to such a context.

[154] The expression is נְעִים זְמִרוֹת יִשְׂרָאֵל. See McCarter 1984:480, who translates it as "the darling of the stronghold of Israel."

[155] nʿmn (UM 64. 41; UM 80 i. 21; UM 311. 6; UM 321 i. 26; UM 321 iv. 2; PRU II 32. 2; 43. 8; 46. 39; 81. 12; in Gröndahl 1967:402. The semantic parallel cited above from the Baal epic is also masculine.

[156] 10. 2; 11. 2; 19. 4; but see Lemaire 1977 who reads here ʾdnʿm.

[157] Vattioni 1969 no. 95.

and Punic,[158] in Ammonite,[159] and in Aramaic.[160] The question of its occurrence in syllabic cuneiform may involve confusion with the root nḥm "to comfort."[161] nʿm may occur in personal names in Amorite,[162] at Ugarit,[163] and in first millennium B.C. cuneiform sources.[164]

Naamah has two possible etymologies, "to sing" or "to comfort." In either case, it has a West Semitic onomastic environment which occurs throughout all periods of the Ancient Near East.

2. Conclusions

---

[158]Some 21 possible instances in Benz 1972:362 including 14 feminine names such as nʿmlkt (CIS 41, 2), nʿmpʿm (CIS 2063, 2), nʿmt (CIS 4987, 1), and mtnʿmt (CIS 4744, 2).

[159]nʿmʾl (Jackson 1983a, Heshbon ostracon 1, 3); in Jackson 1983b:514.

[160]nʿmh (CIS 2, 118); in Vinnikov 1964:211; Maraqten 1988:92, 187.

[161]Thus Sivan 1984:250 finds this root attested in personal names in texts from Taanach (na-ma-di (4. 5); in Gustavs 1927-28:203) and from Alalakh (na-mi-^{d}da-gan (11. 33 [not 32]; 52. 23; 58. 23; 96. r 8; 274. 6); in Wiseman 1953:142; Sivan 1984:250). However, Wiseman also lists some 5 appearances of a na-aḫ-mi-^{d}da-gan, and suggests that both sets of references may reflect the same name. If so, its root may be nḥm rather than nʿm. For nḥm, there are numerous attestations of personal names; e.g. Sivan 1984:235. This also calls into question the Taanach example, and the example suggested, with reservations, by Coogan 1976:78 in the Murashu documents (na-aḫ-ma-nu (BE X 107.12; UM 209.12; TMHC 187.4)).

[162]Bauer 1926:78; Huffmon 1965:237-239; Gelb et al. 1980:26, 329. Among the 51 examples listed by Gelb, there are at least 15 feminine names. For example, there appears na-mi-ia (CT XLV 3. 8, 15, 23); ni-ḫi-ma (ARM IX 291 iii 36′); nu-ḫa-ma (ARM IX 291 ii 28); and a-bi-na-aḫ-mi (ARM 13 1 vii 43).

[163]Gröndahl 1967:163 lists some 12 different names including nu-ma-re-ša-ip; Ug V no. 98. 2; nu-me-nu; PRU IV p. 237 RS 17.251. 23 and Ug V no. 83. 4, 6, 11, 12, 17; nʿmn; UM 64. [CTA 87, KTU 4.33]. 41; 311. [CTA 91, KTU 4.96] 6; 321. [CTA 119, KTU 4.63] i 26; et al.

[164]Zadok 1978a:113, 116 provides two examples:New/Late Babylonian na-aḫ-ma-nu (BE IX 7. 30 lower edge); and Neo-Assyrian la-ni-iḫ-ma-a (ADD no. 365. r 4). Cf. also nim-ia(?)-u (Parker 1954:58 no. ND 2339. 13); in Zadok 1979:99.

This study has provided sufficient data to make some observations concerning the origins of the personal names of Genesis 4:17-24.

1. The etymologies of the names have confirmed our initial predisposition toward West Semitic as a means of identifying the elements. Of the twelve names, only one had no identifiable etymology, i.e. Lamech. Two may have contained geographic names, i.e. Irad and less likely Tubal-Cain. It should be noted that in both cases these names originated outside of the West Semitic geographical world. However, of the remaining nine names (ten if Tubal-Cain is included), all have possible associations with West Semitic elements. Of these, five of the single word names were interpreted as some sort of noun form. These include Cain, Enoch, Adah, Zillah, and Naamah. The names of the three brothers, Jabal, Jubal, and Tubal-Cain, possess verbal elements and may function as shortened forms of names containing a verbal element followed by a divine name. The remaining two names, Mehujael and Methushael, are each made up of two elements. The first was identified as a verbal sentence name and the second as a construct name. Only these two names, among those in Genesis 4:17-24, may have divine names as part of their constructions. If its second element is original, the name Tubal-Cain provides the sole example of a compound name.

2. The onomastic environment represented by these names varies. With respect to Irad and Lamech, we have little or no evidence of any certain parallels among Ancient Near Eastern names. Enoch has one parallel in an Israelite name of the patriarchal period. Cain may have later parallels in South Arabic onomastica. On the other hand, with regards to Mehujael, Adah, Zillah, and Naamah, numerous parallels exist throughout all periods of West Semitic onomastica. Methushael and the three brothers remain. If correctly identified, the mt or mutu element which forms the first part of the name of Methushael, occurs in Canaanite onomastica only in the second millennium B.C. A similar observation can be made of ybl, the root found in the name Jabal, Jubal,

and possibly Tubal-Cain. The only occurrences of this root in West Semitic personal names come from second and possibly third millennium B.C. sources. The preponderance of the evidence points to the early part of the second millennium B.C. as the period in which the names fit most comfortably.[165]

---

165 Such evidence argues against the view of Vermeylen 1991:181-182 that the names of Cain's line are creations of a first millennium redactor.

CHAPTER 4

THE GENEALOGY OF SETH

1. Genesis 4:25-26

a. Adam

As argued above, אָדָם here appears for the first time in Genesis as a personal name. The onomastic environment of the ʾdm element includes a sizeable quantity of material from cuneiform literature of the third and second millennia B.C. In the texts discovered and published from Tell Mardikh, the site of ancient Ebla, adam appears in personal names, divine names, and a month name.[166] As a personal name it appears as a-da-ma, a-da-mi, a-da-mu, a-dam-ma-lik.[167] As a divine name it appears as ^{d}a-da-ma, ^{d}a-da-ma-um, a-dam-ma, ^{d}a-dam-ma, ^{d}a-dam-ma-su, ^{d}a-dam-tum.[168] Several calendars have been published in which the name of a month appears containing the adam element:ITU ^{d}a-dam-ma-um, "month of the god Adama."[169] It may also be added here that, in the Eblaite vocabulary, ʾà-da-um TÚG appears. This seems to be related to the textile industry, but its meaning has not been

---

[166] As the study of the Eblaite script and language has only begun in the past few years, further research may call into question some of the readings proposed here.

[167] Pettinato 1979 Nos. 238, 929, 1671, 4966, 5043; 1980 Nos. 19 v. IX 2, 19 r. IV 4, 34 r. VII 4, 38 r. V 4, 19 r. VII 15; D1981:260, 274; Edzard, 1981 Nos. 3 X 5; 6 I 3; Archi and Biga 1982 Nos. 57 II 1, 335 II 11, 342 r. IV 7, 466 v. III 6, 501 I 2, 521 II 4, 599 r. II 3, 865 II 1, 917 r. I 2; Biga and Milano 1984 Nos. 5 r. II 6, 10 r. II 1, 16 r. VI 1, 16 r. IX 9; Archi 1985 Nos. 5 v. VI 20, 11 r. IV 4, 11 r. VII 15, 11 v. IX 2, 30 r. IX 6; Sollberger 1986 Nos. 521 6, 522 9, 526 24, 539 11, 541 3. See also Dahood 1978:274; 1980:55; 1980:278; Müller 1980:11; Krebernik 1988a:71, 75, 119-120; Gordon 1988:154.

[168] Pettinato 1979 Nos. 18, 55, 57, 82, 88, 90, 122, 140, 148, 158, 167, 181, 198, 203, 228, 1740; Edzard 1981 Nos. 5 I 2, 8 IV 4, 8 VII 3, 8 VIII 3; Archi and Biga 1982 Nos. 185 III 8, 337 v. VI 4, 358 VII 6, 359 II 1, 534 V 3; Biga and Milano 1984:17 v. II 17; Pomponio 1983:143.

[169] Pettinato 1976; 1977. See also Charpin 1982; Shea 1980; 1981a:65-66; 1981b.

determined.[170] The appearance of adam as a personal name in the Ebla texts is the single most significant feature to be observed. Insofar as no context exists for its use outside of personal names, the name a-dam-ma-lik may prove important for understanding the meaning of adam if it is possible to accept the interpretation of the name as "man of (the god) Malik."[171]

The 'dm root appears in Old Akkadian as a personal name in the forms, a-da-mu,'à-da-mu, and a-dam-u.[172] Among the thousands of personal names which have appeared in the publications of the volumes of Mari texts, only one name resembles the adam names, that of a-da-mu, a woman whose name appears once in the published texts.[173] The numerous personal names containing the element, admu, reflect a deity who may be related to the geographic name Admum and derive from the Amorite root 'dm , "red."[174] Probably this is also true of the divine names from the Sargonic and Ur III periods, šu-ad-mu and ^{d}Nin-admu.[175] No other occurrence of the adam root exists in the personal names from Mari. Several additional Amorite personal names with the adam form also occur.[176] The personal name, a-da-ma-nu is found in texts from Mananâ.[177] a-da-mu is found in a collection of texts from Chagar Bazar.[178] The name a-dam-te-lum is found

[170] Edzard 1981:118; Archi and Biga 1982:338; Archi 1985:275. Pettinato 1980:11, reads this vocable as é-da-um túg.

[171] Pettinato 1981:260.

[172] Cf. Gelb 1957:19.

[173] Dossin 1971 text I. 8; as cited in Birot 1979:49.

[174] H. B. Huffmon 1965:158-159; Biggs 1967; Gelb et al. 1980:13-14, 215. Of the 31 names with an 'dm root listed by Gelb, 23 have the ad-ma or ad-mu element, and nearly all of these are from the Mari texts. The exceptions include ad-mu, one name from Tell Harmal and one from Alalakh (cf. below). See also Rasmussen 1981.

[175] J. J. M. Roberts 1972:14; Pomponio 1983:140n34.

[176] These are listed in Gelb et al. 1980:215.

[177] Ruttøn 1960:19, 19 et passim; 28, 12.

[178] Gadd 1940:35, occurrences 989 and 995].

in a text from Dilbat.[179] We may add to these the a-da-mu who is second in the initial group of kings listed in the Khorsabad king list.[180]

What is remarkable is the absence of this form among personal names in West Semitic texts from the late second and first millennia B.C. Thus a brief survey of personal name collections gathered from inscriptions written in Semitic languages of this period reveals more in what is missing than in what is present. The personal names published from the Alalakh,[181] Amarna,[182] and Ugarit[183] texts do not preserve an adam element. Neither Akkadian[184] nor Hittite[185] personal name collections increase the inventory of adam names. When one examines the West Semitic inscriptions of the first millennium B.C., the situation is not much better. There is no evidence for the personal name in Aramaic.[186] A single occurrence of 'dm does appear as a personal name in a Punic text, but the reading is uncertain.[187] It may be 'rm. Two other Punic occurrences, mlk'dm and 'bd'dm, may reflect the existence of a deity, 'dm.[188] Perhaps most

[179] Gautier 1908 no. 31. 6. It may also be of interest to add the occurrence of the name a-du-mu in a Sumerian economic text of the Ur III period from Umma. Kang 1973:161, no. 115, line 8.
[180] Moran 1958:100.
[181] Wiseman 1953; Sivan 1984:195. Cf. however the one ad-mu name identified by Gelb et al.:215 as ia-am-i-id-dam-mu. Gelb cites Wiseman 1953 no. 60, line 4. However, Wiseman does not appear to translate or copy such in text no. 60.
[182] Hess 1984. Note that the a-ta-mu of EA 32. 1 is an incorrect reading. Cf. Hess 1985:162.
[183] Gröndahl 1967; Kinlaw 1967. See also Sivan 1984:195. We should note here the presence of a Hurrian divine name 'adm in a Hurrian text from Ugarit. See Ug V, 499:23. de Moor 1988:110 n29 and the literature cited there.
[184] Tallqvist 1906; 1914; Ranke 1905; Clay 1912; Saporetti 1970; Freydank and Saporetti 1979.
[185] Laroche 1966; 1981.
[186] Vinnikov 1958:189; DISO 4-5, 58; KAI III 53.
[187] Benz 1972:55. Cf. also KAI III 45.
[188] Benz 1972:138, 149, 260. At least in the case of the first example, such an interpretation remains only one among several that are possible.

remarkable of all is the lack of ʾdm as a personal name in Hebrew,[189] in the Biblical text, in extra-Biblical inscriptions of the pre-exilic period,[190] among the Jews in Babylon,[191] and among those at Elephantine.[192]

However, a divine name occurs in the late second millennium B.C. texts from Emar.[193] ^{d}a-dam appears there as a month name.[194] In at least one case, that of ^{d}a-dam-ma-te-[ri],[195] the name may appear as part of a divine name.

The personal name appears to be more at home the earlier one goes. It is quite rare in the late second and in the first millennia B.C. However, it is found earlier in Amorite, in Old Akkadian, and possibly at Ebla (again, if the evidence has been interpreted correctly). These attestations of personal names with spellings related to adam- add evidence to suggest that both a common noun and a personal name formed from the ʾdm root were in use in the third millennium B.C.

A final note considers the question of the relationship of Adam to the a-da-pa figure in Akkadian literature. This is important for consideration of Adam's onomastic environment since an identity of the two names could imply the need to recognize a-da-pa as a variant of Adam. The literary texts in which a-da-pa appears are found throughout the Ancient Near East, but the largest and most important fragment recounting the story of a-da-pa is found among the

---

189 Other than for the name bearer in Genesis 1-5.

190 Lawton 1984; Avigad 1986; Tigay 1986; Fowler 1988. The ʾdm bn yqmyhw in Arad inscription 39, line 1 requires a reconstruction of a missing aleph in the first name (Aharoni, Naveh, et al. 1981:68), something disputed by Lemaire 1977:206 who restores the name as qdm Qiddem.

191 Zadok 1978a; 1979.

192 Silverman 1985.

193 Arnaud 1985, 1986a, 1986b, 1987.

194 No. 110. 38. See also ^{d}a-dama, no. 446. 82′.

195 No. 465. 2′.

Amarna texts.[196] Thus the existence of this myth in the West Semitic world of the second millennium B.C., even if only as a scribal copy text imported from Babylonia,[197] requires consideration of a possible relationship between a-da-pa and אדם. The literary interpretation of the **a-da-pa** story has been debated on many points.[198] Its similarities and differences with the early chapters of Genesis have been noted. For example, G. Buccellati notes four similarities:

(1) "both are faced with the prohibition to partake of a certain food;"

(2) "The occasion to circumvent the prohibition coincides in both cases with a temptation coming from a third party, supernatural in character - and the temptation consists in presenting the forbidden food under an attractive light;"

(3) "Both traditions present the culprit as summoned directly by god into his presence."

(4) "the presumed ignorance of the events on the part of god" occurs in both cases.

Buccellati identifies the main difference between **a-da-pa** and אדם as:"the former remains obedient, whereas the latter betrays his trust." This is based upon a particular interpretation of the myth set forth by Buccellati but challenged by J. D. Bing. N.-E. Andreasen provides a similar set of parallels. The difference he finds in the narratives is based upon a more traditional understanding of the **a-da-pa** myth:

---

[196] For the text fragments and translation, see Speiser 1950 and the bibliography there. For the Amarna fragment, EA 356, see Knudtzon1915:964-969. See also von Soden 1976.

[197] Knudtzon 1915:25; Bing 1984:52n5.

[198] See de Liagre Böhl 1959; Roux 1961; Jacobsen 1970; Kienast 1973; Xella 1973; Buccellati 1973; Foster 1974; Shea 1977; Kienast 1978; Michalowski 1980; Andreasen 1981.

> Adapa is restrained by Ea from seeking immortality (presumptuously or even accidentally) in the court of Anu; Adam is restrained (unsuccessfully) from losing it. However, once Adam has lost his immortality, he too must be kept from seeking it anew (Gen 3:22fl).

An additional parallel, noted by a number of writers, is that both a-da-pa and Adam are prototypes or models of humanity. The role of an a-da-pa who appears in cuneiform texts as a wise man who may be contemporary with the first king may also be significant as a parallel with Adam, a figure portrayed as part of the first generation of humanity and as possessing wisdom to care for the garden and to name the animals.[199] Such relationships are of interest and may suggest a relationship between the two narratives. However, the distinctions must be kept in mind.

Of special interest here is the suggested relationship between the two names. Are a-da-pa and Adam simply two variants of the same name? While earlier attempts to read a-da-pa as a-da-mu$_6$ must be rejected due to the absence of such a value for the sign outside of Sumerian,[200] the question does arise as to the possibility of an interchange between the p and m bilabials. Indeed, there is the example in West Semitic of the Ugaritic špš [ša-ap-šu] corresponding to the Akkadian šamaš, the word for "sun."[201] However, this is the only such example and, if anything, tends to argue for an original m

---

[199]Jensen 1928; Reiner 1961; Hallo 1963:54; 1970:62, Andreasen 1981:188; Shea 1977:35-37. The following cautions should be observed: (1) the designation of a-da-pa as a sage (nun.me) or priest (me) of Eridu first appears only in texts from the Neo-Assyrian period, and the latter appears in a broken context where the name of a-da-pa is restored on the basis of an epithet; (2) the association of a-da-pa with the first antediluvian king appears first in a Neo-Assyrian text. For Adam as sage, see Alonso-Schökel 1976:54. For Adam as symbolic of a king in these chapters, see Wyatt 1981:15, 20.
[200]See de Liagre Böhl 1959:418n3.
[201]See Sivan 1984:37.

which became p. Such an analogy would suggest an original Adam becoming a-da-pa.

Adam in the genealogy of Genesis is a personal name. Its occurrence as the first name in the genealogy, and its role in the stories of Genesis 2-3, may suggest a figure who is presented as the Urvater of the human race, i.e. a mythical figure, a "divine Adam" inserted in what may be a later genealogy of personal names. This may be suggested by the usage of adam or ʾdm as a divine name in the West Semitic world throughout much of the same period as it appears as a personal name, and by a possible relationship to Adapa. However, evidence from Ugaritic and Phoenician, where ʾdm appears in titles (e.g. ʾab ʾadm) and in mythological contexts, suggests that the term consistently is used to distinguish humanity from divinity (Wallace 1992: 62). This implies a "human Adam." The same is true in Genesis. This is important because it argues for the selection of the "human Adam" rather than the "divine Adam" by the author of the biblical text. Such a conclusion would agree with the wordplay with the common nouns, ʾādām and ʾᵃdāmâ, as used in the Genesis text (see below) and with the linguistic and Ancient Near Eastern context in which ʾādām functions as the title of the human in charge of the garden.[202]

b. Seth

The onomastic environment of Seth (šēt שֵׁת) draws upon its etymological relationship to the West Semitic š/śyt "to place." This root appears in many West Semitic languages of the second and first millennia.[203] In personal names, it

---

[202]Cf. Hess 1990b, where the function of the logogram lú as a title to describe leaders of towns and cities is compared with the usage of ʾādām in Genesis 2. Linguistic precedent for a shift from a title to a personal name is also noted. Thus is is more likely that the personal name, Adam, had its origins in the title describing the function of the man in Genesis 2-3 than that it originated some other mythical context.

[203]At Ugarit it is vocalized as ši-tu in the polyglot vocabularies (Ug V 130 iii 10′; Sivan 1984:277; Huehnergard 1987b:181).

occurs in Amorite names from Mari,[204] in names from Ugarit,[205] and in Punic names.[206] In the last, the verb is compounded with what may be the divine name, Baal. In the other names, the shortened verbal forms and hypocoristic endings also invite the view that names with this element regularly have a divine name appended or implied as subject. Thus the wordplay on the name in Genesis 4:25, where אֱלֹהִים "God" forms the subject to the verb שָׁת "has placed."

The possible connection of Seth with the Sutu tribe remains an interesting suggestion.[207] The nature and source of this relationship remains unproven and uncertain, however. In any case, we lack any apparent significance for the use of such a relationship in the text of Genesis.

c. Enosh

Enosh (ʾĕnôš אֱנוֹשׁ) means "human" in Hebrew. It forms a synonym with the Hebrew root underlying the name of Adam (Maass 1973). Its most common usage occurs in poetic texts where parallelism demands a synonym for the more frequent root, ʾdm. Thus both roots have the same meaning and both appear here in the genealogy as personal names but nowhere else in personal names in the Hebrew Bible. In fact,

---

[204] The most common form occurs with a prefix, e.g. ia-ši-tum (ARM XIII 98. 3). Although Huffmon 1965:253 cites no other types in Amorite, Gelb 1980:349 cites ma-ši-it-a-nu-um (an Isin period name cited in Buccellati 1966) and the feminine name ši-ta-tum (ARM XIII 1. iv 74).

[205] Always with suffixes: ša-ta(?)-na (PRU III RS 16.257 3. 58); šty (PRU V 80. 13; 89. 1; 159. 14); in Gröndahl 1967:196.

[206] In compounds: blšt (CIS 2182. 3/4); bʿlšt (CIS 495. 3/4; 3777. 2?); in Benz 1972:426.

[207] On the Sutu and their relationship to Seth see, Heltzer 1982. Mazar 1986:6 n13 comments: "The Šutu tribes (cf. Num 24:17, where the 'sons of Seth' appear as a synonym of Moab) are referred to in the Execration Texts and are known to us from cuneiform sources (beginning in the reign of Rim-sin of Larsa and expecially in the Mari documents) as nomadic tribes in the region of the Euphrates, in the Syrian Desert and in the kingdom of Qaṭna in central Syria."

the root of Enosh, ʾnš, occurs in no other personal name attested in West Semitic. As will be suggested below, its obvious Hebrew etymology serves a literary function as the beginner of a new line of the descendants of Seth; i.e., as a second Adam.

d. Conclusions

1. Wordplay, either implicit or explicit, exists for the three names. The text makes explicit the intended wordplay on Seth's name. It leaves implicit the wordplay on the name Enosh. That Enosh parallels Adam becomes evident from the etymologies of the two names. The role of the two roots in relation to one another elsewhere in Biblical Hebrew may point to the role of Enosh as a second Adam. Implicit wordplay exists for Adam in the relation of that name to Enosh. At the beginning of chapter five the text summarizes the implications of Adam as a personal name and the origins of that name in the earlier chapters of Genesis.

2. The onomastic environment of the three names differs. Adam appears in personal names only in the early West Semitic world, that of the third and second millennia B.C. and perhaps earlier. The root of Seth appears in personal names throughout the second and first millennia B.C. Enosh never occurs as a personal name.

2. Genesis 5:1-32

a.-c. Adam, Seth, and Enosh

On these names, see the above discussion.

d. Kenan

Kenan (qênān קֵינָן) has an initial set of three consonantal signs which are identical to those of Cain. Indeed, the name divides into two parts, Cain (qyn) followed by a nun vocalized as -ān in the MT (and in all versions). This suffix, along with -ōn, commonly occurs in West Semitic personal names of all periods.[208] Noth (1928:38) has proposed that we identify this ending with a diminutive sense and render Kenan as "little Cain," i.e., a second Cain (Diakonoff 1982:17). However, Noth's other examples need not be interpreted as diminutives. Instead, the general identification of -ān as a hypocoristic suffix better accords with the evidence.[209] Note, however, the presence of a deity qynn Kenan(?), in Sabaean inscriptions (Ryckmans 1934:30).

e. Mahalalel

Mahalalel (mahălal'ēl מַהֲלַלְאֵל) seems to have an obvious etymology, related to two roots, hll "to praise" and 'l "god" or the DN "El." The mem preformative on the hll root may suggest an original participial form ("praising god/El") or a nominal form ("praise of god/El"). In either case, the name expresses worship to the deity, perhaps in the context of the birth of the child.

Both roots generate names in many periods of West Semitic. Among biblical examples of the hll root,[210] the name itself recurs as an ancestor of one of the Jerusalemites of Nehemiah 11:4. Elsewhere in the West Semitic world, this root appears in Amorite personal names from Mari and other places in the Old Babylonian period and earlier (Birot 1979:97, 108; Gelb 1980:19, 247). Huffmon (1965:195), however, understands a number of the Mari forms as derived from a ḫll root, which he identifies with the Arabic ḫalīl, "friend."[211] Gröndahl (1967:133) finds one possible name

[208] Noth 1928:38; Huffmon 1965:135-138; Sivan 1984:97; Silverman 1985:125.
[209] For another example of this suffix, see the analysis of Haran in the discussion of the genealogy of chapter eleven.
[210] hll (Judges 12:13, 15); yhll'l (I Chronicles 4:16 and II Chronicles 29:12); in Noth 1928:205; Fowler 1988:342.
[211] Indeed, it is difficult to demonstrate that all of Gelb's examples are from this root, especially those lacking an initial ḫ, e.g. a-li-lu-um, a-li-la-ḫa-du-um, e-la-li. Of special interest for Mahalalel is the prefixed form, ma-aḫ-li-lum.

from Ugarit with a hll root, h(?)lhd. Otherwise, no clear examples of this root exist in West Semitic names. Thus, in addition to the few Biblical examples, we have examples of this root used in West Semitic names from the late third and early second millennia B.C.

f. Jared

Jared (yered יֶרֶד) lacks any notation concerning the name or its meaning. Explanations for the name Jared include: (1) the Hebrew word for "rose" (Noth 1928:231); (2) the Akkadian word for "servant," (w)ardu (HALAT II 416); (3) the Arabic word for "courageous;" (4) the Hebrew root, yrd "to descend." Noth's proposed etymology does not occur elsewhere in Classical Hebrew. While the Akkadian (w)ardu often occurs in personal names, the word does not appear in West Semitic. There it is replaced by the root ʿbd, which is rendered abdu in cuneiform.[212] The suggestion of an Arabic cognate goes even farther afield.

On the other hand, the root, yrd does appear in West Semitic personal names. It appears in at least two Amorite names of the second millennium B.C.: ia-ri-du-um[213] and i-ri-da-nu-um.[214] A possible occurrence has also been suggested in an Alalakh text.[215] Reading the initial PI sign as ya, Sivan 1984:292 identifies the personal name, ya-ra-du. In Hebrew the same spelling for the name occurs as a Yered in I Chronicles 4:18 (Zadok 1988:212). The name yrd, occurs in Old South Arabic.[216] Understood as based upon the root, yrd, "to descend,"[217] Jared is a name with West Semitic parallels in the second and first millennia B.C. The attestations are simply the verbal form. Whether or not this is a shortened

---

[212] Although often in personal names both ardu and abdu are not spelled syllabically, but are represented by the logogram, ÌR.
[213] ARM III 65. 6; in Birot 1979:127.
[214] UCP X/1 109.3; in Gelb 1980:276.
[215] No. 158 lines 5′ and 9′.
[216] RES 4650. 1; in Müller 1963:310.
[217] So also, in their respective examples, Gelb 1980:22 and Sivan 1984:292.

form of a name with a divine element (which would request or give thanks for a heavenly deity descending to aid at the time of birth or some other time), is uncertain.

g. Enoch

The name Enoch (ḥănôk חֲנוֹךְ) has received study above in the section on Genesis 4. We have noted the name's etymology in the root meaning "to introduce, initiate," as well as its limited onomastic environment.

h. Methuselah

Methuselah (mĕtûšelaḥ מְתוּשֶׁלַח) comprises two elements: mt "man, husband," and šlḥ. Scholars have identified the second element as a weapon, a canal, or a divine name (Skinner 1930:131-132; Driver 1948:77, 81). The evidence suggests preference for an association with a divine name. The formula, mt plus DN, occurs in early West Semitic names from Amarna and Ugarit.[218] Scholars have suggested two possibilities for DNs. First, there is Laḥ, coupled with the antecedent relative pronoun š (van Selms 1966:318-326). Second, others have set forth a DN based on the šlḥ root (Tsevat 1954a; Loretz 1975). The first alternative seems unlikely because of the lack of this relative (mt + ša + divine name) elsewhere in personal names (cf. Methushael).[219] The preference for the second alternative, with a construct relationship between two nouns, seems more likely. This would interpret the name as "man (i.e. devotee) of the deity Šalaḥ." In proposing this understanding, Tsevat has identified Šalaḥ as god of the infernal river. However, we do not find such a deity attested outside of personal names.

---

[218]mu-ut-ba-aḫ-l[ù] (EA 255, 3); mu-ut-dIM (EA 256, 2, 5); mu-ut-dU (PRU III p. 205; RS 16.155. 6; PRU IV p. 234; RS 17.112. 6); in Sivan 1984:250. On the 'u' in Methuselah as a nominative case vowel, cf. Layton 1990:73-74.

[219]Cf., however, the suggestion for this element in personal names at Ebla by Gordon 1988:154. He interprets names such as šu-i-lum as "Man of God." Note that this and his other examples have no antecedent to the pronoun, however.

Another difficulty with this approach remains the odd mention of a DN in a line which the text describes as devoted to the worship of Israel's god. However, the interpretation remains plausible. DNs attested only in personal names do occur. The presence of a DN in the names of this line may not be as unique as first seems. The name Kenan, even if related to Cain in its present location in the genealogy, may ultimately find its origin in a DN. As observed above, Mahalalel may also have the DN El present. Further, the minimum information available on this name means we do not know anything about the identity of the figure represented by Šalaḥ. Therefore, we may find here a divine epithet of some sort rather than a DN per se.

i. Lamech

Lamech (lemek לֶמֶךְ) received attention when the same named figure appeared in the line of Cain. We observed the lack of a clear etymology or onomastic environment for the name.

j. Conclusions

These conclusions will take into account all names in the linear genealogy from Adam to Lamech, nine generations.

1. Of the nine names studied, seven had clear etymologies, while two (Kenan and Lamech), though related to names in the Cainite line, had no obvious etymology. From those with etymologies, we learn the following:

(1) the construct formation "man (i.e. devotee) of DN" occurs once in full (Methuselah), and less likely in a shortened form with only the first element (Adam). A third occurrence of "man" or "humanity," Enosh could also reflect such an instance though we have no evidence that here is anything other than the single noun.

(2) Three simple verbal roots exist (Seth, Jared, and Enoch). Evidence exists for Seth that the name occurs with a DN, declaring divine (re)placement of the child. We have not the same onomastic evidence for Jared as a shortened form, omitting a DN, but the same could apply, signaling the declaration of a divine visit. With Enoch, the idea of a divine introduction could reflect the shortening of the name by the omission of a DN. However, the lack of any widespread onomastic environment for this name reduces all hypothesis to conjecture.

(3) One other name (Mahalalel) consists of a participle or noun followed by a noun and thus creating a sentence name. This name declares praise either to a general deity or to El.

2. Of the nine personal names, five have attestation in the onomastica of the West Semitic world (Adam, Seth, Mahalalel, Jared, Methuselah). This number includes Methuselah, though the second element of this name occurs nowhere else as an onomastic element except in a name in the genealogy of Genesis 11. Most of the name elements find their use in names of both the second and first millennia B.C. However, two, Adam and the first element in Methuselah, occur in Canaanite onomastica no later than the second millennium. Thus the best environment for these names, likes those of the line of Cain, seems to be the West Semitic world not later than the second millennium B.C.

CHAPTER 5

THE TABLE OF NATIONS IN GENESIS 10

1. Introduction

We will not examine most of the names listed only in the genealogy of chapter 10. This is due to the nature of these names as place names and gentilics, and therefore not primarily personal names. The purpose of this chapter is to show that the known world at the time of writing the text included all these peoples and places. Implicit in the enumeration lies the observation that all peoples, cities, and nations trace their descent to a common origin, and share a common heritage. Whether we find the divisions in this chapter to suggest linguistic, cultural, or ethnic features, these names reflect a universal consciousness not perceived elsewhere in the contemporary world. Although primarily a simple list of proper names, two notes occur in the genealogy of Ham. One concerns Nimrod in vv. 8-10 and another discusses the boundaries of Canaan in vv. 18-20. The latter has geographical interest first encountered in Genesis 14. It has continued significance as a description of the boundaries of the land which the Israelites are charged with possessing. The former, Nimrod, includes the only obviously personal name among the "descendants" of Japheth and Ham.

2. The Names

a. Nimrod

The note concerning Nimrod (נִמְרֹד nimrōd) contains the one name in the genealogies of Japheth and Ham which seems to be personal. The figure which Nimrod represents in the narrative has been associated with historical figures such as Sargon of Akkad and Tukulti-Ninurta I,[220] with mythological

---

[220] See the equation of Nimrod with Assyria in Micah 5:5.

figures such as Gilgamesh, with deities such as Marduk and Ninurta, and with some ideal of kingship.[221] Von Soden (1960) argued for the association of the name Nimrod with the Sumero-Babylonian god of war and hunting, Ninurta. Ninurta protected the Assyrian kings in war and while hunting.[222] A similarity between the two name and a likeness in their attributes, as well as the association of both with Mesopotamia, may suggest a common origin in the past, connected with a figure who was or became legendary. The particular vocalization of the name is related to its form in Hebrew as a first common plural imperfect Qal stem of the root מרד, i.e. "we will rebel."[223] This root does not occur in West Semitic onomastica until the later Palmyrene and Epigraphic South Arabic inscriptions.[224]

b. Joktan

The genealogy of Shem in Genesis 10 also includes many gentilics and place names. The line from Shem to Abram

---

[221] For a summary of these views, see Wenham 1987:222. Summaries of positions are also found in van der Toorn and van der Horst 1990. While admitting uncertainty as to the philological relationship, van der Toorn argues for an association of Nimrod with the deity Ninurta, whose portrayal as a divine warrior in the Sumerian LUGAL-E, functions as an image of a mighty hunter of mythical beasts, a constructor of dykes, an introducer of agriculture, and ruler of the gods and cosmos. Cf. also Lambert 1965:298-299.

[222] Cf. van der Toorn and van der Horst 1990. While admitting uncertainty as to the philological relationship, van der Toorn argues for an association of Nimrod with the deity Ninurta, whose portrayal as a divine warrior in the Sumerian LUGAL-E, functions as an image of a mighty hunter of mythical beasts, a constructor of dykes, an introducer of agriculture, and ruler of the gods and cosmos. Cf. also Lambert 1965:298-299.

[223] Zimmermann's 1966:319 suggestion to connect this name with the Hebrew word נָמֵר "leopard" seems less likely as it leaves the final daleth unexplained and does not serve the broader context any better. Indeed, the text itself provides no indication that the name should be an animal. If such were the case, it would be the only known example in the onomastica of Genesis 1-11.

[224] For the Palmyrene name, mrd, see Stark 1971:37, 97. However, Stark identifies the name as a substantive, "rebel;" not as a verb. For the Epigraphic South Arabic evidence, see Ryckmans 1934 I 132.

which appears in chapter 11 runs to the fifth generation from Shem in this chapter. These names appear in the midst of the others. The degree to which they are personal names will be considered in our examination of the line for Genesis 11.

Joktan (yoqṭān יָקְטָן) is the only personal name in the genealogy of Shem which appears in chapter 10 but not in 11. The etymology of Joktan has a clear relationship to the West Semitic root qṭn "be small." The presence of South Arabian tribal names in the descendants of Joktan has led to observations concerning the traditional ancestor of these groups (Winnett 1970:181; Simons 1959:48-49). As this name does not appear in written sources until the Islamic period, there is no question of any influence on the name in Genesis 10, whatever Qaḥṭān's own origins may be. A similar conclusion may suggest itself in terms of comparisons with Sabaean name formations based on the qṭn root (Ryckmans I 1934:190; Biella 1982:452).

In Ancient Near Eastern onomastica, a qṭn root occurs in all periods: in the third millennium Old Akkadian period,[225] at second millennium Ugarit,[226] and in first millennium Aramaean[227] and Phoenician/Punic[228] personal names. QATUL, QUTAL, QATIL, and QATLU forms occur; though no prefixed forms, as in Joktan. Although some of the attestations may reflect the Akkadian cognate "to be thin, slender,"[229] or less likely a possible Hurrian word for an implement, qà?-ti-nu-[ma?],[230] the root's presence in West Semitic onomastica argues for a West Semitic etymology in the majority of cases. This suggests that, whatever its origin, Joktan is understood as a common personal name. At the

---

[225] qá-aṭ-núm, D; in Gelb 1957:227.
[226] qa-ṭú-na (PRU III RS 15.168. 4); qu-ṭá-ni, (PRU VI 43 v. 11'); in Gröndahl 1967:177, 349:Kinlaw 1967:97, 314-315; Sivan 1984:262. Sivan also identifies the place name Qaṭna with this root (p. 261).
[227] qà-ṭi-nu (BE 9, 28a.14); in Zadok 1977b:124.
[228] See Benz 1972:403.
[229] Kinlaw 1967:314-315.
[230] PRU VI 157. 11. For discussion of this word see Huehnergard 1987b:174.

same time, the root does occur as a verb in Hebrew. Like Nimrod, Joktan is a prefixed verbal form.

CHAPTER 6

THE GENEALOGY OF SHEM IN GENESIS 11

1. The Names

a. Arpachshad

Arpachshad (*'arpakšad* אַרְפַּכְשַׁד) appears as the only son of Shem named in Genesis 11. In chapter ten, however, Arpachshad appears alongside several "siblings:" Elam, Ashur, Lud, and Aram.[231] Although the identification of Lud has not found agreement among scholars, there is no doubt that these four names are place names. Arpachshad's position in their midst suggests we may find in it a place name as well. Indeed, attempts[232] to find in the first part of Arpachshad the place name *Arrapḫa*, with its identification at Kirkuk, suggest we might have a location which could fit well within the geographic context of Elam, Ashur, and Aram. The second part of the name has been equated with *kaśdîm*, the gentilic for Chaldeans. *Arrapḫa*, a city frequently mentioned in the Nuzi texts, would suggest a Hurrian etymology for this name. Another suggestion would identify the initial letters of Arpachshad with the Hurrian name element, *arip*.[233] Such explanations, while providing a reason for the absence of Babylon from the Table of Nations,[234] require phonological shifts which, though possible, are not certain and remain hypotheses which await a better knowledge of the non-Semitic language.

---

[231] Arpachshad's occurrence as third in the list of Shem's offspring in Genesis 10:22 is not proof that he was not the eldest son as suggested by 11:10. The order of names in the Table of Nations may reflect a geographical or some other organization.

[232] See especially Albright 1924:388-389; Cazelles 1973:22.

[233] Gordon 1962.

[234] Simons 1959:9-10. It does appear in the story of Nimrod in 10:10.

Perhaps we should confess our ignorance as to the etymology of the term. It may be that the earliest writers of the text also held this view. This may help to explain the odd **pataḥ-shewa** pattern which repeats itself three times in the name. It may suggest an artificiality in the pronunciation, reflecting the loss of an original understanding of the name with its six consonants and non-Semitic appearance.[235] Thus the context of Arpachshad among the place names of Genesis 10, the possible relationship to known place names, and the repetitive pattern of the vocalization point to an originally non-Hebrew, possibly non-Semitic, element or elements which reflect a place name. If a Hurrian place name is intended, or even a Hurrian term, the provenance for Arpachshad's origin could be in the Hurrian homeland or a center of its occupation such as northeastern Syria and the **Ḫabur** river valley.

The personal name Arpachshad occurs nowhere else in West Semitic.[236] It therefore has no onomastic environment. As observed, attempts to relate the name to either the Hurrian geographical or linguistic environment rest upon apparent phonological similarities. Attempts to associate the name with place names rest upon its literary context in Genesis 10. Thus, while such possibilities do exist it seems best to reserve judgment until the place of the other names in the genealogy of Shem can be identified.

---

[235]Sagarin 1987:146-147 identifies a mishqal of the form קַלְקֵל which appears in Hebrew. He identifies four Biblical nouns of a quadriliteral form in this pattern, גַּלְגַּל wheel, זַלְזַל shoot, תַּלְתַּל date tree cluster. However, of these, only the first appears in a singular form in the Hebrew text in such a way as to indicate the pattern described here. גַּלְגַּל is a common Semitic word. However, these forms are unlike Arpachshad, with its six consonant pattern. Sagarin provides no example of such a mishqal for Hebrew nouns.

[236]Arpachshad appears as a Median ruler defeated by Nebuchadnezzar in the deuterocanonical/apocryphal account of Judith (Judith 1:1). That this figure has no attestation elsewhere suggests an attempt by a Hellenistic author to fit an otherwise unknown figure in Shem's genealogy into some sort of historical context. The identification of Arpachshad with a Scythian king and an Iranian etymology (Brandenstein 1954:60, 62) is speculative.

b. Shelah

The Masoretic Text defines Shelah (šelaḥ שֶׁלַח) as the son of Arpachshad.[237] The name Methuselah in the line of Seth has as its second element the same triradical element as Shelah. This also applies to its Masoretic vocalization. As noted with the name Methuselah, we may best understand this element as a DN or an epithet which, although unattested elsewhere, does seem a likely way of interpreting the root, especially given the structure of the name Methuselah. Such an understanding would apply to the name Shelah as well. In terms of onomastic environment, a personal name, šlḥn, appears in Old South Arabic,[238] but we lack clear evidence that the root represented here should be understood as the one in the Biblical text. As a personal name the root appears nowhere else in the Biblical text outside Genesis 1-11.[239]

The possibility of a place name as part of the origin of Arpachshad has been noted. Can the same be true for Shelah? On the surface, there seems to be no objection. Even if Shelah represents a deity, the appearance of DNs in place names does occur, though usually not alone. Nor is the existence of a GN in the form reflected by Methuselah without precedent. From Alalakh we have the example mu-ut-ḫa-la-ab, in which the second half of the name represents the place name Aleppo.[240] The only problem with this understanding is the lack of evidence for a place name such as Shelah. The analogy with the second element found in

---

[237] The LXX, the Apocrypha (Jubilees 8:1), and the New Testament (Luke 3:36) place a Cainan in the genealogy between Arpachshad and Shelah. However, in the Masoretic Text the genealogies of Shem and Seth parallel one another in terms of number of generations. This parallel no longer exists if we follow the LXX and later texts. Further, no mention of Cainan occurs in the genealogy of Shem in the Table of Nations.

[238] RES 2687, 1; as in Müller 1963:315.

[239] Neither Shelah, the third son of Judah (Genesis 38:5), nor his descendants, the Shelanites (Numbers 26:20), share the final ḥeth found in the Shelah under consideration here.

[240] Alalakh Text 271. 3; in Wiseman 1959:29; Sivan 1984:250.

Methuselah and its identification as a DN remains more likely.

c. Eber

Eber (ʿēber עֵבֶר) fits in the third slot from Shem after Shelah and before Peleg and Joktan. From the association of the name Eber with the Hebrews of the Bible (Wenham 1987:228),[241] scholars have found several possible explanations for the name: (1) Eber is part of the place name in Akkadian, eber nāri, "beyond the river;"[242] (2) Eber defines an ethnic group (Skinner 1930:218-220; Malamat 1968a:166-167; Koch 1969:39-40, 71-78; Loretz 1984:183-190), especially related to the apiru;[243] (3) Eber refers only to the personal name in a genealogical list (Westermann 1974:700-701); (4) Eber is a socio-political group characterized as nomadic;[244] (5) More recently, the name Eber has been related to the name of Ebrium (eb-rí-um), a king of the third millennium B.C. Syrian city of Ebla (Matthiae 1976:109; Pettinato 1976:47). This last suggestion was considered a possibility (Archi 1979:565; Loretz 1984:190-192) but is becoming increasingly doubtful.[245] These theories involve identifications which span three

---

[241] עִבְרִי[ם] is first applied to Abram in Genesis 14:13 and does not reappear in Genesis until the Joseph story (39:14 and five other times). The association with Abram in Genesis 14, the most international of the Abramic narratives, recalls the Table of Genesis and "all the sons of Eber." Eber's sons included his descendants in Abram at least from the time of the association of chapters ten and fourteen (contra Haran 1970:288 n35).

[242] For this opinion, see as early as Gunkel 1902:80 as well as Cazelles 1973:22. Thompson 1974:305-306 shares this view for the etymology of "Hebrew" though he does not confirm it for Eber.

[243] On this see the review of the evidence for these people in the second millennium B.C. in Bottéro 1954, Greenberg 1955, and Loretz 1984.

[244] Oded 1986:19-22. Oded also notes the parallel with the figures in the line of Cain in Genesis 4. He focuses on Jabal who is the father of the tent-dwellers. For Oded's purposes this figure's "contribution" to culture has a closer affinity with the distinctions he makes in the Table of Nations. However, the phrase which describes the achievements of Jubal remains closer in form to that which describes Eber.

[245] See Krebernik 1988a:39, who now posits a wholly different verbal root for this name.

millennia and include a wide geographical area within the West Semitic environment.

In fact, the etymology of the name enjoys some agreement. The root of Eber, ʿbr, "to cross over (water)," may appear as a verb in West Semitic and Akkadian. As a West Semitic personal name Eber's possible onomastic environment has a broad range. Although it probably does not include third millennium Ebla (unless the identification of the ʿbr root with Ebrium is correct), it is found in second millennium Alalakh and Taanach,[246] and in first millennium Biblical Hebrew.[247] The name here is a personal name, although holding obvious associations with the gentilic for "Hebrew."

d. Peleg

Peleg (peleg פֶּלֶג) occurs fourth in the line after Shem and fifth before Abram. The etymology of Peleg may be traced to three possible sources: (1) a Hebrew root; (2) an Akkadian root; or (3) a place name. As to the first, this is the direction taken by the text itself. The root פלג can mean "to divide" and refer to

[246]This is the case if we accept as from this root DUMU-ḫu-bi-ri (Taanach 3 obv. 8); and ḫa-bu-ri (AT 90. 1); in Gustavs 1927-1928:199; Sivan 1984:205. Although Sivan lists ḥbr, "unite" and "search for," as possible roots, these seem less likely since they lack onomastic attestation elsewhere. The presence of the "u" vowel after the first or second root consonant of both examples suggests that these names are not to be associated with the apiru who are not so spelled in these texts. Sivan's other example, a-ba-ra, seems doubtful due to the absence of indication of the initial ʿayin. Further, ʿbr element(s) appear in contemporary names. Of the examples, the one from Taanach holds particular interest with its DUMU "son of" logogram as the first element. This compares with the phrase "sons of Eber" in Genesis 10.
[247]In the MT, this includes at least three personal names: (1) first among three sons of Elpaal, a Benjaminite (I Chronicles 8:12); (2) second of eleven sons of Shashak, a Benjaminite (I Chronicles 8:22); (3) leader of a priestly clan of Amok among the returnees to Jerusalem after the Exile (Nehemiah 12:20). A personal or clan name from the territory of Gad is mentioned in I Chronicles 5:13. See Zadok 1988:242, 243, 251, 265. It should be noted that in all these examples there are Hebrew manuscripts which, along with the LXX, read as a variant a name reflecting the ʿbd root, "serve; servant." This is probably another example of the ד/ר confusion in copying manuscripts.

the act of division. Here it could function as an appellative (Malamat 1968a:166). As a verb it appears only in the niphal and the piel stems. In Akkadian we find **palgu**, "canal." This occurs throughout all periods in Akkadian as a common noun, from Old Akkadian (Gelb 1957:214) onwards. When compared with Joktan, it provides a third possible explanation for the name, a division between the settled irrigation engineers of early Mesopotamian city origins and the nomadic tribes of the descendants of Joktan. In the context, however, such an explanation seems speculative. The West Semitic root would seem the more likely of the two possibilities, given a similar source for other names in this genealogy.

The third option, as a geographic name, is plausible, not only in terms of the context of the genealogy of Shem already noted, but also because examples of this root have been found in place names of the Ancient Near East. One suggestion for this approach observes the Hellenistic Phalga, lying probably at the junction of the Upper Euphrates and its branch, the Balikh (Thompson 1974:306; HALAT 878). However, we should note that the earliest mention of this place occurs in a Byzantine source which locates it in Seleucia and Mesopotamia.[248] There are other possibilities: Arabian place names (Thompson 1974:306); Old Babylonian **pulukkum** (Hallo 1964:69; Groneberg 1980:186); and New Babylonian **pallukkatu** (Zadok 1985:245-246).

A final conclusion is not possible. There is the explanation of the text which favors a Hebrew root. We have seen that such explanations do not necessarily correspond to the origin or meaning of the name based on its elements. Nevertheless, it at least represents the association made in the text. The Akkadian root seems less likely unless it is associated with a place name such as those suggested. Of course, the same could be true of the West Semitic root. The original meaning of the place name could refer to a division between territories as easily as it could to an irrigation project

[248] PW Band 19. 2, Halbband 38, col. 1668.

in the region. The Akkadian suggestion does link the name with the Euphrates and its tributaries. Taking both possibilities into account, we suggest one of the many sites among the Northern Mesopotamian sources of the Euphrates.

The onomastic environment is limited. One personal name, found on a seventh century text from Ur, pal-gu, remains the only attestation.[249] This name, too, could be either Akkadian or West Semitic (Aramaic).[250] Such a limited onomastic environment points to the unusual aspect of the name as a personal name and to the possibility that it reflects a place name, whether etymologically West Semitic or Akkadian.

e. Reu

Reu (rĕʿû רְעוּ) ranks fifth in line from Shem. Attempts to determine an etymology might begin with a study of the name and possible associations with geographic names. The Neo-Assyrian toponym Til-Ra-ḫa-a-ú-a has been proposed as possibly containing a similar root. However, the vocalization is different. Therefore the possibility of a direct derivation seems doubtful.[251]

We have more success when we try to identify an etymology in the West Semitic inventory of roots. In fact, we can find three possibilities for the consonants rʿw, reflecting a West Semitic root rʿh, and meaning "to give pasture" and so "shepherd," "to associate with" and so "friend," and "to be content" and so "one who is pleasing; pleasing." Unfortunately, both the difficulty of identifying the second and third root letters in cuneiform and other scripts and the

---

[249] Ur Excavation Texts 4. 23. 30; in Zadok 1977b:334. The possible reading plg appears in Damascus Covenant 20. 22. However, the text is broken and the reading and its interpretation are uncertain. Such limited attestation as a place name argues against a West Semitic meaning for the name as referring to the birth of the child, i.e. "division" in the sense of "breach of the womb."

[250] As Zadok observes.

[251] Zadok 1978b:176; Layton 1990:97; see Parpola 1970:354.

wide onomastic attestation of these homonymous roots create problems for identifying one etymology as certain among these possibilities. Note that the attestations of the third option in personal names are all late in the first millennium.[252] Elsewhere in the Bible we find the name compounded with the element for God, אל. This produces the name Reuel, "God/El is a shepherd/friend," which we find as a son of Esau in Genesis 36, as a father-in-law of Moses in Exodus 2, and as a Benjaminite ancestor of one of the returnees in I Chronicles 9:8 (Zadok 1988:267; Layton 1990:91-94). The root also may occur in the name of a tribal leader from Naphtali, אֲחִירַע.[253]

In addition the West Semitic root may appear in personal names from Amorite sources,[254] as well as in Ugaritic,[255] and Aramaic (Zadok 1977b:87, 290)[256] and Punic (Benz 1971:409-410) contexts. Akkadian personal names with these elements occur in many periods (Clay 1912:194; Tallqvist 1914:305, 306; Stamm 1939:189, 214, 223; Gelb 1957:228-229). The names from Mari and Nuzi have a special interest. They include the element re'û "to shepherd," "shepherd" (Rasmussen 1981:347; MacRae 1943:313). The same element appears in Middle Assyrian names (Saporetti 1970:II 152).

---

[252] See footnote below.

[253] Numbers 1:15; 2:29; 7:78, 83; 10:27.

[254] E.g. [Su]-mu-ra-ḫi-e-im, in Bauer 1926:40; Huffmon 1965:260-261; Gelb et al. 1980:29, 343.

[255] rʿy in Gröndahl 1967:178.

[256] In the later periods Zadok (1977) finds the West Semitic root rʿy/w "to be content, pleased" in the following personal names:Neo-/Late Babylonian -ra-ḫa-' (p. 87) as a QAL 3rd masculine singular form in Šamaš-ir-ḫa-n[i]-' (p. 94); as a 2nd masculine imperative singular with -nū/ī in Nabû-ri-ḫi-nu (p. 96); and as an Aramaic passive participle QATĪL + divine name (which has then undergone vowel harmony) in Ri-ḫi-Adad-milki (p. 109; this however may mean "Adad is (my) friend/shepherd" as in Ra-ḫi-i-lu/Ra-ʾil [p. 297]). These names could reflect the West Semitic rʿy "pasture" or "to be friendly," but Zadok (p. 290) finds a lack of evidence for the ḫ/Ø interchange in the Akkadian spellings. Cf. also Ra-'-ú(Tallqvist 1914:186, Neo-Assyrian) which might come from rʿw/y "pasture" (Tallqvist 1914:305), but more likely originates with the Aramean tribe ru-'-u-a (Zadok 1977a:65).

Although any of the etymologies are possible, given the wide onomastic environment, the example of Reuel implies that Reu is a shortened form of a name with the DN omitted. Thus Reu would mean "DN is a friend/shepherd." The name Shelah in the genealogy of Shem could represent an example of a corresponding member of this construct relationship.

f. Serug

We find Serug (śĕrûg שְׂרוּג) sixth in the line from Shem. Unlike his fathers, Serug has had a fairly well accepted identification with a place name in the region of northern Mesopotamian around Harran. The name has been identified with URU sa-ru-gi appearing in texts from the region west of Harran in the seventh century B.C. (Johns 1901:29, 33, et passim; Schiffer 1911:64 n. 3; Albright 1924:385-386; Malamat 1968a:166; Fales 1973:29, 36 et passim; Thompson 1974:306), between Harran and Bîrejik.[257] A sa-ru-gi may be named in a broken context in the annals of Shalmaneser III. Is sa-ru-gi identical with the site described by the later place names Batnai and Sürüç (Kessler 1980:197-202)? To the south, in the region of Ur, there is the Neo-Assyrian name of a meadow Šá/Še-ri-gu-ú. However, this has been identified as possibly Arabic in origin (Zadok 1977b:325-326).[258]

In comparison with the place name attestations, we find no personal names of this sort in the first millennium B.C. A Ša-ru-gi has been observed in a tablet dating from the third dynasty of Ur (Barton 1909:plate 94; Schneider 1952:521). However, it is difficult to know if this is related to whatever

[257] The identification of Serug with a ṣe-er-ki on an Old Babylonian itinerary from Harran to Emar (Hallo 1964:64, 78-79) is no longer acceptable. The site's name should be understood as ṣe-er-di/-da (Dossin 1974:28; Beitzel 1978:212).

[258] We may also observe the Neo-Assyrian place name sa-ar-ra-gi-ti (Parpola 1970:306).

element lies behind the Serug of Shem's line. Wenham has observed a Hebrew root śrg with the meaning "to intertwine" which can refer to a twig or a tendril (Wenham 1987:251-252). Like the root behind Peleg, śrg is not productive of other personal names in Hebrew.

The best option for Serug remains that found in the Assyrian "Doomsday Book," a place name in the region of Harran in northern Syria. If the name of Abram's ancestor could be identified with such a place name, we have evidence for an implicit wordplay suggesting the starting point for the narratives of Abram.[259] If this relationship to a place name does not provide an etymology, it does establish an onomastic environment which is geographically defined. Given the propensity for place names to retain their integrity despite the passage of time and the entrance of new ethnic and linguistic groups into the "neighbourhood," we should not be surprised if the original root behind the name is no longer present. Nor should we expect the date of the texts in which the place name appears to tell us anything about the date of the name.

g. Nahor

Nahor (nāḥôr נָחוֹר) appears as the name of two people in Genesis 11. A Nahor occurs as the seventh in the line of Seth. But there is also a grandson of this Nahor who has the same name. Such papponymy is unique for the book of Genesis. The root, nḥr, appears in Biblical Hebrew with the meaning "to blow."[260] Schneider (1952:519) identified a personal name na-ḫa-ru-um in the Ur III period of the third millennium B.C. However, the context of this name seems

---

[259] Although the region of Ur might be a better place from which to draw such a personal name if this is the intent of the text, we note the key role which the region of Harran continues to play in the pursuit of brides for each of the patriarchs. It, and not Ur, remained the ancestral homeland throughout the book of Genesis.

[260] This is true in the Qal. Its occurrence in the Piel carries the meaning "to pant."

to suggest an etymology in the Akkadian naḫraru/nērāru "to help." This element is more reasonable than a West Semitic one as it generates personal names at Mari (Birot 1979:160) and elsewhere (Gelb 1980:27, 329), including Jewish names from Babylonia of the first millennium B.C. (Zadok 1977b:335, 342). The West Semitic root is not productive of personal names found in West Semitic texts and environments.[261]

A much closer parallel with the personal name Nahor exists in both consonants and vocalisation. This is the place name Nahor. At a place named Nahor Abraham's servant finds a suitable bride for his master's son (Genesis 24:10). The same chapter of Genesis makes the connection between this "city of Nahor" and the personal name Nahor explicit by repeating the proper name three additional times (vv. 15, 24, 47). However, it seems unlikely that the text intends here a place with the name of Nahor. More probable is the connection with Harran, a city mentioned and associated with Abram and his brother Nahor in Genesis 11. From Harran came shepherds acquainted with Laban, son of Nahor (29:4-5). Despite this, the association of Nahor with the region and with urban life seems established.

A population center spelled as na-ḫu-ur or as na-ḫur did exist in the region of Harran. The textual evidence suggests it lies to the east of that city on one of the western branches of the Ḫabur river. It appears in Old Babylonian texts (Groneberg 1980:173), including those from Mari (Kupper 1979:24; Malamat 1989:53), and also occurs in Middle Babylonian and Middle Assyrian documents (Kessler 1980:91; Nashef 1982:201). No first millennium textual evidence for the site exists (Kessler 1980:223-224). This contrasts with the evidence for Serug's place name, sa-ru-gi. It may suggest the degree to which all such place name attestations must remain open to

---

261 Also note the absence of QATŪL/QATŌL forms among these examples; i.e. the sort of forms we would expect for the personal name Nahor. For the textual problem with MT's נחרי, both in II Samuel 23:37 and in I Chronicles 11:39, see McCarter 1984:494.

the continuing emergence of evidence from the publication of texts discovered at sites in this area. This region containing the sources of the Ḫabur was a rich area in ancient times filled with hundreds of tells, only a few of which have been excavated to date. It is premature to use the present evidence, or, more to the point, the present lack of evidence, to date the usage of particular place names. Thus there need be no contradiction in finding there personal names side by side, despite the association of one with a place name which so far appears only in the first millennium B.C., and the association of the other with a place which occurs only in texts from earlier periods. No exact identification of the place name Nahor has yet been made.[262] In addition to the identification proposed, the identification of one of Nahor's sons as Kemuel, the "father of Aram" (22:20-24) supports a location in this region, later to become a stronghold of Aramaean culture and language.[263]

h. Terah

Terah (teraḥ תֶּרַח), the eighth in line from Shem, also has associations with the worship of pagan deities in Joshua 24:2. However, his role in Genesis is of such significance as to assign him his own toledoth (Genesis 11:27 - 12:25). The etymology of the name has been ascribed to the Hebrew word for "ibex, mountain goat," which has the same consonants in its root. This root occurs in personal names of the Amorite period (Gelb 1980:34, 200). A similarity with the West Semitic word ירח "moon," with which it shares the final two consonants, has been proposed in light of the associations of Terah with the lunar cult centers at Ur and Harran. However, these associations should not be pushed beyond the evidence which remains very meagre at this point. Nor

---

[262]Malamat 1989:53n96 follows Beitzel:1976:236-237,377 in locating it on the Upper Habur, north of Amaz (mentioned in the Mari texts) and in the land of Idamarats.

[263]Nahor's twelve offspring, have been compared with the twelve sons of Jacob, whose mothers also include both wives and concubines. If so, the twelve children of Nahor reflect twelve tribes.

is there sufficient basis for the suggestions that a divine name trḥ appears in the Keret myth from Ugarit (Albright 1938; Gordon 1938; Joüon 1938:280-281).[264]

Although Schneider (1952:521) has suggested a Sumerian personal name te-ra in an Ur III period text,[265] such equations remain difficult due to the uncertainty of the presence of Sumerian personal names in Genesis 1-11.[266] A more profitable association for Terah has been found in the place name Til ša turāḫi which occurs in neo-Assyrian texts (from Shalmaneser III in the mid-ninth century B.C.), and is situated in the region of Harran and on the same river, the Balikh (Kraeling 1922-23; Parpola 1970:355-356).[267]

At this point we reach the end of our study of the genealogy of Shem. Abram is not included as he figures primarily in the subsequent narratives and only secondarily in the material of Genesis 1-11. The role of his name in the context thus belongs in the later chapters and lies outside of the consideration of our study here. The same is true of Sarah and Lot whose important roles also occur in later chapters. Of the remaining figures in Genesis 11, only four do not appear in the later narratives and therefore may be considered here in terms of the role they play in the context of Genesis 11. One of these, Nahor, has already received consideration along with his grandfather of the same name. The other three are Abram's brother Haran and his daughters, Iscah and Milcah.

---

[264] Neither can legitimate association be made with a lunar deity named Têr who was identified with the region of Harran in the Neo-Assyrian period and who was found to be present in personal names (Landsberger and Bauer 1926-27:92; Lewy 1945-46:425-426; Zadok 1977b:42). Ter is a form of Šer, Šahar.

[265] King 1900:plate 46 no. 18964.

[266] Or at least the presence of names borrowed directly from Sumerian without any intermediacy.

[267] See also Westermann 1974:749-750. Albright (1924:386-387) finds in this place name, "mound of the ibex," evidence for Aramaeans in the second millennium B.C. Cf. the sons of Nahor the younger, especially Kemuel, father of Aram.

i. Iscah

Iscah (yiskāh יִסְכָּה) appears in Genesis 11:29 as the daughter of Haran and thus apparently the sister of Milcah. We learn nothing more about this figure.[268] The etymology of Iscah seems to reflect a YIQTĀL whose root may be either nsk, "to pour" (referring to perfume; cf. Cassuto 1964:277), or skh, "to see" (referring to divine favor at the birth of the child; cf. Loewenstamm 1958:707). The lack of onomastic parallels for the former means we should prefer the latter option, which does have such parallels in West Semitic.[269] Iscah is a shortened form of a prayer or an expression of hope for the protection of the deity who would look upon the name bearer with loving concern. The name is shortened by the omission of the DN.

j. Milcah

In Genesis 11:29, Milcah (milkāh מִלְכָּה) is another daughter of Haran who becomes the wife of Nahor. Both Haran and Nahor were brothers of Abram.[270] Although Milcah is mentioned later in Genesis as a mother (22:20-33) and as a grandmother (of Rebekah 24:15), we learn little more about the person herself.

As far as the etymology of Milcah is concerned, no suggestions have associated it with any place names. Instead, Westermann (1981:158) has recognized a possible association with Šarratu and Malkatu (= Ishtar), the names of the wife and

---

[268] Attempts to identify Iscah with Sarah lack any textual support.

[269] Note, however, that the root skh is not attested in biblical Hebrew.

[270] The unusual relationship which results for Milcah has led to comparisons with "marriage adoption" contracts from Nuzi (ṭuppi mārtūti, ṭuppi kallatūti, ṭuppi mārtūti u kallatūti, ṭuppi aḫātūti) which refer to "daughter," "daughter-in-law," and "sister" relationships created by law (see Koschaker 1933 and its development by Speiser 1963:25). For criticisms of parallels between these practices and those of Genesis see Thompson 1974:233; Eichler 1977:48-59; Greengus 1975; Selman 1980; Grosz 1987.

daughter of the moon god, Sin. Given the importance of this lunar cult at the sites visited by the patriarchs, Westermann can suggest an identification of these divine names with Sarah and Milcah. This is an intriguing possibility and such an association may lie somewhere in the dim past in terms of the origins of these names. However, the Biblical text before us makes no such association nor does it even hint at the possibility. Instead, the simplest identification of this name is with the Hebrew term for "queen."[271] The name, Milcah, is a feminine form of the root, mlk, "ruler." It carries a meaning similar to that of the root of the name Sarah, and has been understood as a description of the name bearer's position within the family group (Stamm 1967:326). Names with forms of mlk, and carrying the meaning "king,"[272] appear throughout the second and first millennia B.C. Specific examples of the appearance of the name, mlkh, appear in the second millennium B.C. in a feminine name from Mari,[273] and in one from Ugarit.[274] The name also appears at Emar.[275] However, mlkh does not appear in as a personal name in names from the first millennium B.C. Hebrew, Phoenician, and Punic sources. We find only one other Milcah in the Biblical text, one of the daughters of Zelophehad who come to Moses concerning inheritance of their father's property in the case of the absence of a male heir (Numbers 27:1-11).[276]

---

[271] Again, Westermann's objection that such an etymology would mean the relatively obscure Milkah should outrank her sister-in-law Sarah (whose name means "princess") lacks cogency since the terms are not juxtaposed for such a purpose, nor can we know for certain the relative rankings of the two titles at the time of the giving of the names and the creation of this and the following narratives. Stamm (1967:326) does find in these names hints as to the positions of the name bearers as prominent socially; but he does not draw conclusions about the implied relationship between the two.

[272] Rather than refer to the divine name Molech (Heider 1985).

[273] ma-li-ka (ARM IX 291 ii 13; ARM XXIV 224 ii 14'); in Birot 1979:148; Huffmon 1965:231.

[274] mi-il-ka-a (PRU III p. 54 RS 15.92.21); in Gröndahl 1967:157; Kinlaw 1967:80; Sivan 1984:247. However, this name may be a reflection of mlkyy.

[275] [I]mil-ka-ma-[] (53.6'); in Arnaud 1986:67.

[276] On this see the discussions of Ben-Barak 1980; Paradise 1980; 1987; Huehnergard 1985:429-430. Despite this narrative, there is no clear

k. Haran

The name of Haran (hārān הָרָן) occurs in Genesis 11:27-29 as the son of Terah and brother of Abram and Nahor. He is the father of Lot, Milcah, and Iscah. The same name is used of a son of Shimei of the Levites (I Chronicles 23:9). It should be distinguished from the place name Haran. The personal name is spelled with an initial hē, while the place Haran is spelled with an initial ḥēth.[277] Thus despite associations with place names in the region of Harran for earlier members of the line of Shem, the personal name Haran must be kept distinct from the place name.[278] A name bearer, Haran (hārān הָרָן), appears as a Levite in the period of the United Monarchy.[279]

As to the etymology and onomastic environment of the personal name Haran, Cassuto (1964:268) and Wenham (1987:253) suggest a theophoric element, hr, "rock," and a West Semitic suffix, -ān.[280] The element hr appears in personal names in Egyptian Execration texts of the 19th century B.C., in cuneiform writings, in place names such as hr'l (Thutmose III list No. 18) and hr hhr, and possibly in the Old South Arabic personal names hrn and hrm. However, attempts to place the hr root at Mari seem to be based upon a putative name, ḫa-ri-in-ma-lik (Birot 1955:text no. 6, 58), which should now be read, ḫa-ar-šum-ma-lik.[281] Although other Mari personal names exist with ḫa-ri- spellings, neither

---

association of even this Milcah with a place name. Rather, Milcah's inheritance has been associated with the Hammolechet of I Chronicles 7:18, in the region of Tell el-Farah North. See Gray 1896:116; Noth 1948:164-165; Demsky 1982:70-75; Budd 1983:300.

[277] Haran, son of Caleb in I Chronicles 2:46, shares the same spelling as the place name.

[278] Speiser 1964:79, Thompson 1974:304, and Cassuto 1964:268.

[279] I Chronicles 23:9; Zadok 1988:236.

[280] Zadok 1988:159 identifies this suffix as well and observes that it is common in all Semitic languages, and the most common suffix in Amorite and Ugaritic onomastica.

[281] Birot 1979:103; cf. the same spelling in ARM XXI, 399 6.

Huffmon (1965) nor Gelb (1980) identify this spelling as an Amorite root, let alone a theophoric element. Even less certain are the names, ḫa-ra-ì̀a, ḫa-ra-il, and ḫa-ri(?) from Ebla (Pettinato 1979:269).[282] The Egyptian material is summarized by Ward 1976:358-359, who concludes that the evidence is too scarce[283] to confirm the existence of a deity, Har. However, he suggests a relationship with the West Semitic hr, "mountain," which, as Ward observes, occurs in the later Phoenician personal name, hr-bʿl.[284] Benz (1972:303) notes, in addition, the Punic name hr;[285] although this could be a variant of the divine name ḥr (p. 317). If compounded with the divine name Baʿlu, the hr element in hr-bʿl is unlikely to be another divine name. Rather, hr-bʿl is best understood as "Baʿlu is a mountain," i.e. a refuge or sanctuary (cf. Benz, ibid). The same is also true of the Israelite name, hryhw, "Yahweh is a mountain," on a seal from Gibeon.[286] The evidence points to the use of hr in proper names as derived from the common West Semitic word for "mountain," used as a theophoric element. Cf. also Late Bronze Age West Semitic cuneiform ḫa-ar-ri in a letter from Byblos.[287] There it is glossed on the Sumerogram ḪUR.SAG, "mountain." It is possible that this word also appears in a personal name from Alalakh[288] and in a place name from Amarna.[289] Therefore, if

---

[282] Krebernik 1988:88 suggests a ḫyr root for ḫa-ra in personal names from Ebla. W. G. Lambert 1989:116 remains unconvinced by the suggestion by A. Archi 1987:11, 14 of a ḫr'/y/w root with the meaning "choose." He notes that no certainty is possible, observing the additional possibility of a double geminate root, ḫrr.

[283] He finds three personal names:yʿqb-hr, ʿnt-hr, Sm3-hr.

[284] Cf. Dunand 1938, no. 1113.

[285] CIS 2511.5.

[286] Pritchard 1962:119 (Seal 273 in Vattioni 1978; Fowler 1988:342). Pritchard's interpretation of a mistake in the preceding bn seems plausible, rendering the reading of the name likely. Cf. Tigay 1986:51. For the Canaanite PN hōrām (Joshua 10:33) containing a secondary form of hr "mountain, refuge," cf. Loewenstamm 1964:855; Maisler 1947:46; Layton 1990:173.

[287] EA 74. 20.

[288] ḫa-ru (293. 11); in Wiseman 1953.

[289] ḫa-ri (56. 44; although this name is broken and the reading is uncertain); in Sivan 1984:222.

Haran is to be associated with a root in West Semitic, it is best related to the common noun for "mountain," hr, with a noun suffix, -ān(u/i/a), which is not limited to Amorite but occurs throughout West Semitic of the second millennium B.C. (Sivan 1984:97-98).

As in the above example of the Hebrew personal name hryhw "Yahweh is a mountain," Haran may be a shortened form of a similar name with the hr element plus a DN. We find here a clear etymology. The onomastic environment links the name with names throughout much of the Ancient Near East. It encompasses all periods, especially the second millennium B.C.

2. Conclusions

1. Of the eight names, four (Peleg, Serug, Nahor, and Terah) and less likely a fifth and sixth (Arpachshad and Reu) have associations with place names. One, Shelah, is a possible DN. Four (Shelah, Eber, Peleg, and Reu) have identifiable roots in the lexicon of West Semitic. Of these, only Eber, Peleg, and Reu prove useful in understanding either the onomastic environment or the wordplay of the name. Eber appears to anticipate its usage as a gentilic. With the possible exception of the unidentified Arpachshad, all the names are single word names. The overlapping of etymological categories reflects something of the difficulty involved in identifying these names. Except for Shelah, we have nothing similar in etymology with the names in the earlier genealogies. What seems clear is the sense in which the line of Shem is unique in the etymology and structure of its names. In terms of the emphasis on geography and of the presence of a possible gentilic Eber, it most closely resembles the Table of Nations, as noted above.

2. Concerning the onomastic environment of these names, there is little to be said. Only Eber and Reu seem to enjoy much in the way of later attestations in personal names. The remainder have only the occasional rare occurrence in texts

removed from the West Semitic world of the other personal names in Genesis. Many of the geographic associations tend to be rare, occurring only once or a few times in a set of texts from one period.

3. Beyond what has already been noted in terms of geography and pagan religious environment, we learn little about the name bearers themselves from their names. Perhaps in the name Eber we may recognize a movement from one place to another. Does this migration provide a context for the geographical environment of the place names in the second half of Shem's line? Reu provides a hint, if it is indeed a shortened form of a name such as Reuel. Such a name is much closer to the religious values of Seth's line and anticipates those of Terah's family as well as later Israelite personal names.

4. This brings us to the personal names in the family of Terah. Here the etymologies are clear. Of the four names we have considered, Nahor, Haran, Iscah, and Milcah, the latter three have etymologies in the vocabulary of the West Semitic world. Further, these names are all of recognizable structure, comparable with Hebrew names of the Iron Age II period[290] and with names in the earlier genealogies. Both Haran and Iscah may be shortened names. Both would form sentence names, Iscah a verbal sentence and Haran a nominal sentence. Milcah is a single word name.

5. Haran and Milcah have clear onomastic environments. They contain elements which are common throughout the second millennium West Semitic world, though less so in the first millennium. The onomastic environment of Iscah is not apparent and this may be reflected in the single name of this figure and consequent lack of any continuing family. Nahor also lacks an onomastic environment, as already noted.

[290] I.e., 1000 B.C. until 587 B.C.

CHAPTER 7

CONCLUSION

1. Summary

The following material represents a summary of the names studied in Genesis 1-11. On the matter of the grammatical elements found in the names, those unidentified names and those identified as having their origin in place names are not considered. Not all the names catalogued here have had their etymology identified with the same degree of certainty. Only those where their is considerable doubt are marked with a question mark in the summary which follows. For the degree of certainty involved in the etymology of each name, the reader should consult the relevant section in the preceding chapters. Following the summary of grammatical and syntactical information argued for the names, we will consider the similarities and differences suggested by the groups of names in the genealogies and in the narratives.

a. Mishqalim

QĀL	Ham
QATLĀH	Naamah
QĀTĀL	Adam, Adah, Jabal
QĀTÔL	Nahor
QITLĀH	Milcah, Zillah
QĪL	Seth, Shem
QLÛ	Methushael, Methuselah, Reu
QTÔL	Enoch, Enosh
QÛTĀL	Jubal

b. Verbal Forms

Prefixed:
י - Joktan, Iscah(?)
נ - Nimrod

ת - (?)Tubal-Cain
מ - prefixed participles(?) - Mehujael, Mahalalel

c. Lexical Roots

אדם	humanity	Adam
אנשׁ	human	Enosh
הבל	breath, nothingness	Abel
הלל	to praise	Mahalalel
הר	mountain	Haran
חיה	to live, give life	Eve, Mehujael
חם	paternal kinsman	Ham (theophoric)
חנך	to introduce, initiate	Enoch
יבל	to bring	Jabal, Jubal, (?)Tubal-Cain
ירד	to descend	Jared
למך	?	Lamech
מלך	to rule	Milcah
מרד	to rebel	Nimrod
מת	man, husband	Methuselah, Methushael
נוח	to rest	Noah
נעם	to be pleasant	Naamah
נעם	to sing	Naamah
סכה	to see	Iscah
עבר	to cross over	Eber
עדה	to ornament (oneself)	Adah
פלג	to divide	Peleg
צל	shade, protection	Zillah(?)
צלל	to shrill; cymbal	Zillah(?)
קטן	to be small	Joktan
קין	?	Cain, Tubal-Cain
רעה	friend, shepherd	Reu
שׁית	to place	Seth
שׁם	name	Shem (theophoric?)

d. Place Names

Erech	Enoch(?)

Eridu	Irad(?)
Nahur	Nahor
Phalga	Peleg
Til Raḫaua	Reu(?)
Sarugi	Serug
Tabal	Tubal-Cain(?)
Turāḫi	Terah

e. Divine Names or Epithets

אָדָם	Adam	Adam
אֵל	god; El	Mahalalel, Mehujael
שׁאל	Sheol(?)	Methushael
שֶׁלַח	Shelah(?)	Methuselah, Shelah

f. Afformatives

-ān	Haran, Kenan
-āh	(feminine) Zillah, Milcah, Naamah

g. Structures

Single Element
Abel, Adah, Adam, Enosh, Eve, Ham, Haran, Irad, Kenan, Milcah, Naamah, Nahor, Peleg, Reu, Serug, Shem, Shelah, Terah, Zillah, Eber, Enoch, Iscah, Jabal, Jared, Joktan, Jubal, Nimrod, Noah, Seth, Tubal-Cain

Two Elements
Construct Relationship - Methuselah, Methushael
Nominal Sentence - (?)Tubal-Cain
Verbal Sentence
Verb + Noun - Mahalalel, Mehujael
Noun + Verb - none

2. Observations

a. Number of Names

The following figures represent the number of personal names studied in each of preceding chapters: for narratives in Genesis 1-4 and 6-9, 7 names; for the genealogy of Cain, 11 names (not counting Cain); for the genealogy of Seth, 9 names, for the Table of Nations, 2 names; and for the genealogy of Shem, 11 names (not counting Shem or Abram, but including Iscah, Milcah, and Haran). If we take account of the duplication of two names in two genealogies, Lamech and Enoch, we are left with 38 personal names in Genesis 1-11.

b. Two Element Names

Of these 38 names, all but four are single element names. This counts Tubal-Cain as a compound name, but not as a two-element name. These four single elements include two construct names, Methuselah and Methushael; and two verbal sentence names, Mahalalel and Mehujael. Except for the name, Shelah (which may include a divine element or epithet found in Methuselah and may be a shortened form of that name), these four names represent the only names composed of what are probably divine elements. They are similar in sound, composed of an initial "m" consonant and a final or penultimate "el" sound. All four names are made up of one element which is easy to identify and is found in many personal names, either mutu or ēl. They are all composed of another element which is difficult to identify and is not found in personal names (except for Shelah) either as that element (e.g. Šalaḥ and שאל) or in the exact form of the verb found here (e.g. the initial elements in Mahalalel and Mehujael). Two of these names each appear in the genealogies of Cain and of Seth. We have already discussed the similarity of spelling and sound in many of the names in these two lines, noting especially the identity of two names in both lines, Enoch and Lamech.

c. Single Element Names

The large number of single element names is worthy of note. Along with this there is a complete absence of the common hypocoristic suffixes which indicate that a name has been shortened. For example, the -ya suffix, so common at all periods in West Semitic, is entirely missing from the names. Along with this we might note the complete absence of the divine name, יהוה, in any of the names. This includes the shortened forms, יָה and יָהוּ, which are so common throughout the Iron Age period in Israel.[291] Such observations may indicate that the personal names have an origin other than in the general onomastica of the Israelite and West Semitic world of the first millennium B.C. This could suggest (1) an origin for the names in an earlier period, or (2) artificially constructed onomastica which provide wordplays relevant to the didactic purpose of the text.[292]

As to the second alternative, there is the possibility of a narrator taking lexical items reflecting the sort of message to be conveyed and forming these items into personal names. Indeed, such a feature is not unknown and might be expected in narratives such as Genesis 1-11 where wordplay has a significant role. If this were the case, we might expect the narrator to use lexical items which possessed an onomastic environment in the society of ancient Israel. That this often is the case lends support to the hypothesis. The common onomastic environment of elements in names such as Eve, Mahalalel, Shem, and Ham could explain their use in the narratives and genealogies. The narrative uses names which would be readily recognized as the sorts of names which might be personal names.

However, there are problems with this view. If a narrator sought to identify etymologies with the narrative in some cases, it is not clear why it was not done in all cases. In each of the above sections we identified names whose etymologies

[291] I.e., 1200 B.C. until 587 B.C.

[292] A variant to this view argues that a late redactor took an already existing list of names in the line of Cain and modified them slightly to produce the line of Seth. Cf. Vermeylen 1991:184-185.

were uncertain or impossible to find in the Hebrew world or anywhere else we looked. This might be understandable if it happened for one or even two names. After all, we do not possess the full lexicon of Classical Hebrew. However, the recurrence of this phenomenon, coupled with the unusual vocalizations of some names with identifiable roots, suggest that more is involved than an Israelite narrator creating names to suit the narrative.

A second problem lies in the fact that some of the personal names are given specific explanations as to how the name is to be interpreted in light of the narrative. However, these explanations do not reflect the etymology of the name itself. This is certainly true for the explanations or word associations provided with the names of Cain, Noah, and Japheth. If an author felt free to create new names, it could have been done in such a way as to provide an undisputed etymology between the name and its explanation. Consider the cases of Cain and Noah, who play such important roles in the narratives and genealogies. The onomastic environments of the roots associated with their names in the Biblical narrative, i.e. קנה and נחם, yield a rich harvest of names actually containing these roots. The fact is that the names Cain and Noah do not possess these roots in their etymologies. If the names were artificial creations for use in the narrative, it would have been easy enough to select names whose etymologies correspond precisely to the wordplays in the narratives.[293]

Divine names of non-Israelite deities appear in the elements of some of the personal names. Especially in the cases of Shelah, Methuselah and Methushael, we have examples of divine names or epithets which are nowhere else attributed

---

[293]Cf. Hess 1990c. This is an important caution for those studies which rightly emphasize the wordplay of these names, but do so without adequate consideration of (1) their deviation from Classical Hebrew vocabulary (both in consonants and in preserved vocalization) and (2) their Ancient Near Eastern onomastic environment, especially that found in the West Semitic world. Cf. e.g. Radday 1990:74-78 and Vermeylen 1991.

to the God of Israel. In the world of ancient Israel, the only divine name regularly used in personal name is יהוה, normally in an abbreviated form This is true for both the Biblical (Fowler 1988) and extrabiblical (Tigay 1986) personal names. It seems unlikely that a narrator would artificially create personal names made up of names of other deities and insert them into a narrative of the ancestry of the nation credited with the origins of monotheism.

d. Origins of the Names

All this suggests that the personal names in Genesis 1-11 have an origin other than the Iron Age. This study has demonstrated that most of these names have some relation to attested personal names of the West Semitic world. But can we go farther than that? While many of the elements in the personal names have an onomastic environment extending throughout most or all periods of the Ancient Near East, a few are more restricted. Some names have only one or two attestations in the form of a geographic name. These names occur in the latter half of the genealogy of Shem. While their geographic environment may help us to pinpoint the background of that line in Northern Syria, the periods of time are less useful. This is for two reasons, one specific to Shem's line and another general to geographic names. As for Shem's line, we have some geographic names which are attested only in the second millennium and some which are attested only in the first millennium. As these exist side by side in the same genealogy, it suggests that this would not be useful for determining the original period of these names. This is confirmed by a general principle behind place names, that such names rarely change (Gelb 1962). Even in some cases where the site is given a new name, it can revert back to the original soon after those who introduced the new name disappear. A famous example of this is Jerusalem which, under the Romans in the second century, became Aelia Capitolina. This name remained only as long as (pagan) Rome remained. It did not survive, but reverted to Jerusalem once again. The point here is that place names, when used in personal names, say little about their chronological origins. However, they do help to establish the origin of at least some of the names in Northern Syria.

A second group of elements in the names which are more specific are those which occur in personal names only in the second millennium but disappear from West Semitic onomastica and are not attested in the first millennium. This appears to be the case with the root in the name Adam and with the root shared in the first element of the two names, Methushael and Methuselah. Both roots are related to "person" or "man." Both roots are found in common nouns in Hebrew and other West Semitic (or Canaanite in the case of mutu) languages in the first millennium, but not as elements in personal names. However, both appear frequently in personal names of the second millennium. Indeed, the earlier we go in that millennium, the more frequently we find these elements occurring. The same is true for names containing the ybl root, i.e. Jabal, Jubal, and possibly Tubal-Cain. Given the unique wealth of onomastic attestation from this period in comparison with many of the other periods surveyed here, such an observation does not prove an early second millennium date for the origins of all the names in Genesis 1-11. However, it does suggest an environment in which most or all would find congeniality on the basis of our present evidence. The second millennium and especially the earlier part of that millennium would seem, at present, to be the most appropriate time period for the personal names of Genesis 1-11.

Having made this observation, the names of Cain and Nimrod seem to be exceptions to the generalization of an early second millennium origin for the names of Genesis 1-11. The etymologies of both names have attestations in onomastica which are found only in the first millennium. However, both these names present other difficulties. Cain's etymology may involve a root found in Epigraphic South Arabic. If this root has been correctly identified, we are left with the problem that there is no written evidence for Epigraphic South Arabic in the second millennium. There is no attested second millennium antecedent to South Arabic in Arabia. Conclusions concerning the origins of the name, Cain (as well as Kenan and Tubal-Cain), must take into account this absence of evidence. As noted above, the possible Hurrian origins for Tubal as a gloss (or in some other way related) for Cain would imply an earlier origin than has previously been supposed for this name.

Nimrod presents a different problem. It is the only personal name identified among the "offspring" of either Ham or Japheth. Its appearance in Genesis 10 is unique. The fact of first millennium attestations of the מרד root in personal names may suggest a later date for this narrative and its contents. The associations with Ninurta, if accepted, would allow for a much earlier date for the name, while not excluding a first millennium date as well. It is difficult to reach any sort of definite conclusion on the evidence of this isolated name. It is possible to identify a distinction between Nimrod and the other names of Genesis 1-11 in terms of both its onomastic environment and in terms of its immediate context.

It is difficult to assess the value of these conclusions for Old Testament criticism. Care must be taken so that no more is made of the evidence than is warranted. Perhaps the clearest result is that these names cannot be dated to the exilic or post-exilic period, given the present state of onomastic evidence. Nor are they obviously artificially constructed names. Instead, the evidence for most of the names suggests an early date. In itself this says nothing about the date of the genealogies or the narratives in the form in which they appear in the present Hebrew text. However, it does suggest a terminus ad quem to the traditions lying behind the material in the early part of the second millennium. For those who would date the Priestly source of the Pentateuch to the sixth century B.C. or later, allowance must be made for the early date of the personal names contained within the text.[294] From a form critical perspective, the genealogies of Genesis 1-11 remain unique. They are neither related to the early king lists of Mesopotamia and Ugarit, nor to the later Hesiodic "Catalogue of Women" (Hess 1989). Similar observations may also be made for the narratives in Genesis 1-11. Despite attempts to identify them with one or another of the creation and flood stories of the Ancient Near East, no scholarly agreement exists as to their origins. Thus the personal names of Genesis 1-11 bear witness to the presence of early traditions in this literature, without providing clear direction as to the origins of those traditions. As with so much in Genesis 1-11, the comparisons with early Ancient Near Eastern materials raise intriguing possibilities without yielding certain conclusions.

294 The same is true for those who deny the existence of Pentateuchal sources and prefer a single late composition. Cf. e.g., Whybray 1987.

PART II

THE FUNCTION OF THE PERSONAL NAMES IN GENESIS 1-11

WORDPLAY

CHAPTER 8

INTRODUCTION

This section will examine the function of the personal names in the narratives and genealogies of the final form of the Masoretic text of Genesis 1-11. In few other places in ancient literature does one find so many wordplays and associations with personal names. This is easiest to identify in the larger narratives of Genesis 1-4 and 6-9. These will be examined first. Then the function of the names in the genealogies will be considered. As in the study of part I, an attempt will be made to identify patterns or themes in the role of the personal names within each of the genealogies. Items taken into consideration include the etymology of the personal name and any notes or information about the name bearer which is provided by the text, including word associations and folk etymologies.

CHAPTER 9

THE NARRATIVES IN GENESIS 1-4, 6-9, AND 11

1. The Names in the Narratives of Genesis 1-4

a. Eve

If the name, Eve, refers to the role of one who is the giver and nurturer of all life, do we find in the name what is actually a title as has been argued elsewhere for her male counterpart, Adam (Hess 1990b)? The contextual appearances of the name suggests this may be the case. We find no mention of the name Eve until after the incident with the serpent in the Garden in Genesis 3. This is followed by the curses of vv. 14-19. Immediately after these curses we find Eve given her name (v. 20). That part of God's judgment which concerns the woman[295] is found in v. 16. Even if this verse is understood as requiring both subsistence labor and childbirth,[296] the distinctive aspect of the first part of the verse, i.e. the point where woman's fate differs from that of man, lies in the bringing forth of children. It is this role of giving life which is first ascribed to the woman at this point. It is therefore the first opportunity for the man and woman to be informed of that role. Thus it follows that the next statement involving the woman is the attribution of a name which defines that unique aspect of her role in bearing life. The giving of a name in this text reflects a discernment which recognizes a role assigned by God.[297]

---

[295] Neither the woman nor the man are actually "cursed" in Genesis 3. Only the serpent and the ground receive the אָרוּר designation.
[296] Meyers 1983:344-346.
[297] For the act of name giving as one of discernment, see Ramsey 1988. Understanding v. 20 as an insertion, along with most commentators, Westermann 1974:364-366 argues for an origin in a genealogical table (Stammbaumnotiz). If so, this reflects an interplay between genealogy and narrative in the first example of a personal name in Genesis 1-11; something which will continue throughout the remaining chapters and in

The only other occurrence of the name Eve is found in Genesis 4:1 in a context which describes the conception and birth of her first son, Cain. This is followed by the conception and birth of a second son, Abel in v. 2. The verbs in this verse also refer back to the Eve of v. 1. Thus the distinctive role assigned the woman in 3:16 is shown in her name and in the use of that name when she first exercises that role in the Genesis narrative.

b. Cain

Genesis 4:1 provides the biblical text's own basis for understanding the name: קָנִיתִי אִישׁ אֶת־יהוה "I have acquired a man with/from Yahweh."[298] It associates Cain with the root qnh "to create," "to acquire."[299] Although the Cain and Abel narrative provide little in the way of wordplay on this meaning, vv. 17-24 portray Cain and his line as involved in the creation of cities, music, tools and weapons. The line acquires property, wives, and the fruits of vengeance. More directly, the root occurs in the difficult construction[300]

---

which personal names serve as an important means of relating the two forms of literature.

[298] The interpretation of אֶת as a preposition with the meanings of "with" or "from" and the implications for divine maternity (Kikawada 1972:35-37) or divine paternity (Gordon 1988:154-155) rest upon speculations about the origin and prehistory of the narrative and the structure of the Hebrew explanation rather than any clear indication in the text we now have. What is clear is that the interpretation of the name Cain (or Eve for that matter) is not affected by either exegesis. See further below.

[299] Cf. Strus 1978:65 who sees the primary association as one of assonance. Other associations with roots including the letters qoph and mem (pp. 172-173) are not as persuasive. The distinction between "create" and "acquire" does not seem compelling for the context of Genesis 4, contra Westermann 1974:395. It seems that Eve could intend to confess the birth both as God's gift which she acquired through the pain of childbirth, as suggested in the curse of chapter 3, and as God's intent to create through her a new human being. Whether either of these statements suggests a willful assertion by Eve of a role equal to that of God remains uncertain from the text and its context (Wenham 1987:102).

describing the contribution of Jabal (v. 20). Among other things, Jabal is the father of miqneh. A verbal tie appears between the section in which 4:20 occurs and the preceding narrative which begins with 4:1. This tie uses wordplay with the name of Cain, the only explicit wordplay for any name in Genesis 4.

Although the lack of a clear identification for the etymology of the name may mean we are overlooking wordplay with Cain in the story of 4:1-16,[301] this is doubtful as no similar sounding roots appear in the text. Neither the name Cain nor the qnh root has an identifiable role in the narrative. This is unlike the names of Eve and Abel in their narratives.

c. Abel

The third personal name to appear in Genesis is that of Abel (הֶבֶל hebel). The name appears some eight times in Genesis 4 and not again in the Hebrew Bible. It is clear from the beginning that the figure holds out hope for humanity. This hope is recognized by God's acceptance of Abel's gift but then cut short by the murder of Abel at the hands of his brother. The last mention of Abel in v. 25 describes the mother's hope of a replacement for Abel in the birth of a new son, Seth. Throughout the narrative of Genesis 4, Abel plays a passive role. His only activities are those of shepherding and presenting a minḥah to God. The murder which follows, whatever the reason(s) for it, evokes the sense of a life cut short before its intended time and before the accomplishment of its intended goals. In Genesis 1-11 these goals are pre-eminently the continuation of the line which leads to the nation of Israel.

---

[300] The statement in 4:1 is also difficult and has been the source of much speculation, though without consideration of the comparison with 4:20. Especially persuasive is the comparative onomastic material collected by Borger 1959, who identifies אֵת with Akkadian itti, here carrying the meaning "from."

[301] We do not consider here the alliteration in a phrase such as that in v. 8, וַיָּקָם קַיִן "and Cain arose."

The figure of Abel represents the potential inheritor of the hopes and promises of humanity. However, the failure of these hopes to be realized, even though no fault of Abel, casts doubt on this etymology as involving any wordplay in the present text.

There is no explicit wordplay for Abel in the narrative of Genesis. Indeed, the name bearer is described in cursory fashion and has no particular role beyond the occupation of shepherd and the fate of being a victim in the first fratricide. But this very aspect of the name bearer may be a reflection of an implicit wordplay in the name. With the meaning of that which is ephemeral and transitory, the name Abel well describes a figure who remains on the scene only a brief time and then disappears with no descendants or other impact of note upon the human race. This is set in strong contrast to Cain who himself accomplishes great deeds such as (perhaps) city building and whose line continues the invention and acquisition of renowned human achievements.[302] Thus the meaning "breath, nothingness" is an apt description of Abel's role in the narrative and in the course of human development in Genesis 1-11.[303]

It might be intriguing to find in Abel another tie with the narrative, i.e. a well known root unproductive of personal

---

[302] For a survey of the history of scholarly opinion addressing the question as to whether 4:1-16 represents two groups of people, such as the urban and the nomadic, or whether it is intended to describe two primeval individuals, see Westermann 1974:385-388. From an onomastic standpoint, the descriptive nature of the names and their lack of an onomastic environment might seem to point to a symbolism to the story which would argue for an interpretation in which the figures represented something other than what they are in the story, i.e. groups such as urban and nomadic. However, the wordplay of the names, particularly that of Abel whose role in the text is confined to this narrative, has nothing to do with a nomadic people. It rather fits well as the narrative of two individuals and the tragic consequences of their personal conflict.

[303] The commentaries concur with this interpretation of the name. See Cassuto 1961:202; von Rad 1972:104; Westermann 1974:398; Seybold 1977:337-338; Wenham 1987:102.

names coincides with a name bearer who might have played the most important of roles in the future of humanity but who was himself unproductive of any heirs. Perhaps more likely is the view that this feature is a coincidence caused by the reluctance of Israelites and those for whom this story played a significant role in their heritage to assign such a name to their offspring, one which described a figure cut short in his life without heirs.

2. The Names in the Narratives of Genesis 6-9

a. Noah

Noah (**nōaḥ** נֹחַ) occurs more frequently than any other personal name in Genesis 1-11, some forty-one times. Its first appearance is in Genesis 5:29, bringing the line of Seth in Genesis 5 to an end. It recurs throughout the following chapters as the narrative of the Flood progresses. Noah's key role in this text continues in the subsequent narrative concerning his drunkenness. He is mentioned twice in chapter 10, at the beginning and end of the Table of Nations. Thus the figure of Noah links the antediluvian line, reaching back to Adam and Seth, with the postdiluvian expansion of Noah's offspring and the formation of all the families of humanity in the known world.

Although no כִּי clause is used to explain the name of Noah, Lamech's naming of his son is followed by an observation obviously intended to associate a verbal root with the name:

וַיִּקְרָא
אֶת־שְׁמוֹ נֹחַ לֵאמֹר זֶה יְנַחֲמֵנוּ מִמַּעֲשֵׂנוּ וּמֵעִצְּבוֹן יָדֵינוּ מִן־הָאֲדָמָה אֲשֶׁר אֵרְרָהּ
יהוה

"He called his name Noah, saying, 'This one will console us from our work and from the toil of our hands from the ground which the Lord cursed'."

The root נחם, "comfort," "console," which shares two consonants with נוח, and sounds similar,[304] occurs in many West Semitic names throughout all periods.[305] Except as a personal name, נוח does not appear in the Flood story and its sequel in Genesis 6-9, with the exception of a cognate form, in רֵיחַ הַנִּיחֹחַ, "the pleasing aroma" of Noah's sacrifice which Yahweh smells in 8:21. This is probably not an intentional wordplay because (1) the comfort given is not directed toward humanity, as in the prophecy, but toward God; and (2) the term forms part of a formulaic phrase used for divinely acceptable burnt sacrifices. The נחם root does occur in Genesis 6-9.

The נוח root occurs in the hiphil stem in Genesis 2:15. There it describes God's placement of הָאָדָם in the garden to tend it. There is a correspondence with Noah who is also to have a positive effect upon the land. The hiphil stem carries two nuances of meaning; the sense of providing rest and the sense of settling down. Genesis 2:15 uses the hiphil nuance of settling down, which is different from that used to explain the name of Noah in 5:29.

In Genesis 6:6-7, the root נחם appears twice in the story of the "sons of God" and "daughters of men" in the niphal stem. Unlike the piel in 5:29, it does not emphasize a provision of comfort. Rather, it describes the opposite experience; how grieved God becomes when viewing the wickedness of humanity. However, this has not prevented scholars from observing irony in the wordplay.[306] Lamech's hoped for

---

[304] See Strus 1978:66 for details.

[305] Amorite: na-aḫ-ma-nu, na-aḫ-mi-im, na-aḫ-mi-e-ra-aḫ JCS 11:29 no. 17.5; in Huffmon 1965:237-239; na-aḫ-mi-^{d}da-gan; Wiseman 1953: pl. VI, 7, seal b, a-bi-na-aḫ-mi (fem.); ibid, no. 455.4, 13. Amarna: ia-an-ḫa-mu/mi/ma (EA 83.31,39,40 85.23,48); in Hess 1984:331. Ugarit: ia-an-ḫa-(am)-mu (PRU III RS 16.257-III-5,41,46, etc.); in Gröndahl 1967:165; Kinlaw 1967:307; Sivan 1984:253.

[306] Cassuto 1961:289, 303, 307; Strus 1978:158-162; Zakovitch 1980a:38-41. The latter also observes the simlarity between the נחם of v. 6 and the נח

comfort turns into God's repentance for the creation of humanity. This leads to the Flood in which Noah continues to play a key role. From the standpoint of wordplay, it invites comparison between נֹחַ and a word whose consonants are spelled in reverse, חֵן "grace", which Noah found before God in v. 8 of chapter 6. One may also observe the already mentioned "pleasing aroma" of 8:21 which contrasts with the divine grief of 6:6-7. However, this last comparison depends upon two different roots which are related by Lamech's explanation of Noah's name.

The roots נוח and נחם serve to tie Noah with the experience and role of אָדָם in the Garden, and with the subsequent events of Genesis 6:1-8. As with the explanation of the name, so the relation to 2:15 may suggest that, as with אָדָם, Noah's name describes an occupation or role. The occupation is one of comforter, and the comforting is related to the relief of the toil required to work the land. While it may be that the Flood and Noah's subsequent sacrifice lead to promises from God regarding the world, this does not seem to fulfill the explanation of the name. God alone is responsible for the blessings. In addition, none of the promises or commands deal with the question of relief from the toil required to work the soil. We turn to the story of Noah's planting a vineyard. Perhaps the comfort from the toil of the land is implied here. Indeed, this expectation seems to be the case in the initial effects of Noah's drunkenness which lead to sleep. However, such a hope is shortlived as the incident results in the cursing of one of his sons and a grandson. In fact, the meaning of Genesis 5:29 is one of hope to reset the proper order of the world which was lost in the events of chapter 3. That the hope is not fully realized in the earthshaking events of Genesis 6-9 does not terminate it. Rather, it simply moves us forward to continue the expectation in the offspring of Noah and the generations which follow in his line. In a sense its frustration in the

---

plus חן of v. 8. For other parallels of assonance with Noah in chapters 6-9 see Strus.

incident with Noah's drunkenness serves only to focus the hope in future generations, for Noah curses the line of Canaan but blesses the line of Shem.[307]

The failure of the hope to be realized in the generation of Noah also frustrates the possible wordplay in the meaning of the name and in its explanation by Lamech. In the end Noah does not provide comfort for his generation. Thus although likely etymology and onomastic environments exist for the name and for its explanation (נחם), the single example of a wordplay on the root is removed from the narrative of Noah and hidden back in chapter 2.

b. Shem

The names of Shem, Ham, and Japheth, all form a link between the genealogies of chapters 5 and 10. They also tie in the intervening narratives. Shem, however, is unique in that he alone serves as the ancestor of the genealogy of chapter 11, the one which leads forward to the figure of Abram and the fulfillment of the hopes unrealized in the generation of Noah. Along with this, Shem's name calls to mind the acts of naming which take place in Genesis 1-11. There the first "namer," the אָדָם, names the living creatures and Eve. Eve herself names her sons. Lamech, Shem's grandfather, names Noah. If, as argued elsewhere, these incidents of naming serve to express discernment as to the role played by the individuals involved,[308] the name of Shem may express a culmination of these expectations. Shem's relation to what follows becomes clear, not in the naming of his line in chapters 10-11, but in the desire of the builders of Babel's Tower to make a name for themselves (11:4; also Moye 1990: 589). This is contrasted with the desire of God to make a name for Abram (12:2) in the promise which introduces the narratives following Genesis 1-11.

---

[307] Cf. Wallace 1990:24-29.

[308] See Ramsey 1988. Note Clines' 1990:39 n3 observation that an exercise of authority is still involved in the naming process.

c. Ham

For this name two etymologies have been suggested. Either is possible.[309] The Egyptian root of Ham exhibits a possible wordplay in the story of the curse of Canaan. In this story, Ham's son Canaan is doomed to be a servant of Ham's brothers (Genesis 9:25-27). The repetition of the word "servant" three times in the curse may suggest an implicit wordplay with the Egyptian name. A remembrance of Ham as Egyptian in origin may be reflected in the descendants attached to Ham in the Table of Nations in Genesis 10. In addition to מִצְרַיִם "Egypt," we find other nations associated with the region of northeast Africa; i.e. Cush and Put (10:6). Thus wordplay which depends on the Egyptian etymology of Ham is found in the names of his descendants, a fact which would suggest that the name may have had an original association with the peoples of Egypt.

As to the West Semitic etymology "paternal kinsman," we find a possible wordplay between the role of Ham as "paternal kinsman" and the line of his brother Shem in Genesis 11. Along with Japheth, Ham is the prototypical "paternal kinsman" of the members of the line of Shem and its descendants, i.e. of Israel. With its West Semitic etymology, this interpretation would have direct appeal to early readers of the Hebrew narratives and genealogies. If the Egyptian etymology is accepted as the original one for the name of Ham in Genesis 9 and 10, the West Semitic etymology serves as a reinterpretation providing a convenient explanation for the role of this figure in Genesis 11 and, by extension, in the following chapters.

In addition to these semantic relationships, there is the alliteration between חָם and the חָמָס "violence" which fills

---

[309] It is unlikely that an Egyptian etymology would be found in word plays in a West Semitic text. However, Ham is an exception. Like Japheth, his tie with the Table of Nations in chapter 10 suggests an international aspect to this figure. This aspect provides a context for an Egyptian etymology and word play.

the earth in Genesis 6:10-11.[310] This identification is valuable insofar as it ties Ham in with the Flood narrative, something which the previous wordplays do not do.

d. Japheth

Noah's blessing of Japheth appears to make reference to a future event and probably one which is not so much a part of the individual Japheth as it is a part of the people who represent his descendants. Tied in with the following Table of Nations, it may suggest that group of peoples at the edge of the known world of the Hebrews. Their extent would seem large, if not uncounted. Alternatively, the wordplay may refer to a future event when the descendants of Japheth would be driven from their home lands, perhaps through increase in their population and the inadequacy of resources to provide for their numbers. They then would come to the land where the descendants of Shem lived. There they would dwell. Whatever historical circumstances this event may refer to, the implications are that the explicit wordplay on the name Japheth, unlike that of others in these narratives (i.e. Eve, Cain, and Noah), represents a characteristic of a people rather than an individual. This should not be surprising in light of what we have observed about the names in the narratives and their tendency to provide connections between the various texts in Genesis 1-11, and beyond. Like brothers Shem and Ham, Japheth serves to tie the narratives of chapters 6-9 with what follows in the Table of Nations. Unlike them, however, this figure represents the most obscure of the three and his descendants remain the least known to the Hebrew readers of the text. The one feature apparently known to the author is the number and size of the descendants. This is the feature which also fits easily with a Hebrew word which sounds like the name Japheth.

3. Conclusions

---

[310] See Strus 1978:91.

1. As noted in part one, five names have identifiable etymologies in West Semitic and particularly in Hebrew; Eve, Abel, Noah, Shem, and Ham. The two names which do not share this characteristic, Cain and Japheth, represent two lines of descendants which do not continue the main part of our story; i.e. neither stand in the line which leads from Adam to Abram.

2. Four names have some sort of explicit wordplay associating the name and a Hebrew root with which, except in the case of Eve, it is not related in terms of etymology. These four are Eve, Cain, Noah, and Japheth.

3. Thus all seven names (Eve, Cain, Abel, Noah, Shem, Ham, and Japheth) have some sort of etymological character in Hebrew; either in obvious roots behind the names, or in explicit wordplay in the narrative, or in both. In fact, the only two which seem to have both are Eve and Noah, two parents of the remaining name bearers in our narratives.

4. Among the four names with explicit wordplay in the text, only Japheth is identified with a Hebrew root which seems to be unproductive of personal names. As in the first point, Japheth represents a figure who does not stand in the line from Adam to Abram, but represents someone outside of that line.

In general, it is evident that wordplay associates the name with the narrative, providing the name bearer with a role or characteristic which becomes integral to the narrative in which the bearer is functioning. This is most obvious where the name receives an explicit statement associating it with a Hebrew root. Thus Eve is the one who gives life; Cain is the one who acquires the fruits of civilization (for good and for ill); Noah is the one who comforts humanity through attempts at viticulture and through continuing the line; Japheth is the one who enlarges his family to extend beyond its former borders.

The remaining names also suggest roles in the meanings associated with the elements which comprise each name. Abel is the shortlived son; Shem is the prototype of all the "names" in the genealogy which leads to Abram; Ham, with his Egyptian-like name, is the paternal kinsman of the figures in Shem's line. However, we may note a difference with these latter three. Unlike Eve, Cain, Noah, and Japheth, the wordplays on the names Abel, Shem, and Ham, reflect less what they do and more what they become through no particular action on their own. Abel's short life is not his fault! Shem's role at the head of the line leading to Abram and Ham's role as his brother are also matters which lie outside his control. These three name bearers also play a passive role in general in the narratives. They are less the focus of the author's attention. True, Abel's sacrifice receives God's blessing; but Cain is the one addressed by God. Cain acts in the murder and goes on to dialogue with the deity and to migrate to a new life. Shem, Ham, and Japheth all appear to play equal roles throughout the Flood narrative. Indeed, Ham is the actor in bringing on Noah's curse, while Shem plays the key role as head of the line leading to Abram. Japheth, however, is the only one of the brothers mentioned in Noah's curse of 9:26-27 who is said to do something. Ham does not even appear. Shem appears but only as the one who would be served by Canaan and who would allow Japheth to dwell in his tents.[311] Thus, Japheth is described as a doer in this text, while his brothers remain absent or passive. The remaining name bearers, Eve and Noah, have entire narratives focusing on their activities (chapters 4 and 6-9). They are the most active of all.

These distinctions are reflected in the etymologies of the names. Where an explicit wordplay is made, it is always with a finite verb (so Cain, Noah and Japheth), or a related

---

[311]This observation raises the interesting question as to whether the insertion of Canaan in the curse of Noah, in place of the expected figure of Ham, might relate to an intent to diminish the significance of the latter in importance in the narrative and consequently to suggest the upcoming role assigned to Canaan and the Canaanites in the history of Israel.

form of a verb (Eve). With the remaining three names, the etymologies most easily derived from the Hebrew spellings and Masoretic vocalizations of the names are always nouns. Further, these nouns are invariably unattached to any identifiable verbal roots, at least any known to be in frequent use in Classical Hebrew.

Thus the roles of the name bearers in the narratives concur with the explicit or implied etymologies of names themselves in suggesting the degree of activity and significance assigned to the name bearer. In these ways the West Semitic etymologies and wordplays available to each of the names provide a suggestion of their role and importance in the text. The etymology and related wordplay integrate the name, the name bearer, and the narratives of which they are a part.

CHAPTER 10

THE GENEALOGY OF CAIN IN GENESIS 4

1. Introduction

Six of the name bearers mentioned in vv. 17-24 appear with notes. These include Cain, Enoch, Lamech, Jabal, Jubal, and Tubal-cain. Two others, Adah and Zillah, are addressed in Lamech's song but we learn nothing more about them. In the linear genealogy, three names have no further information supplied. They are Irad, Mehujael, and Methusael. In the segmented genealogy, there are also three names with no further information supplied. They are Adah, Zillah, and Naamah. These are all the feminine names in vv. 17-24. There are thus 6 name bearers with additional information about them and 6 name bearers whose names are restricted to genealogical information. For wordplay suggested by the names Cain, Enoch, and Lamech, see the relevant sections of part I and of chapters 9 and 11.

2. The Names

a. Jabal

The text describes Jabal as the father of tent dwellers and miqneh. This latter term has occasioned some discussion. Some understand it as livestock and use this interpretation to find here a description of nomadic life.[312] Others have associated miqneh with the meaning "possessions," and thereby understood Jabal as a trader (Sawyer 1986:160). This would support the association of this occupation with an

---

312 Wilson 1977:142 n10; Wenham 1987:95 n20d. Cf. Amynos and Magos, whom Philo of Byblos associates with the origin of villages and sheep herding (Cassuto 1961:235; Attridge and Oden 1981:45). On the association of Cain's descendants with the Kenites, cf. above under Cain, and Miller 1974:168.

urban culture as advocated by some interpretations of Genesis 4:17-24 (Wallis 1966:134-135).

miqneh, from the root qnh, shares two consonants with the name of Jabal's ancestor, Cain, qyn. As already noted, it also possesses the same root as that found in the statement of Genesis 4:1, relating the name Cain to the root qnh. The name Jabal seems to share the same root with the names of his brothers, Jubal and Tubal-Cain. Related as brothers, only these three (in Genesis 4:17-24) receive designations either as the "father" of various cultural manifestations (Jabal and Jubal) or as one who possesses an occupation (Tubal-Cain). Cain and Abel, the one earlier set of brothers described in Genesis 4, also hold specific occupations. In addition to the wordplay between the three brothers and Cain already noted, we find a similarity of two consonants of the ybl root to the name of the first caretaker of livestock, Abel (hbl).

Wordplay associated with the name of Jabal and his occupation relate Jabal to his brother and half-brother through the alliteration of the roots of the names Jubal and Tubal-Cain, and through the similarity of glosses on each of the figures describing their occupations. Again, the similarity of the roots of the names Jabal, Jubal, Tubal-Cain, and Abel further associate Cain and Abel with this later generation.

b. Jubal

The text designates Jubal as the father of lyre- and pipe-players.[313] The name Jubal may connect his musical occupation with (1) the yôbēl "ram's horn," used to proclaim special days and seasons, and containing the same consonants as Jubal; and (2) Naamah, Jubal's half-sister whose name may also relate to music (Cassuto 1958; Gabriel 1959:417; cf. below under Naamah).

[313] For associations with the Greek shepherd deity Pan, credited with the invention of the lyre, cf. Westermann 1974:450 and Wenham 1987:113.

c. Tubal-Cain

The text describes his occupation with the term lōṭēš "sharpener." In its context this suggests the work of a metal smith (Sawyer 1986:160-164). Implicit wordplay occurs in the name, associating the first element with the similar sounding half-brothers of Tubal-Cain, Jabal and Jubal. The second part of the name, Cain, identifies it with the ancestor of the line. This ties together the first and last generations in the genealogy of Genesis 4:17-24 with the name of the last male mentioned in the line. In addition, to understand Cain as "smith" creates an obvious connection between Tubal-Cain's name and his occupation.[314]

d.-f. Adah, Zillah, and Naamah

Wordplay seems to occur in both interpretations of the name Naamah. The first meaning, "to be pleasant, lovely," suggests the name Adah, which may also convey the idea of that which pleases the eye. The second meaning, related to singing, recalls the other feminine name in this passage, Zillah, Naamah's mother. If Zillah means "cymbal" then both names suggest music. In the case of the latter, Cassuto has discovered an interesting parallel in the Ugaritic myth of Baal where the roots of Zillah and Naamah appear together, "He rose, improvised a poem and sang, the gracious lad (held) the cymbals in his hands, the sweet-voiced youth sang before Baʿlu in the highlands of Sapanu."[315] The Ugaritic for "cymbals" and "gracious" reflects the roots of Zillah and Naamah and suggest their association in West Semitic literature.

---

[314] For qyn as "smith" see above under Cain, with the cautions expressed there. Josephus, Pseudo-Philo, and Jubilees do not transliterate Cain in Tubal-Cain. Instead, they substitute a gloss on its meaning, "metal smith."
[315] Cassuto 1961:234. Cf. also Garsiel 1987:25. The parallel referred to is V AB [CTA 3; KTU 1.3] A col. I lines 18-22a: (18) qm . ybd . w yšr (19) mṣltm . bd . nʿm (20) yšr . ǵzr . ṭb . ql (21) ʿl . bʿl . b ṣrrt (22) ṣpn. The translation followed is that of de Moor 1987:4.

3. Conclusions

1. Although only Cain has wordplay explicitly mentioned in the text, wordplay with the roots of the names may appear in the case of every name with the exceptions of Mehujael and Methushael, who serve only to fill genealogical slots. Even here, however, the similarity of the sound in pronouncing the names suggests their association with one another. This wordplay serves to link together the names and name bearers in various ways.

2. Within Genesis 4:17-24 wordplay links together Jabal, Jubal, and Tubal-Cain, the three sons of Lamech. It associates Adah, Zillah, and Naamah, the three women mentioned in the text. It also links the three brothers with Cain.

3. Wordplay also provides a means of associating the narrative section of 4:1-16 and the names of Cain and Abel there with the Cain of 4:17-24 and also with the three brothers in the genealogy. On the other hand, it does not seem to play a significant role in associating the genealogy of Genesis 5 with that of 4:17-24.

4. With respect to what these names may tell us about the name bearers, Irad and, less likely, Tubal-Cain may describe something of geographical origins. Cain, Enoch, Zillah, and Naamah may suggest occupations. Adah and (again) Naamah may reflect physical characteristics. Although it is difficult to determine, Jabal, Jubal, and Tubal-Cain could imply expressions of thanksgiving in the bringing forth of the child at birth. Other suggestions include associations with being led forth in a procession, perhaps religious or military, though the idea of a procession is not necessarily implicit in the verb. In these cases, however, we do not know the identity of the deity. Methushael, if interpreted correctly, does designate the name bearer as the devotee of a specific underworld deity. Mehujael confesses the life-giving power of either the West Semitic deity El or of an unspecified deity.

5. Both the study of the origins of these names and the investigation into their wordplay confirm Cain's line as one concerned with representatives of a range of cultural skills.

CHAPTER 11

THE GENEALOGY OF SETH

1. Genesis 4:25-26

a. Adam

As argued above, אָדָם here appears for the first time in Genesis as a proper name. This serves to attach Adam to the line of Seth and to implicitly disassociate him from the line of Cain. The failure to mention Eve's name contrasts with her appearance in 4:1, where Adam's name does not appear. This might seem to associate Eve with Cain's line were it not for her statement of v. 26, which refers to both Seth and Abel as her offspring (זֶרַע), but omits any reference to kinship when mentioning Cain. Whatever the tie at the beginning of chapter four, the events of the chapter have separated her from Cain. The use of אָדָם as a personal name for the first time serves as an indication that something new is about to happen, something which contrasts with the mistakes and failures of chapters three and four. It signals the movement of this figure from a generic representative of humanity through the titular caretaker and husband into the realm of a participant in the toledoth of Genesis and thus in the memory of humanity in general and of Israel in particular.

b. Seth

Discussions concerning the **kî** particle which introduces the second half of the verse must allow for an asseverative force in the particle.[316] This renders possible a translation such as, 'She called his name Seth, "God has (indeed) provided another seed for me in place of Abel whom Cain slew."' However, comparison with other wordplay in Genesis 1-11, especially 3:20, where **kî** also appears, requires some

[316]See the discussion in Muraoka 1985:158-164 on the emphatic use of this particle. Muraoka argues that this was the original use of the particle.

connection between the name and the statement of Eve which follows it. Whatever the precise relationship to the name Seth intended by the statement of Eve which follows, clearly the text intends a wordplay on the name itself. As Strus (1977:66) observes, the assonance of the proper name Seth and the verb *šāt* expresses how this birth brings to an end one line and begins a new line of descent.

זֶרַע אַחֵר "another offspring" conveys the key idea of v. 25. It insists that what follows serves as a substitute or replacement for the line which Abel might have engendered had he lived.[317] Despite the implications of the Sethite line as intended to contrast with the line of Cain, this verse emphasizes the role it plays in relation to the line which would have belonged to Abel. In this way, the text of v. 25 understands the name of Seth as primarily associated with his own generation and its events. Seth becomes the replacement for Abel. On the other hand, his line, as we will see, provides a greater thematic focus in comparison with that of Cain. Later biblical and extrabiblical emphasis on the righteousness of Seth[318] reflects the conviction of tradition that the birth of Seth represents a change in the order of things. The culmination of the line in Noah, the divinely favored one, suggests we may find here the "placing" or setting forth of a line which contrasts with Genesis 4:17-24.

---

[317] The עוֹד "again" at the beginning of the v. also serves to emphasize the replacement for Abel which this text describes. Abel (not Cain) is the last son born to Adam and Eve before the birth of Seth. Further, associations of Seth with the line of Cain (Wilson 1977:158-166) have no support in the text. Nor does Seth have any clear relation to the figure of Alalgar, the second named figure in the antediluvian line of the Old Babylonian king list with whom he has been associated (cf. Zimmern 1924:24; Westermann 1974:472-475).

[318] The expression, "children of Seth" (*bĕnê šēt*), appears in Num 24:17 in what may be a reference to humanity in general, or to the Sutu, a term used to describe nomadic groups. See Rouillard 1985:436-438. Rouillard rejects the Sutu identification arguing that this is a general nomadic designation incompatible with the specific region of Moab. Sir 49:16 describes Seth as highly honored among humanity. For further significance to Seth and his righteousness in later Jewish, Gnostic, and Christian writings, see Klijn 1977.

c. Enosh

The introduction of such a name in v. 26 would point to several implications. First, the semantic parallel with Adam would lead the reader to expect Enosh to fulfill a parallel role, starting the human race anew. Second, as the son of Seth, the bearer of the name Enosh would point to the beginning of a line which would replace that which Abel had not lived to engender. Third, the appearance of an offspring of Seth with this name would suggest that the reader may now expect a new line which will also provide an alternative to the line of Cain. In Enosh, we anticipate the new or second Adam, a parallel to the first, not only in terms of beginning anew but also in terms of finding in this figure the hopes and aspirations for a future humanity which were first founded in Adam (Cassuto 1961:246-247; Sasson 1978:175; Rendsburg 1986:24).

We therefore find in the generation of Enosh that people began to call upon the name of Yahweh.[319] The problem of the mention of Yahweh as used by individuals at this point has provoked discussion in light of its apparent introduction in Exodus 3 and 6. Although this problem may appear to lie outside of the study of personal names in Genesis, it does raise redactional questions concerning the history of the text. A number of explanations have been suggested.[320] Whichever proves correct, the importance of the name of Yahweh as a particular revelation of the divine character (whether or not the actual name then appeared) remains a valid exegetical point in Genesis 4:26. It agrees with the approach argued for understanding the personal names, one in which the implications of the name itself interact with the narrative so as to reinforce the intent of the text. Drawing attention to the name of Yahweh at this, the beginning of a

---

[319] Accepting the verb as it is commonly understood and not as possessing a meaning "to profane" as earlier suggested. For surveys of the interpretation of this passage, see Sandmel 1961; Fraade 1984.

[320] For a summary, see Hess 1992 "Enosh."

new line and at the conclusion of Genesis 4, also draws our attention to the fact that God is not mentioned in the Cainite genealogy of Genesis 4:17-24. Even where we would expect to find the name of God, in the song of Lamech, there appears the odd use of the passive construction in v. 24, perhaps revealing an intentional desire to avoid a divine name. Indeed, searching the text, we find the last reference to Yahweh in 4:16, where Cain leaves the presence of Yahweh. Such a statement not only explains the lack of God's presence in the Cainite genealogy. It also points to the contrast anticipated in the line of Seth, a line in which the first offspring, the new/second Adam, experiences the beginning of a new era of worship of the Lord.[321]

d. Conclusions

This text concludes the story of Cain and Abel and forms a transition from the genealogy of Cain in Genesis 4 to that of Seth in Genesis 5. The personal names serve to reinforce this in several ways already noted. The names also help us to interpret the two verses:

1. Five personal names appear. Of these, three occur as personal names for the first time: Adam, Seth, and Enosh. The other two, Cain and Abel, provide a segmented aspect to what otherwise serves as a linear genealogy with notations. Only the name Seth appears twice; Seth, who forms the key in the kinship relations of all the named figures, as son, father, and brother. Seth alone receives an explanation for his name. In the light of chapter five, we find a relationship of three brothers at the beginning and end of the line of Seth. In the line of Cain, the text suggests two brothers at the beginning (Cain and Abel) but three at the end (Jabal, Jubal, and Tubal-Cain) of the line.

---

[321] See von Rad 1964:112. Perhaps the difficult form of the verb in this phrase in v. 26 intended to reflect a new beginning of worship of Yahweh after the cessation during the generation of Cain.

2. Noteworthy is the absence of Eve's name. Of the other three personal naming episodes of Genesis 1-11, only one includes the name of the name giver in the sentence describing the naming (4:1). However, in one of the other two instances the text locates the name of the name giver in close proximity (5:28). Only in Adam's naming of Eve does the text omit Adam's name, but there Adam does not appear as a personal name, and the title, הָאָדָם, serves as a substitute for the personal name. The reason for the absence of the name Eve remains a mystery. We only observe that in the parallel incident in 4:1, Eve is named but not Adam. In 4:25, Adam is named but not Eve.

3. Wordplay, either implicit or explicit, exists for the three names. The text makes explicit the intended wordplay on Seth's name. It leaves implicit the wordplay on the name Enosh. That Enosh parallels Adam becomes evident from the etymologies of the two names. The role of the two roots in relation to one another elsewhere in Biblical Hebrew may point to the role of Enosh as a second Adam.

2. Genesis 5:1-32

a. Introduction

In Genesis 5 we have the genealogy of Seth, extending from Adam to Noah's sons, although (as we will see) coming to a conclusion of its own in the generation of Lamech. Of the eleven generations described, six have a form which does not vary. Besides its concern with the father and son of each generation, the form also notes the ages at which the fathers begat their offspring and the age at which they died.

The form of the text invites comparison with that of the Cainite line in chapter four: (1) Twelve names occur in 4:17-24;[322] thirteen personal names appear in 5:1-32. (2) A

---

[322] Again, this number remains twelve even if Tubal-Cain is understood as two personal names. Cain has already appeared as a personal name.

recurring genealogical formula appears over three generations in 4:18. Another form extends over six generations in 5:6-20, 25-27 and, with minor variations, over two more in 5:21-24, 28-31. (3) The genealogy of Cain is half linear and half segmented. That of Seth is entirely linear except for Noah's three sons, mentioned as the last words of the chapter. (4) Both genealogies contain notes on specific individuals; that of chapter four includes notes on nine of the persons named. The genealogy of Seth includes notes on three or four of the figures, but only of those at the beginning and end of the line.

This brief comparison of the two genealogies demonstrates the greater order and regularity of the one in chapter five. This is not an accident. It serves in a formal way to distinguish the two lines which have also experienced a distinction by the text in its evaluation of the actions of their members. Within the context of genealogies which thrust forward in time with father-son relationships (Hess 1989), we have in Genesis 5 a demonstration of that movement with a minimum of impediment. This serves to contrast with the line of Cain which does not move forward with the same speed and efficiency and finally stalls in the generations of Lamech and his offspring, with no continuation anywhere in narrative or genealogy.

We will not treat the issue of the meaning of toledoth in these texts, except indirectly through a study of the contexts in which this term appears in Genesis 1-11. Indeed, an appropriate understanding should arise out of its usage in context. Toledoth does divide the text and thus Genesis 5 begins a new division in the book. We have already observed how the last two verses of chapter four bring to a conclusion the preceding material and prepare for what follows in chapter five. In the light of this, the observation deserves emphasis that, while we may ascribe both the lines of Cain and Seth to Adam on the basis of the present text, chapter five moves us on to see the line of Seth as pre-eminently that of Adam. Perhaps more accurately, the line of Seth serves as the new hope for the future of humanity and thus as the line of the new Adam (as observed above), whether in the sense of Seth the Substitute or of Enosh the (new) Human.

b.-d. Adam, Seth, and Enosh

As names, these three have already received discussion. We have also noted the role of vv. 1-3 in reviewing the development of the name of Adam in the opening chapters of Genesis from a generic term to a personal name. It remains only to observe how this passage encapsulates key aspects of the nature and role of humanity as described in chapters one through four, and thereby prepares the reader to begin anew with a second line. However we understand בִּדְמוּתוֹ כְּצַלְמוֹ "in his image as his likeness," the verbal tie with God's creation of humanity in Genesis 1:26-27 demonstrates that the line of Seth will continue something of the divine purpose set forth at creation.

e. Kenan

As with Seth and Enosh in this genealogy, Kenan (qênān קֵינָן) fills a slot in a neatly structured genealogy. No note exists. However, this does not mean that no comparison exists. Comparisons of the name Cain with Kenan yield a similarity distinguished only by an afformative on the latter. We have already seen a possible example of an addition to Cain in the name Tubal-Cain, if we can accept the latter as a two-element name rather than two separate names. If these names do share the same root, then a comparison of Cain with Kenan seems natural. As with Cain, Kenan lacks an onomastic environment and a clear etymology. On the other hand, the figure of Kenan parallels that of Cain insofar as both serve as offspring of two figures whose names possess identical meanings, Enosh and Adam (Wilson 1977:161 and n. 63). Although we know nothing about the figure Kenan, we do know something about both of the fathers of Cain and Kenan. The comparison between Adam and Enosh had already appeared from several angles. This similarity in the names of their offspring draws one more link, again an onomastic one, between the two figures.

We may still question why, if the text intends a comparison, it does not provide the same name. Why do we have the difference in the two names? This observation ties in with differences we have already noted between other names in the two genealogies, names which sound similar and differ by only one or two letters. We will consider this question in summarizing the conclusions on this chapter.

f. Mahalalel

Mahalalel (**mahălal'ēl** מַהֲלַלְאֵל) also serves to fill a genealogical slot, with no apparent significance for the name bearer or wordplay for the name. We have already noted the similarity and difference in the pronunciation and spelling of Mahalalel and the Mehujael of Genesis 4.

g. Jared

Jared (**yered** יֶרֶד) lacks any notation concerning the name or its meaning.

h. Enoch

Enoch (**ḥănôk** חֲנוֹךְ) appears in Genesis 4:17-18 as a son of Cain and as the father of Irad. The same name also occurs in Genesis 5:18-24, where Enoch is the son of Jared and the father of Methuselah. The Enoch of chapter 5 "walked with **hā'ĕlōhîm**," and was taken by God. The Enoch of Genesis 4 receives a notice in the text in which Cain builds a city and names it after Enoch. Dispute has arisen regarding this note.[323] What is clear in the present text is the position of the

[323] Many scholars find in the fact that the phrase is placed after Enoch, the suggestion that Enoch (rather than Cain) may have been the builder of the city. Enoch then would have named the city after his son, Irad (Cassuto 1961:229-231; Wilson 1977:139-141; Sasson 1978:174; Miller 1985:241-242 n. 9; cf. however Sawyer 1986:164). However, a textual displacement of the

note associating it with Enoch in some way. Wordplay remains absent from the text. It seems unlikely that the present text equates the two Enochs in chapters 4 and 5. Instead, the placement of Enoch seventh from Adam in the line of Seth in Genesis 5 (Sasson 1978) corresponds to Lamech, seventh in the line of Cain. Enoch's life of piety contrasts with that of Lamech, whose life is one of bloodshed (Gen 4:23-24). Enoch's heavenly wisdom, elaborated in the prophecies of I Enoch and of Jude 24, also contrasts with Lamech's earthly wisdom (cf. Reiner 1961). Thus the Enoch of Genesis 5 is more closely associated with the Lamech of Genesis 4 than with the Enoch of Genesis 4.

i. Methuselah

As with Mahalalel, Methuselah has been related to a name in the line of Cain, Methushael. The LXX also renders both names mathousala. For the differences in spelling, see under the discussion on Methushael. Such distinctions do not render the observations on the similarity invalid. Neither do they necessitate a common source for the two names (Finkelstein 1963:50; Wilson 1977:150-151). Instead, they may suggest an attempt to focus on similar elements in both lines, a conscious decision to provide a contrast by observing the similarities in the names and yet also the distinctions in the name bearers.

j. Lamech

Lamech acts as a pivotal figure in Seth's genealogy. His lifespan of 777 years surely reflects the number 7, so important in the Lamech of chapter four. In addition, in chapter five Lamech figures as seventh in the line from the new Adam, Enosh, just as Enoch received a position seventh in the line from Adam (Jacob 1934:166-167; Cassuto 1961:243).

---

phrase is as likely as a textual change in the name (from an original Irad to Enoch). The relation of Irad to Eridu is not clear and the background to this name may be closer to the West Semitic world. Cf. above under Irad.

This serves to signal the completion of the line with its formulaic repetition.

With Lamech we find a break in the genealogy in the form of a note (as with Enoch). Here the text provides a reason for the naming of Noah. We have considered the meaning of this statement under the study of Noah. We also find a rationale for the giving of the name. This occurs with only two other name givers, Adam (for Eve) and Eve (for Cain and Seth). In all these cases, the name giver designates the first of a new line (the case of the naming of Eve involves the first named figure of the line of the entire human race). As with the number of years and position in the line, Lamech's act of name giving implies the end of one line and the beginning of a new one. In fact, from the perspective of the text, the line of Seth ends with Lamech. Noah picks up with a new line in chapters ten and eleven. Meanwhile, in chapters six through nine, he and his sons serve as the major characters in a narrative context. For this reason, the genealogical formula ceases with Lamech. Noah and his sons receive cursory notice in the last verse of the chapter. Much more than in chapter five, they form part of the narrative which begins in six. We will examine them separately as names connected with this narrative.

Considering the pivotal role of Enoch in the genealogy of Seth, it may be of interest to compare his position in the genealogy of Cain. Although not in the same way, he also serves as a figure whose generation marks a transition. Cain's line forms of linear genealogy until Lamech's generation. His offspring are described in terms of a segmented genealogy. Thus the structure of Cain's genealogy changes with Lamech. The transitional nature of Lamech in both genealogies may be suggested by the name itself. Although possessing no known etymology, it has the unusual feature of containing the three consonants in Hebrew which lie at the centre of the alphabet and serve to divide the alphabet into two halves on some West Semitic abecedaries.[324]

j. Conclusions

As with the first section, these conclusions will take into account all names in the linear genealogy from Adam to Lamech, nine generations. They will also include allusions to 4:25-26.

1. Explicit wordplay occurs with Seth. As argued above, a possible wordplay exists for both Lamech and Enoch and the comments which appear with these names. We become more speculative with the remaining names, though even here we have observed associations. On the one hand, we may see a relationship between two names (Mahalalel and Jared) and an earlier note concerning the beginnings of some sort of special relationship to Yahweh during their "generations." On the other hand, we may see how parallel associations in function betray a parallel name in terms of its meaning (Enosh).

2. The question remains as to the reason for the similarities of many of the names in the lines of Cain and of Seth. It has been argued: (1) that these similarities do not require a common origin for the two lines; (2) that, except for Enoch and Lamech, significant differences exist in the spellings of the related names; (3) and that these differences produce distinct etymologies.

Yet, the similarities do exist. Even where spellings differ, the structure of the names may remain parallel, as, for example, with Methushael and Methushelah. Further, we do not have so many names to contend with, that we can easily dismiss the identical spellings of two of them. Yet the distinct purposes and directions of the two lines also remain. The line of Cain (1) accelerates in its lifestyle of murderous vengeance; (2) focuses on civilization and culture in its

[324] Cf. Hess 1991 for a comparison with the relevant abecedaries.

various manifestations; and (3) terminates with no further reference. The line of Seth (1) preserves and may enhance concern for and practice of relationship with the divine; (2) omits any reference to murder or to any human culture (unless found implicitly in Lamech's statement on the naming of Noah); and (3) ends as a genealogy but continues in terms of its descendants through the remainder of Genesis and of the Hebrew Bible.

In addition, both lines begin with the same figure, Adam, both include the figure of Enoch, and both end with a figure who bears the same name, Lamech. With this in mind, we would tentatively suggest that, whatever the origins of the two lines of Cain and Seth, the texts of Genesis 4 and 5, and particularly the recurrent similarity in names, invite an examination of their relationship. Thus the text attaches Cain's Enoch to a city but Seth's Enoch moves beyond human culture to the world of the divine. As noted above, both Lamechs play pivotal roles in their lines and both have statements recorded in the text. But Cain's Lamech utters a cry of vengeance and with that terminates his line; while Seth's Lamech expresses the hope for a better life for his descendants, and with that introduces the offspring who will continue his line and play a role in trying to fulfill his wish. There is the suggestion of a special relationship in this genealogical doublet. This will be considered further with the examination of the doublet of chapters ten and eleven.

CHAPTER 12

THE TABLE OF NATIONS IN GENESIS 10

1. Introduction

Noah and his sons, Shem, Ham and Japheth, introduce the genealogical material and narratives of chapters ten and eleven. These names provide a link between these chapters and the preceding material in Genesis. Both the story of the Flood and the smaller but related narrative of Noah's drunkenness and subsequent pronouncements are tied together by the figures who bear these names. The line from Adam to Noah ends in chapter 5 with the mention of Noah, the explanation of his name, and the enumeration of the names of his three sons. The four names occur together five times in the accounts just mentioned; once at the end of the genealogy of Seth (5:32), twice at the beginning of the Flood narrative (6:10; 7:13), once at the beginning of the account of Noah's drunkenness (9:18), and once in the first verse of the passage under consideration here.

In all these occurrences, the order is always the same; Noah, Shem, Ham, and Japheth. That the order here is not one of honor seems clear from the account of the cursing of Ham's son in 9:18-29. Rather, it appears to suggest the common practice of listing the offspring according to their age with the eldest first. It may therefore seem surprising that the discussion of the segmented genealogy of these three sons which appears in chapter ten should begin with Japheth and proceed to Ham, with Shem assigned to the last position. The explanation lies in the method already used in the genealogies of chapters 4 and 5. There Seth's genealogy is the last one named and it is Seth's line which carries on the story in the following chapters. As noted above, Cain's line terminates with chapter 4. Here the concern is not the relative ages of the two, although in the context Cain appears to be the older (see the naming of Seth). The principle that the line which continues always appears last dictates Shem's position as last. We find this principle in chapters 10 and 11, as well. The text assigns Shem's line, which alone continues through the remainder of the book of Genesis, to the final position. This principle remains throughout the book. With each appearance of a set of genealogies, we find the continuing line positioned last in order.

2. The Names

a. Nimrod

We have no explicit wordplay present with Nimrod. As the only personal name in the genealogies of Ham and Japheth in chapter 10, it seems that the Hebrew association of the name with the root, mrd, suggests a relationship with the rebellion of Genesis 11 and forms the primary tie between the Table of Nations and this narrative.[325]

b. Joktan

The structure of the Table of Nations, something long studied in order to understand the reason for the divisions of the gentilics and place names, may suggest an implicit wordplay for Joktan. A third personal name appears in the Table of Nations which, although it does not itself contain a prefixed verbal root, does participate in wordplay in the pronouncements of Noah at the end of chapter 9. The wordplay there assumes a verbal root with a yodh prefix. The name is Japheth. Both Joktan and Japheth have descendants named in the chapter. Japheth's name is related to the concept of enlarging (ptḥ) in the wordplay of Gen 9:27. In chapter 10 Japheth enlarges his family with the enumeration of some fourteen descendants. Joktan, whose

[325]van der Toorn 1990:15, who identifes Nimrod with the deity Ninurta, finds in the figure "the archetype of the Babylonian deity, a symbol of Mesopotamian civilization." Thus there is a conscious contrast with Abram who sets aside Mesopotamian religion and civilization, in obedience to the call of a different deity. Cf. also von Soden 1960.

name would be related to the Hebrew word for making smaller, is given thirteen descendants, one less than Japheth. With these names, Joktan and his descendants cease to appear in the Hebrew Bible.[326] On the other hand, Joktan's brother, Peleg, proceeds to enlarge his own family in the perspective of the Biblical text, as the genealogy of chapter 11 seeks to demonstrate (not to mention the promises of innumerable descendants to Peleg's descendant Abram). This contrast between the names of Japheth and Joktan serves to emphasize the constriction in importance of the latter's descendants from the standpoint of the role they play in the Biblical text.

[326]We might consider the possible relationship to יָקְשָׁן Jokshan, the son of Abraham and Keturah in Gen 25:2, 3. Note that this distinction in the spellings is attested by all ancient versions. Linguistically, the two names remain different despite the similar spellings of names of two of their "sons," Sheba and Dedan.

CHAPTER 13

THE GENEALOGY OF SHEM IN GENESIS 11

1. Introduction

When we examine the genealogy of Genesis 11:10-26 we observe its regularity. The linear genealogy includes the repetition of a formula eight times reaching to nine generations. The formula includes: (1) the name of the line's representative for that generation; (2) the age at which this figure fathered the next generation's representative; (3) the name of the offspring, always a male; (4) the number of years which the first figure lived after fathering the next in the line; and (5) a statement that additional children of both sexes were fathered by the figure. At the ninth generation, that of Terah, the genealogy segments and loses this formulaic character. Although an attempt is made to recapture it with the note in v. 32, the final verses of this chapter are distinct in form and purpose from the remainder of the genealogy. They serve to provide the kinship relations for the family of Abram, relations which will play an important role in the following narratives.

Unlike the genealogy of Shem, the Table of Nations (1) has a segmented genealogy; (2) includes no formula of repetition, omitting any note of ages for the fathering of offspring or for death, and also leaving out all mention of the fathering of additional sons and daughters; and (3) never extends for as long as nine generations. Indeed, the genealogy of Japheth extends for three generations, that of Ham extends for five, and that of Shem, which follows the line of chapter eleven where it takes on a linear aspect, extends for only six generations.

Two observations may suggest reasons for these differences in form. First, the presence of recognizable place names and gentilics throughout the Table of Nations suggests the text was intended as different in form and purpose from the genealogy of chapter eleven. Rather, this is a description of the known world (or much of it) of the period when composition took place. Thus ages of the name bearers and statements about the birth of additional sons and daughters would seem out of place. The names were never intended to be understood as personal; those of chapter eleven were.

Second, the coupling of these two genealogies, separated only by an excursus on the Tower of Babel (itself an extension of the Table of Nations), shows similarities in form with the earlier coupling of two genealogies in chapters 4 and 5. As with the genealogies of Cain and Seth, so the Table of Nations and the genealogy of Shem possess the following features: (1) the first genealogy has a universal context, whether in the descriptions of cultural forms possessed by all peoples (chapter four) or in a listing of those peoples and their cities (chapter ten); (2) the second genealogy has a context which connects it with what follows as well as what precedes in Genesis; i.e. it serves to provide the background for the ancestry of Abram; (3) the first genealogy has less of a fixed form, i.e. whether containing notes on the characters or simply listing descendants without any connecting form, it always moves into a segmented form well before the end of the genealogy; (4) the second genealogy has a much more ordered form, with few or no notes, a clearly identifiable and repetitive formula, and the avoidance of a segmented form until the end of the genealogy; 5) the first genealogy always contains fewer generations, at most about half as many as the second genealogy.

Such observations invite a comparison of the lines of Seth and of Shem.

(1) We notice the extraordinary similarity in form between the two. a) Both use virtually the same formula for each generation in the line, with chapter eleven's text omitting only the final notes about the total years lived and the death of the name bearer. b) Both have lines running nine generations, omitting Adam in chapter five and the generation of Abram in chapter eleven. c) Both have

virtually no interruption in their texts; only a few notes (at the beginning and end of the line, except for Enoch) in Seth's line and none at all in Shem's.

(2) There is also a similarity in content. a) In both, the names in the genealogies and the order of those names have been anticipated with the appearance of some of the names in a preceding genealogy or notice. This is true in Seth's line with the similar and, in two cases, identical spellings of names in Cain's line. It is also true in the genealogical notice which appears at the end of chapter four (vv. 25-26) which includes the names of Seth and Enosh, the first two figures in the line. In Shem's line, the genealogy is anticipated in the Table of Nations with the first five names included in vv. 21-25. All notes on the figures in Shem's line appear in this section rather than the genealogy of chapter eleven. b) Both lines assign to their name bearers incredibly long lifespans. At this point, however, a difference does appear. The lengths of the lifespans diminish as each line progresses, but those of Seth's line remain above 500 years and often approach 1,000 (except for Enoch). On the other hand, the lifespans of Shem's line remain below 500 years (except for Shem) and gradually reduce to the allotted 120 years predicted in 6:3. As significant is the number of years at which the name bearer fathers the next generation. In Genesis 5 this is regularly higher than normal human expectations, from a low of 65 years for Enoch to a high of 187 for Methuselah. On the other hand, the figures in Shem's line, with two exceptions, father their children at ages between 29 and 35. The exceptions are at the beginning and end of the line. Shem, as a member of the pre-Flood era, fathers Arpachshad at the age of 100.[327] Terah, perhaps in

[327] A second reason for Shem's age at the birth of Arpachshad may have to do with a problem which arises in relating the period of the Flood and some of the ages suggested in earlier chapters of Genesis to the notice in 11:10 in which Arpachshad is born two years after the Flood when Shem was 100 years. Genesis 5:32 seems to suggest that the birth of Shem occurred in Noah's 500th year. Genesis 7:6 and 11 place the Flood 100 years later in Noah's 600th year. If Arpachshad was born two years later it should have occurred in Shem's 102nd year. However, the text of Genesis

anticipation of Abram's own age when he fathered Isaac, fathers his sons at 70 years of age.

What do these comparisons and contrasts have to do with the names in Shem's line? First, the close formal association with the line of Seth suggests that, as with that line, the names in Genesis 11 are intended as personal names first and foremost. They reflect name bearers whom the text understood as real people and intended to present that way. Second, the strict adherence to a form, like that of Seth's line, again emphasizes the movement forward with a minimum of stopping for notes or narratives. The purpose of Shem's line is to move the reader as quickly as possible from the preceding material to what lies ahead. This may also suggest a reason for the omission of the final tally of age and notice of death for each name bearer; an essential part of the form in chapter five. Third, an additional reason for this omission and for the introduction of ages which approach those of mortals in subsequent ages is the indication that, with these name bearers we as readers approach our own time. We have left behind the distant past, whose treatment by neighboring cultures as a period of divine-human intermingling may have motivated the emphasis in chapter five that all the ancestors in the line of Seth were mortal and did indeed die, however long they lived.

Finally, the formal similarities between the genealogical "doublet" of Cain and Seth in chapters four and five, and that of the Table of Nations and Shem in chapters ten and eleven allow us to anticipate a possible similarity in content. Cain's line demonstrated aspects of human endeavor and culture available to the whole of humanity while Seth's

---

5:32 could allow for the birth of Shem a year or two after Noah's 500th year. A temporal interpretation of the waw-consecutives in Gen 5:32, in which the second verb of begetting takes place subsequent to the first verb describing Noah's 500th year (Cryer 1985:247-248), combined with Shem's position as second born (Cassuto 1964:260-261), allows for this period of two years. Shem was born in Noah's 502nd year and Arpachshad in Noah's 602nd year (Wenham 1987:250).

genealogy narrowed the focus with its emphasis on one descendant and on one aspect of human concern, as reflected in the meanings of many of the personal names. The concern is that of faith and religious experience with the divine, something which the etymology, structure, wordplay, and onomastic environment of the names suggested. Can we find a similar narrowing of focus in chapter eleven? The Table of Nations clearly provides a universal geographical perspective with its place names and gentilics. Does this suggest that the personal names of chapter eleven will focus this perspective to one region of the world? We shall seek an answer as we proceed to examine the personal names in this line.

2. The Names

a. Arpachshad

Arpachshad (ʾarpakšad אַרְפַּכְשַׁד) has no obvious wordplay.

b. Shelah

Shelah was identified as a divine name. As with Methuselah, the name seems uncertain in its position in the context of the other personal names. Whether as a pagan deity in a line whose names express concern for a relation with the divine, or as a DN in a line whose names suggest a geographical interest, the שֶׁלַח-names represent an enigma in terms of their purpose. They link the genealogies of Seth and Shem. שֶׁלַח is the only element which both lines share.

c. Eber

In Genesis 10:21 the text designates Shem as אֲבִי כָּל־בְּנֵי־עֵבֶר "father of all the sons of Eber." We have encountered the expression אֲבִי כָּל "father of all of" once before, in Genesis 4:21. There the text describes Jubal as the father of all of those who play the lyre and pipe. The expression suggests other than direct paternity. In Genesis 4 Jubal is grouped with those who introduce new cultural forms, so Eber in the context of Genesis 10 may suggest a group related in some way similar to the other gentilics or place names in that chapter. Therefore, we may find in the name Eber a gentilic or a place name, as well as a personal name. Its position at this point in the line and its etymology may suggest a migration during this early generation, a movement to the geographical vicinity specified by those names which appear later in the genealogy.

It is this latter point which serves as the only clue for any implicit wordplay. Yet, beyond the note concerning the sons of Eber, nothing is made of this material in Shem's genealogy. Rather the name forms a link between the genealogy of Shem and Abram the Hebrew in Genesis 14 as well as the Hebrews of the Joseph story.[328] As Shem and Shelah link the line of Genesis 11 with the genealogy and narratives of chapters six through nine, so Eber anticipates the narrative and genealogical material which lies beyond Genesis 1-11 and serves as an onomastic link with it.

d. Peleg

Peleg is the last of Shem's line who is noted in the Table of Nations. There he appears along with his brother Joktan (10:25). If we understand the כִּי-clause which follows the name of Peleg as an explanation of the name, then Peleg represents the last figure in the genealogies whose name receives an explanatory note. The note is כִּי בְיָמָיו נִפְלְגָה הָאָרֶץ "for in his days the earth was divided."[329] Whether this refers to (1) the division between the descendants of Peleg and his brother Joktan,[330] or (2) the division caused by the

[328]It is not necessary that "Eber" and "Hebrew" share the same root from an etymological standpoint. The word play could merely rely on two names whose apparent roots identical consonants.

[329]This etymology is the only one in Genesis 1-11 which Strus 1978:55-56 includes under the category of "les étymologies simples."

[330]Skinner 1930:220; Cassuto 1964:221; Moye 1990:590.

introduction of different languages in the subsequent incident concerning the Tower of Babel (Genesis 11:1-9),[331] the verb with its **plg** root plays upon the name of Peleg, spelled with the same three consonants.

e. Reu

Reu's name bears witness to a continued interest in religious matters in the line and, less likely, may provide an example of a geographical name.

f. Serug

Serug is an identifiable geographic name, probably located in the vicinity of Harran.

g. Nahor

Joshua 24:2 describes both the elder Nahor and his son Terah as polytheists. The Bible also alludes to the religion of the younger Nahor. This time the reference occurs closer to our text, in Genesis. There, in 31:53, we read how Jacob and Laban concluded their agreement by swearing by the deities representative of their ancestors;[332] by the God of Abraham and by the god(s) [ʾĕlōhê] of Nahor. Although we do not know the specific identity of these deities, we may observe the association of both Nahors with Ur and Harran, both of which held a tradition in the Ancient Near East as cult centers of the lunar deity Sin (Edzard 1965:102).

Nahor is a place name in the region of Harran. We also find here an implicit means by which the name fits into the immediate context of Genesis 11 and the broader context of the early Biblical narrative. It fits into the former by

---

[331] Gunkel 1902:80; Driver 1948:130; Wenham 1987:231.

[332] For the role of this action in the inheritance of property rights and family responsibilities, see Morrison (1983:163) and the parallels in invoking deities of the deceased in inheritance rights as suggested in the Late Bronze Age texts from Emar (Huehnergard 1985:429-431).

associating the background of Terah and Abram with the region of Harran. It fits into the broader context of Genesis insofar as the associations of the name bearer with cult centers of an important pagan deity point to the worship of a god different from that of Abram and his descendants.

h. Terah

With Terah we have another example of a place name which finds its way into the genealogy of Shem, a place name located in the region of Harran. But perhaps this is not the sequence of transmission. Perhaps the personal name predated the place name.

i. Haran

We have no connection between the personal name Haran and the place name Harran in the Biblical text. However, the name may have a geographic location in the same area as those already identified in the line of Shem; the northern Euphrates region with its river valleys, plains, and significantly its mountains. It also fits as a religious confession, something already observed with the personal names of Haran's two daughters. Haran thus remains another testimony to the religious sensitivities of the family of Terah.

3. Conclusions

1. The wordplay is largely confined to providing the reader with a geographical area or setting from which Abram emerges in the following chapters and to which his family returns from time to time in order to find appropriate spouses from among their relatives. The name Shelah may suggest something of a pagan environment, but only the note on Nahor later in Genesis renders this conclusive. With such a distinct set of names, the additional ties provided by Shelah with Methuselah of Seth's line and by Eber with the Hebrews of later chapters of Genesis may have

appeared necessary to establish the text in its context as the transition between the worldwide events of Genesis 1:1 - 11:9 and the nationalistic stories which follow.

2. The wordplay of the names Haran and Iscah points to the possible religious interest of the family of Terah. Likewise the name Milcah describes the expectation of a role and status assumed for one who is a forebearer of nations and peoples. Thus all the names speak of an anticipation of what is to come, both of religious expectation and of the hope of many and great descendants.

With these observations we return to those made at the beginning of this chapter. The suggestions concerning a possible thematic relationship between the Table of Nations and the line of Shem have been reinforced. It may be observed that with the segmentation of the line at the end of chapter 11, we reach another turning point. The presence here of feminine names and of marriages with more than one child named most closely resembles the line of Cain in chapter four. Here, however, the line does not terminate but continues into the narrative of Abram and the remainder of Genesis. Indeed, the onomastics at the end of the line of Shem suggest a profound and perhaps intended contrast with those at the end of Cain's line. In chapter four, the names focussed on human accomplishments and on continuing and repeating the ancestor's name, i.e. Cain. In chapter eleven, the sort of names found at the end of the line contrast with what preceded. There is no repetition of the old. Nor do we find here the focus on human accomplishments. Rather, the names suggest religious confession and values as well as expectation of greater things to come in the generations which follow. Thus the text of the genealogy of Shem anticipates a religious, geographic,and social break with the past.

CHAPTER 14

CONCLUSION

Having considered something of the wordplay of the personal names in Genesis 1-11, it is possible to summarize the role which they play in the development of the narrative and genealogies of the text itself.

The names in the narrative sections examined in part II, chapter 2 serve as descriptions of roles or characteristics of the name bearers. As such the appearance and repeated use of these personal names function as refrains in the narratives. They remind the reader of the intent of the story and the significance of the name bearer. The key roles of Eve, Noah, and Shem, in the line from the first generation to Abram, may be enhanced by their names, all of which have plausible etymologies, onomastic environments, and clear wordplay in the narrative. Thus meanings identified in roots associated with Eve and Noah correspond to the Biblical meaning of the promises of life, rest, and comfort to reverse God's curse of death and unremitting toil. The name of Shem prepares the reader for the chosen means of making a name for humanity, through Abram's call and blessing of Genesis 12, rather than through that proposed in the incident of the Tower of Babel. The meanings of the names of the additional figures of Abel and Ham reinforce this focus on the chosen line throughout the narratives, whether by way of contrast as in the case of Abel, "the shortlived," versus the longlived antediluvian line, or by complement as in the case of Ham, "paternal uncle" of the line of his brother Shem. As for Cain and Japheth, neither name has a clear etymology, but the former does describe the acquisitive nature of his own line through the wordplay associated with his name. As for Japheth, he too has associated wordplay in which Noah blesses him through the enlargement of his own line, a feature which anticipates the aspect of blessing promised to Abram in the increase of his descendants.

Thus the personal names of the narratives provide an "onomastic commentary" parallel to the events within the narratives. Tying these stories together are the genealogies. From both a literary perspective and from a comparison with Ancient Near Eastern king lists, the genealogies move the narrative toward the descriptions of the patriarchs in Genesis 12-50.[333] In terms of their relation with the surrounding narratives, the genealogies have their most important links in the personal names which occur in both with no change in their spelling. But when we move into the genre of Biblical genealogy we find a reversal of the roles of the names and their context. In the narratives of Genesis 1-11, the prose, which serves as a context for the names, functions to provide the meaning and direction for the text. The names reinforce this through their repetition. In the genealogies, however, the names function to provide meaning and direction for the text, while their literary context reinforces this through the repetition of its form. Thus the etymologies of the names are no less important in the genealogies than they are in the narratives. In the narratives, it was often necessary to find some vehicle of wordplay to tie the name into the story. In the genealogies, despite the occasional note, this is not the case. Rather, the names themselves point to the significance of the line.

For example, Cain's line begins with basic elements of civilization reflected in urban (Irad) and wisdom (Enoch) names, as well as in names associated with religion (Mehujael and Methushael). Halfway through, however, it turns into a mini-narrative, suggesting a crucial turning point (Lamech). The cultured environment of art and music (Adah, Zillah, and Naamah) and the sophistication of religious procession (Jabal, Jubal, and Tubal-Cain), fail to

[333]For the literary aspect, see Gabriel 1959:421; Johnson 1969:3-36; Westermann 1974:465-467; Clines 1976:491-494; Fishbane 1979:27-39; Robinson 1986:595-608. For the Ancient Near Eastern king lists and this aspect as a fundamental point of contrast with their own "backward looking" ideology, see Hess 1989:244-250.

overcome the murderous vengeance of Cain as manifested with increased ferocity in his descendant.

We may "read" the line of Seth similarly. For here, hope is expressed both for the substitution (Seth) and renewal of the first person (Enosh), with the expectation of even recasting the figure where the line turned away from God (Kenan). Religious sentiment characterizes this line, with praise (Mahalalel), prayer for divine descent [and aid] (Jared), and with a wisdom figure (Enoch), whose note emphasizes a divine rather than human wisdom. The name Methuselah may fit into this group of the pious, though as a devotee of an alien deity. However, the uncertainty of the second element's meaning continues to leave a question mark. Lamech is found at the end of this line, at a crucial turning point insofar as the next generation provides hope for the future. His role anticipates the continuation of Seth's line in the line of Shem in chapter 11.

This last line, although also problematic in some of its names (Arpachshad and Shelah), focuses on the movement (Eber) into the land of Abram's ancestry (Peleg, Serug, Nahor, and Terah) with a brief pause for continued recognition of the line's religious sentiment (Reu). These perspectives suggest a change from the earlier genealogies of Genesis four and five. The three genealogies, as indicated by the personal names they contain, each represents a different thematic emphasis, whether it be cultural with the line of Cain, or religious with the line of Seth, or geographic with the line of Shem. The comparisons and contrasts have already been noted in the chapters on the lines of Seth and Shem. In sum, we find in the genealogies specific themes which emphasize those fundamentals which will comprise the basic elements of the promises made to Abram and the patriarchs in Genesis.

The theme of geography in Shem's line is repeated again and again in the return of the patriarchs to find wives in their homeland of northern Syria. It is refocussed in the promise to Abram of land in Canaan. A second theme, that of the religious piety which appears in the line of Seth, is also found in the experience of Abram and in each of the narratives throughout the remainder of Genesis. As for the theme reflected in the line of Cain, that of culture and civilization, this theme remains a constant challenge to the descendants of Seth's line. There are the leaders of cities and states which Abram confronts in Genesis 14 and continue to struggle with. The contrast of human construction of the Tower of Babel by civilizations which stand opposed to God is summed up in the constant struggle with Egypt, perhaps the best representative of this image in the later chapters of Genesis. But its most vivid expression comes with God's call to Abram to leave his homeland and the cities of Ur and Harran and to journey to a foreign land. This call is made at the beginning of chapter 12. With it come promises which, after the great test of faith in chapter 22, culminate in the promise of possession of the gates of the enemies of Abram and his descendants.

A final theme concerns the overall structure of the genealogies in the context of Genesis 1-11 and throughout the remainder of Genesis. We have already noted the tendency for the genealogies in chapters 4 and 5 to be grouped together, and for this also to occur in Genesis 10 and 11. We have also seen how the names and notes in these two groups of genealogies demonstrate a common tendency. The first of the two genealogies, the A genealogy, contains names which reflect a general consideration, whether of human culture and endeavor in Genesis 4 or of human geography in Genesis 10. The second genealogy, the B genealogy, narrows its subject matter to reflect a specific element of the A genealogy, a concern which will form an important part of the character and background of Abram and his descendants. We have found this to be a religious sentiment in chapter 5 and a North Syrian geographic context in chapter 11.

Having made this observation, we may go on to ask whether this is not a characteristic of the toledoth in Genesis 1-11? The one other example we have is that of Genesis 1 and 2.

Genesis 2:4 refers to the creation account as a toledoth. This would appear to apply specifically to Genesis 1, with its structured form and its progressive movement from one day to the next. Indeed, this may suggest a reason for the use of "days" as dividing points in Genesis 1; they serve a similar function as the years do in the other genealogies, distinguishing one item from the next and relating them in time by use of a repetitive formula. Further, as has long been noticed, the account of Genesis 2 serves as a specification of Genesis 1. It provides a focus from the more generalized account of the creation of the universe to a particular concern with the creation of humanity along with the context in which the first generation of persons can be nurtured.[334]

This brings us to consider whether the whole of Genesis 1-11 does not serve in a similar fashion, as a general statement about the world and all humanity. From this we may expect to move as the text does, into a specific consideration of one part of the world and of one part of humanity, i.e. Abram and his descendants. Thus, although the whole of Genesis 1-11 may not need to be identified as toledoth, the building blocks of the text lead us to ask whether we have here a key principle and rationale for the structure of the whole of Genesis, one which ultimately resides in the wordplay of the personal names in the text.

We have argued that the interaction of the personal names with the literary text of Genesis has been central to understanding the meaning of the text. Perhaps we may also find here something about the role of personal names themselves in ancient Israel. It is insufficient to suggest that personal names merely refer to their name bearers. In fact, more is taking place. The etymology and wordplay of the personal names serve to carry the narrative forward and to provide important clues as to its theme and direction. Yet, as the narratives of Genesis also show, the name bearers themselves carry forward their own historical situation and

---

[334] See Hess 1990a.

provide the centers from which the theme and direction of the narratives and of the entire book may be understood. Therefore, it would appear that the personal names play a role in the literary environment of Genesis 1-11 which corresponds to the role exerted by the name bearers in their history. In neither case is this a passive role wherein the surrounding text or the events of the narrative act upon the names and name bearers. Instead, it is the active involvement of the names in the literature and of the name bearers in their "history" which drive and direct the themes and significance of Genesis 1-11. The key to understanding Genesis 1-11 lies in appreciating the role of the name as well as the name bearer, and thereby in understanding something of the relationship of the name to the name bearer.

With such themes the genealogies of Genesis 1-11 prepare the reader for what is to come in the rest of Genesis. In addition to similar names, which appear with the same spellings in Genesis 1-11 and in the later chapters, and the obvious connection of the name bearers at the end of Shem's line with those portrayed in chapters 12 and what follows, we find a similarity of themes expressed through the names themselves. These move the narrative, with its characters and its drama, forward in the book; and provide a summary of the work itself.

BIBLIOGRAPHY

Abbadi, S.

1983 Die Personennamen der Inschriften aus Hatra. Texte und Studien zur Orientalistik 1. Hildesheim: Georg Olms.

Abou-Assaf, A., Bordreuil, P., and Millard, A. R.

1982 La statue de Tell Fekherye et son inscription bilingue assyro-araméenne. Etudes Assyriologiques. Paris: Éditions Recherche sur les civilisations.

Aharoni, Y.

1979 The Land of the Bible. A Historical Geography. Revised edition. Trans. A. F. Rainey from Hebrew. Philadelphia: Westminster.

Aharoni, Y., Naveh, J., et al.

1981 Arad Inscriptions. Edited and revised A. F. Rainey. Trans. J. Ben-Or from Hebrew. Jerusalem: Israel Exploration Society.

Aḥituv, Sh.

1968 mĕtûšā'ēl. Cols. 643-644 in vol. 5 of Encyclopedia Biblica, eds. U. Cassuto et al. Jerusalem: Bialik Institute. Hebrew.

Aistleitner, J.

1963 Wörterbuch der Ugaritischen Sprache. Berichte über die Verhandlungen der sächsischen Akademie der Wissenschaften zu Leipzig, Philologisch-historische Klasse, 106, 3. Berlin: Akademie Verlag.

Akinnaso, F. N.

1980 The Sociolinguistic Basis of Yoruba Personal Names. Anthropological Linguistics 22: 275-304.

1981 Names and Naming Principles in Cross-Cultural Perspective. Names 29: 37-63.

1983 Yoruba Traditional Names and the Transmission of Cultural Knowledge. Names 31: 139-166.

al-Ansary, A. R.

1969-73 Lihyanite Personal Names: A Comparative Study. Annual of Leeds University Oriental Society 7: 5-16.

Albright, W. F.

1921-22 Contributions to the Historical Geography of Palestine. Annual of the American Schools of Oriental Research 2-3: 1-46.

1924 Contributions to Biblical Archaeology and Philology. JBL 43: 363-393.

1931 Mittannian maryannu, "chariot-warrior," and the Canaanite and Egyptian Equivalents. AfO 6: 217-221.

1938 Was the Patriarch Teraḥ a Canaanite Moon-God? BASOR 71: 35-40.

1944 A Prince of Taanach in the Fifteenth Century B.C. BASOR 94: 12-27.

Alonso-Schökel, L.

1976 Sapiential and Covenant Themes in Genesis 2-3. Pp. 468-480 in J. L. Crenshaw, ed., Studies in Ancient Israelite Wisdom. Library of Biblical Studies. New York: Ktav.

Anderson, B. W., ed.

1984 Creation in the Old Testament. Issues in Religion and Theology 6. Philadelphia: Fortress.

Anderson, M.

1984 Proper Names, Naming, and Labeling in Saami', Anthropological Linguistics 26: 186-201.

Andreasen, N.-E.

1981 Adam and Adapa: Two Anthropological Characters. AUSS 19: 179-194.

Archi, A.

1979 The Epigraphic Evidence from Ebla and the Old Testament. Bib 60: 556-566.

1985 Testi Amministrativi: Assegnazioni di Tessuti (Archivio L. 2769). Archivi Reali de Ebla Testi 1. Rome: Missione Archeologica Italiana in Siria.

1987 Ebla and Eblaite. Pp. 7-17 in C. H. Gordon, G. A. Rendsburg, and N. H. Winter, eds., Eblaitica: Essays on the Ebla Archives and Eblaite Language. Vol. I., Publications of the Center for Ebla Research at New York University, Winona Lake, IN: Eisenbrauns.

Archi, A., and Biga, M. G.

1982 Testi Amministrativi de vario Contenuto (Archivio L. 2769: T.M.75.G.3000-4101). Archivi Reali de Ebla Testi 3. Rome: Missione Archeologica Italiana in Siria.

Archi, A., Biga, M. G., and Milano, L.

1988 Studies in Eblaite Prosopography. Pp. 205-306 in Eblaite Personal Names and Semitic Name-Giving. Papers of a Symposium held in Rome July 15-17, 1985, ed. A. Archi. Archivi Reali di Ebla Studi 1. Rome: Missione Archeologica Italiana in Siria.

Arnaud, D.

1985a Textes sumériens et accadiens. Recherches au pays d'Aštata Emar VI. 1. Éditions Recherche sur les Civilisations "synthèse" n° 18. Paris: A.D.P.F.

1985b Textes sumériens et accadiens. Recherches au pays d'Aštata Emar VI. 2. Éditions Recherche sur les Civilisations "synthèse" n° 18. Paris: A.D.P.F.

1986 Textes sumériens et accadiens. Recherches au pays d'Aštata Emar VI. 3. Éditions Recherche sur les Civilisations "synthèse" n° 18. Paris: A.D.P.F.

1987 Textes de la bibliothèque: transcriptions et traductions. Recherches au pays d'Aštata Emar VI. 4. Éditions Recherche sur les Civilisations "synthèse" n° 28. Paris: A.D.P.F.

Astour, M. C.
1973 A North Mesopotamian Locale of the Keret Epic? UF 5: 29-39.

Attridge, H. W., and Oden, R. A., Jr.
1981 Philo of Byblos The Phoenician History. Introduction, Critical Text,Translation, Notes. CBQ Monograph Series 9. Washington, D.C.: Catholic Biblical Association of America.

Avigad, N.
1986 Hebrew Bullae from the Time of Jeremiah. Remnants of a Burnt Archive. Jerusalem: Israel Exploration Society.

Barnett, R. D.
1975 Phrygia and the Peoples of Anatolia in the Iron Age. Chapter XXX. Pp. 417-442 in The Cambridge Ancient History Volume II Part 2, eds. I. E. S. Edwards, N. G. L. Hammond, and E. Sollberger. Third edition. Cambridge: University Press.

Barr, J.
1968 Comparative Philology and the Text of the Old Testament. Oxford: Clarendon.
1969-70 The Symbolism of Names in the Old Testament. Bulletin of the John Rylands Library 52: 11-29.
1974 Etymology and the Old Testament. Oudtestamentische Studien 19: 1-28.
1990 Review of J. D. Fowler, Theophoric Personal Names in Ancient Hebrew, JSOT Supplement Series 49, Sheffield: JSOT, 1988, in JTS 41 (1990) 137-139.

Barton, G. A.
1909 Haverford Library Collection of Cuneiform Tablets or Documents from the Temple Archives of Telloh. Part II. Philadelphia: John C. Winston; London: Deadley Brothers.

Bauer, T.
1926 Die Ostkanaanäer. Eine philologisch-historische Untersuchung über die Wanderschicht der sogenannten "Amoriter" in Babylonien. Leipzig: Verlag der Asia Minor.

Bean, S.
1980 Ethnology and the Study of Proper Names. Anthropological Linguistics 22: 305-316.

Beek, G. van
1962 Abel. P. 4 in vol. 1 of IDB.

Beeston, A. F. L., Ghul, M. A., Müller, W. W., and Ryckmans, J.
1982 Sabaic Dictionary (English-French-Arabic). Publication of the University of Sanaa, YaR. Louvain-la-Neuve: Éditions Peeters; Beyrouth: Librairie du Liban.
Beitzel, B. J.
1976 The Placenames in the Mari Texts: An Onomastic and Topographic Study. Ph. D. dissertation, The Dropsie University.
1978 From Ḫarran to Imar Along the Old Babylonian Itinerary: The Evidence from the Archives Royales de Mari. Pp. 209-219 in G. A. Tuttle, ed., Biblical and Near Eastern Studies. Essays In Honor of William Sanford LaSor. Grand Rapids: William B. Eerdmans.
Ben-Barak, Z.
1980 Inheritance by Daughters in the Ancient Near East. JSS 25: 22-33.
Ben Iehuda, E.
1926 Thesaurus Totius Hebraitatis et Veteris et Recentioris. Jerusalem and Berlin, G. Landenscheidt. Hebrew.
Benz, F. L.
1972 Personal Names in the Phoenician and Punic Inscriptions. Studia Pohl 8. Rome: Biblical Institute Press.

Biella, J. C.
1982 Dictionary of Old South Arabic. Sabaean Dialect. Harvard Semitic Studies 25. Chico, California: Scholars Press.
Biga, M. G., and Milano, L.
1984 Testi Amministrativi: Assegnazioni di Tessuti (Archivio L. 2769). Archivi Reali de Ebla Testi 4. Rome: Missione Archeologica Italiana in Siria.
Biggs, R. D.
1967 Semitic Names in the Fara Period. Or NS 36: 55-66.
1988 The Semitic Personal Names from Abu Salabikh and the Personal Names from Ebla. Pp. 89-98 in A. Achi, ed., Eblaite Personal Names and Semitic Name-Giving. Papers of a Symposium held in Rome July 15-17, 1985. Archivi Reali di Ebla Studi 1. Rome: Missione Archeologica Italiana in Siria.
Bing, J. D.
1984 Adapa and Immortality. UF 16: 52-56.
Birot, M.
1955 Textes économiques de Mari (III), RA 49: 15-31
1979 Noms de personnes. Pp. 43-249 in M. Birot, J.-R. Kupper, and O. Rouault, eds., Répertoire analytique (2e volume) Tomes I-XIV, XVIII et textes divers hors-collection.

Première partie. Noms propres. ARM XVI/1. Paris: P. Geuthner.

Black, M.
1985 The Book of Enoch or I Enoch. A New English Edition. Leiden: E. J. Brill.
1987 The Strange Visions of Enoch. Bible Review 3/2 (Summer) 20-23, 38-42.

Bordreuil, P., and Lemaire, A.
1976 Nouveaux Sceaux Hébreux, Araméens et Ammonites. Semitica 26: 45-63.

Borger, R.
1959 Gen. iv 1. VT 9: 85-86.
1974 Die Beschwörungsserie Bīt Mēseri und die Himmel-fahrt Henochs. JNES 33: 183-196.

Bottéro, J.
1954 Le problème des Ḫabiru à la 4e rencontre assyriologique internationale. Cahiers de la société asiatique 12. Paris: Imprimerie nationale.

Brandenstein, W.
1954 Bemerkungen zur Völkertafel in der Genesis. Pp. 57-83 in Sprachgeschichte und Wortbedeutung. Festschrift Albert Debrunner. Berlin: Francke.

Brauner, R. A.
1974 A Comparative Lexicon of Old Aramaic. Ph.D. dissertation, The Dropsie University. Ann Arbor, Michigan: University Microfilms.

Brockelmann, C.
1895 Lexicon Syriacum. Edinburgh: T. & T. Clark; Berlin: Reuther & Reichard.

Buccellati, G.
1966 The Amorites of the Ur III Period. Pubblicazioni del Seminario di Semitistica. Ricerche, vol. 1. Naples: Istituto orientale.
1973 Adapa, Genesis, and the Notion of Faith. UF 5: 61-66.

Budd, P. J.
1983 Numbers. Word Biblical Commentary 5. Waco, Texas: Word.

Burrows, E.
1925 Notes on Harrian. Journal of the Royal Asiatic Society pp. 277-284.

Carucci, L. M.
1984 Significance of Change or Change of Significance: A Consideration of Marshallese Personal Names. Ethnology 23: 143-155.

Cassin, E., and Glassner, J.-J.
1977 Anthroponymie et Anthropologie de Nuzi. Volume Premier: Les Anthroponymes. Malibu: Undena.
Cassuto, U.
1958 yābāl. Cols. 451-452 in vol. 3 of Encyclopedia Biblica, eds. U. Cassuto et al. Jerusalem: Bialik Institute. Hebrew.
1958 yûbāl. Col. 582 in vol. 3 of Encyclopedia Biblica, eds. U. Cassuto et al. Jerusalem: Bialik Institute. Hebrew.
1961 A Commentary on the Book of Genesis. Part I. From Adam to Noah. Genesis I-VI 8. Trans. I. Abrahams from Hebrew (1944). Jerusalem: Magnes.
1964 A Commentary on the Book of Genesis. Part II. From Noah to Abraham. Genesis VI 9 - XI 32 with an Appendix: A Fragment of Part III. Trans. I. Abrahams from Hebrew (1949). Jerusalem: Magnes.
Cassuto, U., et al.
1971 ṣillāh. Col. 733 in vol. 6 of Encyclopedia Biblica, eds. U. Cassuto et al. Jerusalem: Bialik Institute. Hebrew.
1965 hārān. Col. 856 in vol. 2 of Encyclopedia Biblica, eds. Cassuto, U. et al. Jerusalem: Bialik Institute. Hebrew.
Cazelles, H.
1973 The Hebrews. Pp. 1-28 in D. J. Wiseman, ed., Peoples of Old Testament Times. Article trans. M. C. de Murville. Oxford: Clarendon.
Charpin, D.
1982 Mari et le calendrier d'Ebla. RA 76: 1-6.
Cheyne, T. K.
1897 Arpachshad. ZAW 17: 190.
Childs, B. S.
1974 The Etiological Tale Re-Examined. VT 24: 387-397.
Clay, A. T.
1912 Personal Names from Cuneiform Inscriptions of the Cassite Period. Yale Oriental Series 1. New Haven: Yale University Press; London: Henry Frowde; Oxford: University Press.
Clines, D. J. A.
1972-73 Noah's Flood, 1: The Theology of the Flood Narrative. Faith and Thought 100/2: 128-145.
1976 Theme in Genesis 1-11. CBQ 38: 483-507.
1990 What Does Eve Do to Help? and Other Readerly Questions to the Old Testament. JSOT Supplement Series 94. Sheffield: Academic Press.
Coogan, M. D.
1974 Alphabets and Elements. BASOR 216: 61-63.
1976 West Semitic Personal Names in the Murašû Documents. Harvard Semitic Monographs 7. Missoula, Montana: Scholars Press.

Cross, F. M.
1974 אֵל ʾēl. Pp. 242-261 in eds. G. J. Botterweck and H. Ringgren, Theological Dictionary of the Old Testament. Volume I אָב–בָּדַד. Revised edition. Translator J. T. Willis. Grand Rapids: William B. Eerdmans.

Cryer, F. H.
1985 The Interrelationships of Gen 5,32; 11,10-11 and the Chronology of the Flood (Gen 6-9). Bib 66: 241-261.

Curtis, E. L. and Madsen, A. A.
1910 Critical and Exegetical Commentary on the Books of Chronicles. International Critical Commentary. Edinburgh: T. & T. Clark.

Dahood, M.
1963 Proverbs and Northwest Semitic Philology. Rome: Biblical Institute Press.
1975 Four Ugaritic Personal Names and Job 39 5. 26-27. ZAW 87: 220.
1978 Ebla, Ugarit and the Old Testament. The Month 239: 271-276.
1980a Are the Ebla Tablets Relevant to Biblical Research? Biblical Archaeology Review 6/5: 54-60.
1980b Ebla Discoveries and Biblical Research. The Month 241: 275-281.

de Liagre Böhl, F. M. Th.
1959 Die Mythe vom weisen Adapa. WO 2/5-6: 416-431.

de Vaux, R.
1978 The Early History of Israel. Trans. D. Smith. Philadelphia: Westminster.

Del Monte, G. F., and Tischler, J.
1978 Répertoire Géographique des Textes Cunéiformes. Band 6. Die Orts-und Gewässernamen der hethitischen Texte. Beiehfte zum TAVO B 20. Wiesbaden: Dr. Ludwig Reichert.

Demsky, A.
1982 The Genealogies of Manasseh and the Location of the Territory of Milcah Daughter of Zelophehad. Eretz-Israel 16: 70-75. Hebrew, English summary, p. 254*.

Diakonoff, I. M.
1982 Father Adam. AfO Beiheft. 28. R.A.I. Wien 6.-10. Juli 1981.19: 16-24.

Dietrich, M., and Loretz, O.
1969-70 Die soziale Struktur von Alalaḫ und Ugarit. II. Die soziale Gruppen -ḫupše-namê, ḫaniaḫḫe-ekû, eḫele-šūzubu und marjanne nach Texten aus Alalaḫ im 15. Jahrhundert. WO 5: 57-93.
1970 Die soziale Struktur von Alalaḫ und Ugarit (IV). Die É = bītu-Listen aus Alalaḫ IV als Quelle für die Erforschung der

gesellschaftlichen Schichtung von Alalaḫ im 15. Jh. v. Chr. ZA 60: 88-123.
1990a Hurritisch-ugaritisch-hebräisch tbl "Schmied." UF 22: 87-88.
1990b mt "Môt, Tod" und mt "Krieger, Held" im Ugaritischen. UF 22: 57-66.

Dillman, A.
1865 Lexicon Linguae Aethiopicae. New York: Frederick Ungar.

Donnellan, K. S.
1974 Speaking of Nothing. Philosophical Review 83: 3-31

Dossin, G.
1971 Deux listes nominatives du règne de Sûmu-Iamam. RA 65: 37-66.
1974 Le site de Tuttul-sur-Baliḫ. RA 68: 25-34.

Driver, G. R.
1965 Review of M. Dahood, Proverbs and Northwest Semitic Philology, Rome: Biblical Institute Press, 1963, in JSS 10: 112-117.
1973 Affirmation by Exclamatory Negation. Journal of the Ancient Near Eastern Society of Columbia University 5: 107-114.

Driver, S. R.
1948 The Book of Genesis with Introduction and Notes. Fifteenth edition. London: Methuen & Co.

Drower, E. S., and Macuch, R.
1963 A Mandaic Dictionary. Oxford: Clarendon.

Dunand, M.
1938 Fouilles de Byblos I. Paris.

Durand, J.-M.
1991 L'emploi des toponymes dans l'onomastique d'époque amorrite (I). Les noms en Mut-. SEL 8: 81-97.

Edzard, O.
1965 Mesopotamien. Die Mythologie der Sumerer und Akkader. Pp. 17-139 in H. W. Haussig, ed., Wörterbuch der Mythologie. Band I. Götter und Mythen im Vorderen Orient. Stuttgart: Ernst Klett.
1981 Verwaltungstexte verschiedenen Inhalts (aus dem Archiv L.2769). Archivi Reali de Ebla Testi 2. Rome: Missione Archeologica Italiana in Siria.

Eichler, B. L.
1977 Another Look at the Nuzi Sistership Contracts. Pp. 45-59 in M. De Jong Ellis, ed., Essays on the Ancient Near East in Memory of J. J. Finkelstein. Memoirs of the Connecticut Academy of Arts & Sciences 19. Hamden, Connecticut: Archon.

Emerton, J. A.
1987 An Examination of Some Attempts to Defend the Unity of the Flood Narrative in Genesis. Part I. VT 27: 401-420.
1988 An Examination of Some Attempts to Defend the Unity of the Flood Narrative in Genesis. Part II. VT 28: 1-21.
1989 Review of J. D. Fowler, Theophoric Personal Names in Ancient Hebrew, JSOT Supplement Series 49, Sheffield: JSOT, 1988, in VT 29 (1989) 246-248.

Engnell, I.
1967 Studies in Divine Kingship in the Ancient Near East. 2nd edition. Oxford: Basil Blackwell.

Eph'al, I.
1982 The Ancient Arabs. Nomads on the Borders of the Fertile Crescent 9th - 5th Centuries B.C. Jerusalem: Magnes; Leiden: E. J. Brill.

Fales, F. M.
1973 Censimenti e Catasti di epoca neo-Assira. Studi Economici e Tecnologici 2. Roma: Centro per le antichità e la storia dell'arte del Vicino Oriente.
1974 West Semitic Names from the Governor's Palace. Annali della facoltà di lingue e letterature straniere di ca'foscari 13: 179-88.
1977 On Aramaic Onomastics in the Neo-Assyrian Period. OA 16: 41-68.
1978 L'onomastica aramaica in età neo-assira: Raffronti tra il corpus aflabetico el il materiale cuneiforme. Pp. 199-229 in Atti del 1º Convegno Italiano sul vicino oriente antico (Roma, 22-24 Aprile 1975). Orientis antiqui collectio 13. Roma: Centro per le antichità e la storia dell'arte del Vicino Oriente.
1979 A List of Assyrian and West Semitic Women's Names. Iraq 41: 55-73.
1982 Note di semitico nordoccidentale. VO 5: 75-83.
1984 Assyro-Aramaica: Three Notes. Or NS 53: 66-71.

Falkenstein, A.
1959 Sumerische Götterlieder. I. Teil. Heidelberg: Carl Winter.

Finkelstein, J. J.
1966 The Genealogy of the Hammurapi Dynasty. JCS 20: 95-118.

Finkelstein, J. J.
1963 The Antediluvian Kings: A University of California Tablet. JCS 17: 39-51.

Fishbane, M.
1979 Text and Texture: Close Readings of Selected Biblical Texts. New York: Schocken.

Fitzmyer, J. A.
1966 The Genesis Apocryphon of Qumran Cave I. A Commentary. Rome: Biblical Institute Press.

Foster, B. R.
1974 Wisdom and the Gods in Ancient Mesopotamia. Or NS 43: 344-354.

Fowler, J. D.
1988 Theophoric Personal Names in Ancient Hebrew. A Comparative Study. Journal for the Study of the Old Testament Supplement Series 49. Sheffield: JSOT Press.

Fraade, S. D.
1984 Enosh and His Generation. Pre-Israelite Hero and History in Postbiblical Interpretation. Society of Biblical Literature Monograph Series 30. Chico, California: Scholars Press.

Frege, G.
1952 On Sense and Reference. Pp. 56-78 in P. Gleach and M. Black, eds., Translations from the Philosophical Writings of Gottlob Frege. Oxford: Basil Blackwell.1952. Originally published in Zeitschrift für Philosophie und philosophische Kritik 100 (1892): 25-50.

Freydank, H., and Saporetti, C.
1979 Nuove attestazioni dell'onomastica Medio-Assira. Publicazione dell'istituto per gli studi Miceni ed Egeo-Anatolici del consiglio nationale delle ricerche. Incunabula Graeca LXXIV. Rome: Edizioni dell'Ateneo & Bizzari.

Gabriel, J.
1959 Die Kainitengenealogie Gn 4, 17-24. Bib 40: 409-427.

Gadd, C. J.
1940 Tablets from Chagar Bazar and Tell Brak. Iraq 7: 22-66.

Gardiner, A.
1957 The Theory of Proper Names: A Controversial Essay. London: Oxford University Press. Second ed.

Garsiel, M.
1987 Midrashic Names Derivations in the Bible. Ramat-Gan Israel: Revivim. Hebrew.

Gautier, J. E.
1908 Archives d'une famille de Dilbat au temps de la première dynastie de Babylone. Mémoires publiés par les membres de l'Institut Français d'Archéologie Orientale du Caire, 26. Cairo.

Geertz, C.
1973 The Interpretation of Cultures. New York: Basic Books.

Gelb, I. J.
1954 Two Assyrian King Lists. JNES 13: 209-230.

1957 Glossary of Old Akkadian. Materials for the Assyrian Dictionary 3. Chicago: University Press.
1961 Old Akkadian Writing and Grammar. Materials for the Assyrian Dictionary 2. Second edition. Chicago: University Press.
1962 Ethnic Reconstruction and Onomastic Evidence. Names 10: 42-52.

Gelb, I. J., Bartels, J., Vance, S.-M., and Whiting, R. M.
1980 Computer-Aided Analysis of Amorite. Assyriological Studies 21. Chicago: Oriental Institute of the University of Chicago.

Gelb, I. J., Purves, P. M., and MacRae, A. A.
1943 Nuzi Personal Names. University of Chicago Oriental Institute Publications 57. Chicago: University Press.

Gerhardt, D.
1977 Zur Theorie Eigennamen. Beiträge zur Namen-forschungen NF 12: 398-418.

Gevirtz, S.
1963 Lamech's Song to His Wives. Pp. 25-34 in Patterns in the Early Poetry of Israel. Studies in Ancient Oriental Civilization 32. Chicago: University Press.

Gibson, J. C. L.
1971 Textbook of Syrian Semitic Inscriptions. I Hebrew and Moabite. Oxford: Clarendon.
1975 Textbook of Syrian Semitic Inscriptions. II Aramaic Inscriptions Including Inscriptions in the Dialect of Zenjirli. Oxford: Clarendon.

Gispen, W. H.
1966 Schepping en paradijs. Verklaring van Genesis 1-3. Kampen: J. H. Kok.

Glück, J. J.
1970 Paronomasia in Biblical Literature. Semitics 1: 50-78.

Goedicke, H.
1985 Adam's Rib. Pp. 73-76 in A. Kort and S. Morschauser, eds., Biblical and Related Studies Presented to Samuel Iwry. Winona Lake, IN: Eisenbrauns.

Golka, F. W.
1976 The Aetiologies in the Old Testament: Part 1. VT 26: 410-428.
1977 The Aetiologies in the Old Testament: Part 2. VT 27: 36-47.

Goodenough, W.
1965 Personal Names and Modes of Address in Two Oceanic Communities. Pp. 266-367 in M. Spiro, ed., Context and Meaning in Cultural Anthropology. New York/London: Free Press/Collier-Macmillan.

Gordon, C. H.
1938 TRH, TN and NKR in the Ras Shamra Tablets. JBL 57: 407-410.
1955 Ugaritic Manual. Analecta Orientalia, 35. Rome: Biblical Institute Press.
1962 Arpachshad. P. 231 in vol. 1 of IDB.
1988 Notes on Proper Names in the Ebla Tablets. Pp. 153-158 in A. Archi, ed., Eblaite Personal Names and Semitic Name-Giving. Papers of a Symposium Held in Rome July 15-17, 1985. Archivi Reali di Ebla Studi 1. Rome: Missione Archeologica Italiana in Siria.

Gray, G. B.
1896 Studies in Hebrew Proper Names. London: Adam and Charles Black.

Grébaut, S.
1952 Supplément au Lexicon Linguæ Æthiopicæ de August Dillmann (1865) et Édition du Lexique de Juste d'Urbin (1850-1855). Paris: Imprimerie nationale.

Greenberg, M.
1955 The Hab/piru. American Oriental Series 39. New Haven: American Oriental Society.

Greengus, S.
1975 Sisterhood Adoption at Nuzi and the "Wife-Sister" in Genesis. HUCA 46: 5-31.

Grelot, P.
1958 La légende d'Hénoch dans les apocryphes et dans la Bible: son origine et signification. Recherches de science religieuse 46: 5-26, 181-210.

Greßman, H.
1907 Mythische Reste in der Paradieserzählung. Archiv für Religionswissenschaft 10: 345-367.

Gröndahl, F.
1967 Die Personennamen der Texte aus Ugarit. Studia Pohl 1. Rome: Biblical Institute Press.

Groneberg, B.
1980 Répertoire Géographie des Textes Cunéiformes Band 3 Die Orts- und Gewässernamen der altbabylonischen Zeit. Beihefte zum Tübinger Atlas des vorderen Orients B7. Wiesbaden: Ludwig Reichert.

Grosz, K.
1987 Some Aspects of the Adoption of Women at Nuzi. Pp. 131-152 in D. I. Owen and M. A. Morrison, eds., Studies on the Civilization and Culture of Nuzi and the Hurrians. Volume 2. General Studies and Excavations at Nuzi 9/1. Winona Lake, Indiana: Eisenbrauns.

Guemple, D. L.
1965 Saunik: Name Sharing as a Factor Governing Eskimo Kinship Terms. Ethnology 4: 323-335.

Guillaume, A.
1964 Paronomasia in the Old Testament. JSS 9: 282-290.

Gunkel, H.
1902 Genesis übersetzt und erklärt. Handkommentar zum Alten Testament III, 1. Göttingen: Vandenhoeck und Ruprecht.

Gustavs, A.
1927-28 Die Personennamen in den Tontafeln von Tell Ta'annek. Eine Studie zur Ethnographie Nordpalästinas zur El-Amarna-Zeit. ZDPV 50: 1-18; 51: 169-218.

Hallo, W. W.
1963 Beginning and End of the Sumerian King List in the Nippur Recension. JCS 17: 52-57.
1964 The Road to Emar. JCS 18: 57-88.
1970 Antediluvian Cities. JCS 23: 57-67.

Hamilton, V. P.
1990 The Book of Genesis Chapters 1-17. The New International Commentary on the Old Testament. Grand Rapids, MI: Eerdmans.

Haran, M.
1970 The Religion of the Patriarchs: Beliefs and Practices. Chapter XII. Pp. 219-245, 285-288 in B. Mazar, ed., Patriarchs. Volume II. The World History of the Jewish People. First Series: Ancient Times (Patriarchs and Judges). Tel-Aviv: Massada.

Harding, G. L.
1971 An Index and Concordance of Pre-Islamic Arabian Names and Inscriptions. Near and Middle Eastern Studies 8. Toronto: University Press.

Harris, R.
1955 The Archive of the Sin Temple in Khafajah (Tutub). JCS 9: 31-58, 59-88, 91-120.

Heider, G. C.
1985 The Cult of Molek. A Reassessment. JSOT Supplement Series 43. Sheffield: JSOT Press.

Heller, J.
1958 Der Name Eva. Archiv Orientalni 26: 636-656.
1967 Namengebung und Namendeutung. Grundzüge der alttestamentlichen Onomatologie und ihre Folgen für die biblische Hermeneutik. Evangelische Theologie 27: 255-266.

Heltzer, M.
1982 šēt, bĕnê šēt. Cols. 268-270 in vol. 8 of Encyclopedia Biblica, eds. U. Cassuto et al. Jerusalem: Bialik Institute. Hebrew.

Hess, R. S.
1984 Amarna Proper Names. Ph.D. dissertation, Hebrew Union College. Ann Arbor, Michigan: University Microfilms.
1985 Personal Names from Amarna: Alternative Readings and Interpretations. UF 17: 157-67
1988 'ĀDĀM as 'Skin' and 'Earth': An Examination of Some Proposed Meanings in Biblical Hebrew. Tyndale Bulletin 39: 141-149.
1989 The Genealogies of Genesis 1-11 and Comparative Literature. Bib 70: 241-254.
1990a Genesis 1-2 in Its Literary Context. Tyndale Bulletin 41: 143-153.
1990b Splitting the Adam: The Usage of 'ĀDĀM in Genesis i-v. Pp. 1-15 in J. A. Emerton, ed., Studies in the Pentateuch. Vetus Testamentum Supplement XLI. Leiden: E. J. Brill.
1990c A Comparison of the Onomastica in Genealogical and Narrative Texts of Genesis 1-11. Pp. 67-74 in Proceedings of the Tenth World Congress of Jewish Studies: Jerusalem, August 16-24, 1989: Division A: The Bible and Its World. Jerusalem: World Union of Jewish Studies.
1991 Lamech in the Genealogies of Genesis. Bulletin of Biblical Research 1: 21-25.
1992 Enosh. P. 526 in vol. 2 of ABD.
Amarna Personal Names, forthcoming.

Hoffner, H. A.
1980 jbl. Cols. 390-393 in Band III, Lieferung 4/5 of TWAT. Stuttgart, Berlin, Köln, Mainz: W. Kohlhammer.

Huber, E.
1907 Die Personennamen in den Keilschrifturkunden aus der Zeit der Könige von Ur und Nisin. Leipzig: J. C. Hinrichs.

Huehnergard, J.
1985 Biblical Notes on Some New Akkadian Texts from Emar (Syria). CBQ 47: 428-434.
1987a Northwest Semitic Vocabulary in Akkadian Texts. JAOS 107: 713-725.
1987b Ugaritic Vocabulary in Syllabic Transcription. HSS 32. Atlanta: Scholars Press for the President and Fellows of Harvard College.

Huffmon, H. B.
1965 Amorite Personal Names in the Mari Texts: A Structural and Lexical Study. Baltimore: Johns Hopkins.
1985 Cain, the Arrogant Sufferer. Pp. 109-113 in A. Kort and S. Morschauser, eds., Biblical and Related Studies Presented to Samuel Iwry. Winona Lake, IN: Eisenbrauns.

Israel, F.
1979 Miscellanea Idumea. Rivista biblica 27: 171-203.

1987a Quelques précisions sur l'onomastique hébraïque féminine dans l'épigraphie. SEL 4: 79-92.

1987b Studi Moabiti I: Rassegna di epigrafia moabiti e sigilli moabiti. Pp. 101-38 in G. Bernini and V. Brugnatelli, eds., Atti della 4a Giornata di Studi Camito-Semitici e Indoeuropei (Bergamo, Istituto Universitario, 29 novembre 1985). Milano.

1987c Supplementum idumeum I. Rivista biblica 35: 337-56.

Jackson, K. P.

1983a The Ammonite Language of the Iron Age. Harvard Semitic Monographs 27. Chico, California: Scholars Press.

1983b Ammonite Personal Names in the Context of West Semitic Onomasticon. Pp. 507-521 in C. L. Meyers and M. O'Connor, eds., The Word of the Lord Shall Go Forth. Essays in Honor of David Noel Freedman in Celebration of HIs Sixtieth Birthday. Winona Lake, IN: Eisenbrauns, for the American Schools of Oriental Research.

Jacob, B.

1934 Das Erste Buch der Tora. Genesis Übersetzt und Erklärt. Berlin: Schocken. Reprinted, New York: Ktav, 1974.

Jacobsen, T.

1970 The Investiture and Anointing of Adapa in Heaven. Pp. 48-51 in W. L. Moran, ed., Toward the Image of Tammuz and Other Essays on Mesopotamian History and Culture. Cambridge: Harvard. Reprinted from American Journal of Semitic Languages and Literatures 46 (1930): 201-203.

Jastrow, M.

1950 A Dictionary of the Targumim, the Talmud Babli and Yerushalmi, and the Midrashic Literature. New York, Pardes.

Jensen, P.

1928 Adapa. Pp. 33-35 in vol. 1 of RLA. Berlin and Leipzig: Walter de Gruyter.

Johns, C. H. W.

1901 An Assyrian Doomsday Book or Liber Censualis of the District Round Ḫarran; in the Seventh Century B.C. Copied from Cuneiform Tablets in the British Museum. Assyriologische Bibliothek 17. Leipzig: J. C. Hinrichs.

Johnson, M. D.

1969 The Purpose of the Biblical Genealogies with Special Reference to the Setting of the Genealogies of Jesus. Cambridge: University Press.

Jongeling, K.

1984 Names in Neo-Punic Inscriptions. Groningen.

Joüon, P.
1938 Trois noms de personnages bibliques à la lumière des Textes d'Ugarit (Ras Shamra), trḥ yśśkr dnʾl. Bib 19: 280-285.

Kang, S. T.
1973 Sumerian Economic Texts from the Umma Archive. Sumerian and Akkadian Cuneiform Texts in the Collection of the World Heritage Museum of the University of Illinois, Vol. II. Urbana, Chicago, and London: University of Illinois.

Kapelrud, A. S.
1977 חַוָּה. Cols. 794-798 in vol. 2 of TWAT.

Kaufman, S.
1982 Reflections on the Assyrian-Aramaic Bilingual from Tell Fakhriyeh. Maarav 3: 137-175.
1989 Assyro-Aramaica. JAOS 109: 97-102.

Kessler, K.
1980 Untersuchungen zur historischen Topographie Nordmesopotamiens nach keilschriftlichen Quellen des 1. Jahrtausends v. Chr. Beihefte zum TAVO B26. Wiesbaden: Ludwig Reichert.

Key, A. F.
1964 The Giving of Proper Names in the Old Testament. JBL 83: 55-59.

Kienast, B.
1973 Die Weisheit des Adapa von Eridu. Pp. 234-239 in M. A. Beek, A. A. Kampman, C. Nijland, and J. Ryckmans, eds., Symbolae Biblicae et Mesopotamicae Francisco Mario Theodoro de Liagre Böhl dedicatae. Leiden: E. J. Brill.
1978 Überlegungen zum "Fluch" des Adapa. Pp. 181-200 in B. Hruška and G. Komoróczy, eds., Festschrift Lubor Matouš. Assyriologia 4. Budapest.

Kikawada, I. M.
1972 Two Notes on Eve. JBL 91: 33-37.
1983 The Double Creation of Mankind in Enki and Ninmah, Atrahasis I 1-351, and Genesis 1-2. Iraq 45: 43-45.

Kikawada, I. M. and Quinn, A.
1985 Before Abraham Was. The Unity of Genesis. Nashville: Abingdon.

King, L. W.
1900 Cuneiform Texts from Babylonian Tablets in the British Museum Part X. London: Trustees of the British Museum.

Kinlaw, D. F.
1967 A Study of the Personal Names in the Akkadian Texts from Ugarit. Ph.D. dissertation, Brandeis University. Ann Arbor, Michigan: University Microfilms.

Kitchen, K. A.
1977 The King List of Ugarit. UF 9: 131-142.

Klijn, A. F. J.
1978 Seth in Jewish, Christian and Gnostic Literature. NTS 46. Leiden: E. J. Brill, 1977.

Knauf, E. A.
1988 Midian: Untersuchungen zur Geschichte Palästinas und Nordarabiens am Ende des 2. Jahrtausends v. Chr. Abhandlungen des Deutschen Palästinavereins. Wiesbaden: Otto Harrassowitz.

Knudtzon, J. A.
1915 Die El-Amarna-Tafeln mit Einleitung und Erläuterungen. 2 Teilen. Leipzig: J.C. Hinrichs. Neudruck der Ausgabe 1915. Aalen: Otto Zeller, 1964.

Koch, K.
1969 Die Hebräer vom Auszug aus Ägypten bis zum Großreich Davids. VT 19: 37-81.

Koenig, J.
1982 L'herméneutique analogique du judaïsme antique d'après les témoins textuels d'Isaïe. VTS 33. Leiden: E. J. Brill.

Kornfield, W.
1978 Onomastica Aramaica aus Ägypten. Vienna: Österreichische Akademie der Wissenschaften, Philosophisch-historische Klasse Sitzungsberichte, Band 333. Vienna: Österreichische Akademie der Wissenschaften.

Koschaker, P.
1933 Fratriarchat, Hausgemeinschaft und Mutterrecht in Keilschriftrechten. ZA 41: 1-89.

Kraeling, E. G.
1922 Terach. - Methuselach. ZAW 40: 153-155.
1953 The Brooklyn Museum Papyri. New Haven: Yale University Press.

Krebernik, M.
1988a Die Personennamen der Ebla-Texte. Eine Zwischenbilanz. Berliner Beiträge zum Vorderen Orient Band 7. Berlin: Dietrich Reimer.
1988b Prefixed Verbal Forms in Personal Names from Ebla. Pp. 45-69 in A. Archi, ed., Eblaite Personal Names and Semitic Name-Giving. Papers of a Symposium held in Rome July 15-17, 1985. Archivi Reali di Ebla Studi 1. Roma: Missione Archeologica Italiana in Siria.

Kripke, S. A.
1972 Naming and Necessity. Pp. 253-355 in eds., D. Davidson and G. Harman, Semantics of Natural Language. Dordrecht and Boston: D. Reidel.

Kühne, C.
1974 Mit Glossenkeilen markierte fremde Wörter in Akkadischen Ugarittexten. UF 6: 157-167.
Kupper, J.-R.
1979 Noms géographiques. Pp. 1-42 in M. Birot, J.-R. Kupper, and O. Rouault, eds., Répertoire analytique (2e volume) Tomes I-XIV, XVIII et textes divers hors-collection. Première partie. Noms propres. ARM XVI/1. Paris: P. Geuthner.
Kuryłowicz, J
1960 La position linguistique du nom propre. Pp. 182-192 in Esquisses Linguistiques. Wroclaw-Krakow: Wydawnictwo Polskiej Akademii Nauk.
Kutscher, Y.
1967 Jewish Palestinian Aramaic. Pp. 52-76 in F. Rosenthal, ed., An Aramaic Handbook Part I/2. Porta Linguarum Orientalium. Wiesbaden: Otto Harrassowitz.
Kuzminski, A.
1979 Names, Descriptions, and Pictures. Review of Metaphysics 32: 453-470.
Lambdin, T. O.
1953 Egyptian Loan Words in the Old Testament. JAOS 73: 145-155.
Lambert, W. G.
1967 Enmeduranki and Related Matters. JCS 21: 126-138.
1980 Babylonien und Israel. Pp. 67-79 in vol. 5 of Theologische Realenzyklopädie.
1989 Review of C. H. Gordon, G. A. Rendsburg, and N. H. Winter, eds., Eblaitica: Essays on the Ebla Archives and Eblaite Language. Vol. I., Publications of the Center for Ebla Research at New York University, Winona Lake, IN: Eisenbrauns, 1987, in Bulletin of the School of African and Oriental Studies 52: 115-116.
Lambert, W. G., and Millard, A. R.
1969 Atra-Ḫasīs: The Babylonian Story of the Flood. Oxford: Clarendon.
Landersdorfer, S.
1916 Sumerisches Sprachgut im Alten Testament. Eine Biblisch-Lexikalische Studie. Beiträge zur Wissenschaft vom Alten Testament 21. Leipzig: J. C. Hinrichs.
Landsberger, B. and Bauer, T.
1926-7 Zu neuveröffentlichten Geschichtsquellen der Zeit von Asarhaddon bis Nabonid. ZA 37: 61-98.
Lane, E. W.
1968 An Arabic-English Lexicon. Part I. Beirut: Librairie du Liban.

Laroche, E.
1966 Les noms des Hittites. Études linguistiques IV. Paris: C. Klincksieck.
1976-77 Glossaire de la langue Hourrite. RHA 34-35.
1981 Les noms des Hittites: supplément. Hethitica 4: 3-58.
Lawton, R.
1984 Israelite Personal Names in Pre-exilic Hebrew Inscriptions. Bib 65: 330-346.
Layton, S. C.
1990 Archaic Features of Canaanite Personal Names in the Hebrew Bible. Harvard Semitic Monographs 47. Atlanta: Scholars Press.
Lemaire, A.
1972 Le "pays de Hepher" et les "filles de Zelophehad" à la lumière des ostraca de Samarie. Semitica 22: 13-20.
1977 Inscriptions Hébraïques. I Les Ostraca. Paris: Les Éditions du Cerf.
Leslau, W.
1969 Hebrew Cognates in Amharic. Wiesbaden: Otto Harrassowtiz.
Lévi-Strauss, C.
1966 The Savage Mind Chicago: University Press.
Lewy, J.
1945-6 The Late Assyro-Babylonian Cult of the Moon and Its Culmination at the Time of Nabonidus. HUCA 19: 405-489.
Limet, H.
1968 L'anthroponymie sumérienne dans les documents de la 3e dynastie d'Ur. Bibliothèque de la Faculté de Philosophie et Lettres de l'Université de Liège - Fascicule CLXXX. Paris: Société d'Édition 'Les Belles Lettres'.
1976 Textes administratifs de l'époque des šakkanakku.. ARM XIX. Paris: P. Geuthner.
Lipiński, E.
1980 Etudes d'onomastique ouest-sémitique. Bibliotheca orientalis 37: 5-10.
Liverani, M.
1962 Antecedenti dell'onomastica aramaica antica. RSO 37:65-76.
Loewenstamm, S.
1964 hōrām. Col. 855 in Encyclopedia Biblica. Volume 2. Eds. U. Cassuto et al. Jerusalem: Bialik. Hebrew.
1958 yiskāh. Col. 707 in Encyclopedia Biblica. Volume 3. Eds. U. Cassuto et al. Jerusalem: Bialik. Hebrew.
Loretz, O.
1975 Der Gott ŠALAḤ, He. ŠLḤ I und ŠLḤ II. UF 7: 584-585.

1984 Habiru-Hebräer. Eine sozio-linguistische Studie über die Herkunft des Gentiliziums ʿibrî vom Appellativum ḫabiru. Berlin and New York: Walter de Gruyter.

Lubetski, M.

1987 ŠM as a Deity. Religion 17: 1-14.

Maass, F.

1973 ʾaenôš. Cols. 373-375 in G. J. Botterweck and H. Ringgren, eds., Theological Dictionary of the Old Testament. Volume I אָב–בָּדָד. Revised edition. Trans. J. T. Willis. Stuttgart, Berlin, Köln, Mainz: W. Kohlhammer.

McCarter, P. K., Jr.

1984 II Samuel. A New Translation with Introduction and Commentary. The Anchor Bible 9. Garden City, New York: Doubleday.

MacRae, A. A.

1943 Akkadian and Sumerian Elements. Pp. 281-318 in Nuzi Personal Names, by I. J. Gelb, P. M. Purves and A. A. MacRae. Chicago: Universtiy Press.

Maisler, B.

1947 Palestine at the Time of the Middle Kingdom in Egypt. Revue de l'histoire juive en Egypte 1: 33-68.

Malamat, A.

1968a King Lists of the Old Babylonian Period and Biblical Genealogies. JAOS 88: 163-173.

1968b nāḥôr. Cols. 805-809 in Encyclopedia Biblica. Eds. U. M. D. Cassuto et al. Jerusalem: Bialik Institute. Hebrew.

1989 Mari and the Early Israelite Experience. The Schweich Lectures 1984. Oxford: University Press.

Maraqten, M.

1988 Die semitischen Personennamen in den alt- und reichsaramäischen Inschriften aus Vorderasien. Texte und Studien zur Orientalistik 5. Hildesheim: Georg Olms.

Martin, W. J.

1955 Sytlistic Criteria and the Analysis of the Pentateuch. Tyndale Monographs 2. London: Tyndale.

Matthiae, P.

1976 Ebla in the Late Early Syrian Period: The Royal Palace and the State Archives. BA 39: 94-113.

Mazar, B.

1986 The Early Biblical Period. Historical Studies. Jerusalem: Israel Exploration Society.

Meyers, C. L.

1983 Gender Roles and Genesis 3: 16 Revisited. Pp. 337-354 in C. L. Meyers and M. O'Connor, eds., The Word of the Lord Shall Go Forth. Essays in Honor of David Noel Freedman in Celebration of His Sixtieth Birthday. Winona Lake, IN: Eisenbrauns.

Michalowski, P.
1980 Adapa and the Ritual Process. Rocznik Orientalistyczny 41/2: 77-82.

Milik, J. T., ed.
1976 The Books of Enoch. Aramaic Fragments of Qumran Cave 4. Oxford: Clarendon Press.

Mill, J. S.
1846 A System of Logic. Reprint of 1843 ed. New York: Harper.

Millard, A. R.
1973 The Canaanites. Pp. 29-52 in D. J. Wiseman, ed., Peoples of Old Testament Times. Oxford: Clarendon.

Miller, P. D., Jr.
1978 Genesis 1-11. Studies in Structure and Theme. JSOT Supplement Series 8. Sheffield: JSOT.
1985 Eridu, Dunnu, and Babel: A Study in Comparative Mythology. Hebrew Annual Review 9: 227-251.

Miller, J. M.
1974 The Descendants of Cain: Notes on Genesis 4. ZAW 86: 164-174.

Moor, J. C. de
1987 An Anthology of Religious Texts from Ugarit. Nisaba 16. Leiden, New York, København, Köln: E. J. Brill.
1988 East of Eden. ZAW 100: 105-111.

Moore, M. S.
1990 The Balaam Traditions: Their Character and Development. SBL Dissertation Series 113. Atlanta: Scholars Press.

Moran, W. L.
1958 Review of C. Schedl, Geschichte des Alten Testaments, I. Band, Urgeschichte und altes Orient, xiv-374,II. Band, Das Bundesvolk Gottes, xiii-327, 1956, in Bib 39: 97-100.
1961 The Hebrew Language in Its Northwest Semitic Background. Pp. 54-72 in G. E. Wright, ed., The Bible and the Ancient Near East. Essays in Honor of William Foxwell Albright. London: Routledge & Kegan Paul.

Moritz, B.
1926 Edomitische Genealogien. I. ZAW 44: 81-93.

Morrison, M.
1983 The Jacob and Laban Narrative in Light of Near Eastern Sources. BA 46: 155-166.

Moye, R. H.
1990 In the Beginning: Myth and History in Genesis and Exodus. JBL 109: 577-598.

Müller, H.-P.
1980 Religionsgeschichtliche Beobachtungen zu den Texten von Ebla. ZDPV 96: 1-19.
Müller, W. W.
1963 Altsüdarabische Beiträge zum hebräischen Lexikon. ZAW 75: 304-316.
Muraoka, T.
1985 Emphatic Words and Structures in Biblical Hebrew. Jerusalem/Leiden: The Magnes Press/E. J. Brill.
Nashef, K.
1982 Répertoire Géographique des Textes Cunéiformes. Band 5. Die Orts-und Gewässernamen der mittelbabylonischen und mittelassyrischen Zeit. Beiehfte zum TAVO B 7/5. Wiesbaden: Ludwig Reichert.
Negev, A.
1991 Personal Names in the Nabatean Realm. Qedem Monographs of the Institute of Archaeology, The Hebrew University of Jerusalem 32. Jerusalem: The Institute of Archaeology, The Hebrew University of Jerusalem.
Neiman, D.
1973 The Two Genealogies of Japhet. Pp. 119-126 in H. A. Hoffner, Jr., ed., Orient and Occident. Essays Presented to Cyrus H. Gordon on the Occasion of His Sixty-Fifth Birthday. AOAT Band 22. Kevelaer: Butzon & Bercker; Neukirchen-Vluyn: Neukirchener.
Nöldeke, Th.
1888 Review of F. Baethgen, Beiträge zur semitischen Religionsgeschichte. Der Gott Israels und die Götter der Heiden. Berlin, 1888, in ZDMG 42: 470-487.
North, R.
1964 The Cain Music. JBL 83: 373-389.
Noth, M.
1928 Die Israelitischen Personennamen im Rahmen der Gemeinsemitischen Namengebung. Beiträge zur Wissenschaft vom Alten und Neuen Testament III, 10. Stuttgart: W. Kohlhammer. Reprinted, Hildesheim: Georg Olms, 1966.
1948 Überlieferungsgeschichte des Pentateuch. Stuttgart: W. Kohlhammer.
Nougayrol, J.
1957 Comptes Rendus de l'Académie des Inscriptions et Belles-Lettres, p. 82.
Oded, B.
1986 The Table of Nations (Genesis 10) - A Socio-cultural Approach. ZAW 98: 14-31.

Offord, J.
1916 Archaeological Notes on Jewish Antiquities. Palestine Exploration Fund Quarterly Statement 138-148.
Olyan, S. M.
1988 Asherah and the Cult of Yahweh in Israel. SBL Monograph Series 34. Atlanta: Scholars Press.
Oosterhoff, B. J.
1953 Israelietische Persoonsnamen. Exegetica Oud- en Nieuw-Testamentische Studien. Delft: Uitgeverij van Keulen.
Paradise, J.
1980 A Daughter and Her Father's Property at Nuzi. JCS 32: 189-207.
1987 Daughters as "Sons" at Nuzi. Pp. 203-213 in D. I. Owen and M. A. Morrison, eds., Studies on the Civilization and Culture of Nuzi and the Hurrians. Volume 2. General Studies and Excavations at Nuzi 9/1. Winona Lake, Indiana: Eisenbrauns.
Pardee, D.
1989 Les textes para-mythologiques de la 24e campagne (1961). Ras Shamra-Ougarit IV. Éditions Recherche sur les Civilisations mémoire n° 77. Paris: A.D.P.F.
Parker, B.
1954 The Nimrud Tablets, 1952 - Business Documents. Iraq 16: 29-58.
Parker, S. B.
1976 Deities, Underworld. Pp. 222-225 in Supplementary Volume of IDB.
1979-80 Some Methodological Principles in Ugaritic Philology. Maarav 2: 7-41.
Parpola, S.
1970 Neo-Assyrian Toponyms. AOAT 6. Kevelaer: Butzon & Bercker; Neukirchen-Vluyn: Neukirchener.
Parunak, H. Van Dyke
1975 A Semantic Survey of NḤM. CBQ 56: 512-532.
Paustian, P. R.
1978 The Evolution of Personal Naming Practices among American Blacks. Names 26: 177-91
Pettinato, G.
1976a Il calendario de Ebla al tempo del re Ibbi-Sipiš sulla base di TM 75.G.427. AfO 25: 1-36.
1976b The Royal Archives of Tell-Mardikh-Ebla. BA 39: 44-52.
1977 Il calendario semitico del 3. millennio riconstruito sulla base dei testi di Ebla. OA 16: 257-285.
1979 Catalogo dei testi cuneiformi de Tell Mardikh - Ebla. Materiali epigrafici di Ebla 1. Naples: Istituto universitario orientale.

1980 Testi Amministrativi della Biblioteca I. 2769, Parte 1. Materiali epigrafici di Ebla 2. Naples: Istituto universitario orientale.
1981 The Archives of Ebla. An Empire Inscribed in Clay. Garden City, New York: Doubleday.

Pomponio, F.
1983 I nomi divini nei testi di Ebla. UF 15: 141-156.

Postgate, J. N.
1976 Fifty Neo-Assyrian Legal Documents. Warminster: Aris and Phillips.

Pritchard, J. B.
1962 Gibeon, Where the Sun Stood Still. The Discovery of the Biblical City. Princeton: University Press.

Pulgram, E.
1954 Theory of Names. Berkeley: American Name Society.

Rad, G. von
1964 Genesis. A Commentary. Revised ed. Trans. J. H. Marks from German. Old Testament Library. Philadelphia: Westminster.

Radday, Y. T.
1990 Humour in Names. Pp. 59-97 in Y. T. Radday and A. Brenner, eds., On Humour and the Comic in the Hebrew Bible. JSOT Supplement Series 92. Bible and Literature Series 23. Sheffield: Almond.

Rainey, A. F.
1977 Verbal Usages in the Taanach Texts. IOS 7: 33-64.
1983 The Biblical Shephelah of Judah. BASOR 251: 1-22.

Ramsey, G. W.
1988 Is Name-Giving an Act of Domination in Genesis 2: 23 and Elsewhere? CBQ 50: 24-35.

Ranke, H.
1905 Early Babylonian Personal Names from the Published Tablets of the So-Called Hammurabi Dynasty (B.C. 2000). The Babylonian Expedition of the University of Pennsylvania Series D: Researches and Treatises Volume III. Philadelphia: University of Pennsylvania.
1935 Die ägyptischen Personennamen: Band I. Verzeichnis der Namen. Glückstadt: J. J. Augustin.

Raper, P. E.
1982 Sociology and the Study of Names. Onoma 26: 63-74.

Rasmussen, C. G.
1981 A Study of Akkadian Personal Names from Mari. Ph. D. dissertation, Dropsie University. Ann Arbor, Michigan: University Microfilms.

Reif, S. C.
1972 Dedicated to ḥnk. VT 22: 495-501.

Reiner, E.
1961 The Etiological Myth of the 'Seven Sages'. Or NS 30: 1-11.

Rendsburg, G.
1986 The Redaction of Genesis. Winona Lake, Indiana: Eisenbrauns.

Rendtorff, R.
1983 Das Alte Testament: Eine Einführung. Neukirchener-Vluyn: Neukirchener.

Ribichini, S.
1982 ’Udm e Šmk, due toponimi <<mitici>>, Materiali lessicali ed epigrafici 1: 51-52.

Ricks, S. D.
1989 Lexicon of Inscriptional Qatabanian. Studia Pohl 14. Rome: Pontifical Bible Institute.

Roberts, J. J. M.
1972 The Earliest Semitic Pantheon. A Study of the Semitic Deities Attested in Mesopotamia before Ur III. Baltimore and London: Johns Hopkins University Press.

Robinson, R. R.
1986 Literary Functions of the Genealogies of Genesis. CBQ 48: 595-608.

Roth, M. T.
1987 Homicide in the Neo-Assyrian Period. in F. Rochberg-Halton, ed., Language, Literature, and History: Philological and Historical Studies Presented to Erica Reiner. New Haven: American Oriental Society.

Rouillard, H.
1985 La péricope de Balaam (Nombres 22-24). La prose et les "oracles." Études bibliques nouvelle série, no. 4. Paris: J. Gabalda.

Roux, G.
1961 Adapa, le vent et l'eau. RA 55: 13-33.

Rummel, S.
1981 Narrative Structures in the Ugaritic Texts. Pp. 221-332 in Ras Shamra Parallels. Volume III. Rome: Pontificium Institutum Biblicum.

Russell, B.
1905 On Denoting. Mind 14: 479-93.

Russell, H. F.
1985 The Historical Geography of the Euphrates and Habur According to the Middle- and Neo-Assyrian Sources. Iraq 47: 57-74.

Rutten, M.
1958-60 Un lot de tablettes Manânâ. RA 52: 208-225; 53: 77-96; 54: 19-40, 147-152.

Ryckmans, G.
1934-35 Les noms propres sud-sémitiques. Bibliothèque du Muséon 2. 3 volumes. Louvain: Bureau du Muséon.

Sagarin, J. L.
1987 Hebrew Noun Patterns (Mishqalim) Morphology, Semantics, and Lexicon. Scholars Press Handbook Series. Atlanta: Scholars Press.

Sandmel, S.
1961 Genesis 4: 26b. HUCA 32: 19-29.

Saporetti, C.
1970 Onomastica Medio-Assira. Volumes I and II. Studia Pohl 6. Rome: Biblical Institute Press.

Sarna, N.
1970 Understanding Genesis. The Heritage of Biblical Israel 1. New York: Schocken.

Sasson, J. M.
1978 A Genealogical "Convention" in Biblical Chronography? ZAW 90: 171-185.

Sawyer, J. F. A.
1986 Cain and Hephaestus. Possible Relics of Metalworking Traditions in Genesis 4. Abr-Nahrain 24: 155-166

Schiffer, S.
1911 Die Aramäer Historisch-Geographische Untersuchungen. Leipzig: J. C. Hinrichs.

Schneider, N.
1952 Patriarchennamen in zeitgenössischen Keilschrifturkunden. Bib 33: 516-522.

Schneider, T.
1987 Die semitischen und ägyptischen Namen der syrischen Sklaven des Papyrus Brooklyn 35.1446 verso. UF 19: 255-82.
1992 Asiatische Personennamen in Ägyptischen Quellen des Neuen Reichs. Orbis Biblicus et Orientalis 114. Freiburg, Switzerland: Universitätsverlag; Göttingen: Vandenhoeck und Ruprecht.

Schoors, A.
1972 Literary Phrases. Pp. 1-70 in L. R. Fisher, ed., Ras Shamra Parallels. Volume I. Rome: Biblical Institute Press.

Selman, M. J.
1980 Comparative Customs and the Patriarchal Age. Pp. 93-138 in A. R. Millard and D. J. Wiseman, eds., Essays on the Patriarchal Narratives. Leicester: Inter-Varsity.

Selms, A. van
1966 A Forgotten God: LAḤ. Pp. 318-326 in W. C. van Unnik and A. S. van der Woude, eds., Studia Biblica et Semitica Theodoro Christiano Vriezen. Wageningen: H. Veenman.

Seybold, K.
1977 hæbæl. Cols. 334-343 in G. J. Botterweck, H. Ringren, and H.-J. Fabry, eds., Theologisches Wörterbuch zum alten Testament. Band II. Stuttgart, Berlin, Köln, Mainz: W. Kohlhammer.

Shea, W. H.
1977 Adam in Ancient Mesopotamian Traditions. AUSS 15: 27-41.
1980 The Calendars of Ebla. Part I. The Old Calendar. AUSS 18: 127-137.
1981a The Calendars of Ebla. Part II. The New Calendar. AUSS 19: 59-69.
1981b The Calendars of Ebla. Part III: Conclusion. AUSS 19: 115-126.

Silverman, M. H.
1985 Religious Values in the Jewish Proper Names at Elephantine. AOAT 217. Kevelaer: Butzon & Bercker; Neukirchen-Vluyn: Neukirchener.

Simian-Yofre, H.
1985 nḥm. Cols. 366-384 in vol. 5 of TWAT.

Simons, J.
1937 Handbook for the Study of Egyptian Topographical Lists Relating to Western Asia. Leiden: E. J. Brill.
1954 The 'Table of Nations' (Gen. X): Its General Structure and Meaning. Oudtestamentische Studien 10: 154-184
1959 The Geographical and Topographical Texts of the Old Testament. A Concise Commentary in XXXII Chapters. Studia Francisci Scholten Memoriae Dicata, 2. Leiden: E. J. Brill.

Sivan, D.
1984 Grammatical Analysis and Glossary of the Northwest Semitic Vocables in Akkadian Texts of the 15th-13th C.B.C. from Canaan and Syria. Alter Orient und Altes Testament 214. Kevelaer: Butzon & Bercker; Neukirchen-Vluyn: Neukirchener.

Sjöberg, Å. W.
1984 Eve and the Chameleon. Pp. 217-225 in W. B. Barrick and J. R. Spencer, eds., In the Shelter of Elyon. Essays on Ancient Palestinian Life and Literature in Honor of G. W. Ahlström. JSOT Supplement Series 31. Sheffield: JSOT Press.

Skinner, J.
1930 A Critical and Exegetical Commentary on Genesis. Second edition. International Critical Commentary. Edinburgh: T. & T. Clark.

Smith, R. P.
1903 A Compendious Syriac Dictionary. Oxford: Clarendon.

von Soden, W.
1960 Nimrod. Cols. 1496-1497 in vol. 4 of RGG.
1976 Bemerkungen zum Adapa-Mythos. Pp. 427-433 in B. L. Eichler, J. W. Heimerdinger, and Å. W. Sjöberg, eds., Kramer Anniversary Volume. AOAT 25. Kevelaer: Butzon & Bercker; Neukirchen-Vluyn: Neukirchener.

Sollberger, E.
1986 Administrative Texts Chiefly concerning Textiles (L. 2752). Archivi Reali de Ebla Testi 8. Rome: Missione Archeologica Italiana in Siria.

Sørensen, H. S.
1963 The Meaning of Proper Names. Copenhagen: Gad.

Speiser, E. A.
1950 Adapa. Pp. 101-103 in J. B. Pritchard, ed., Ancient Near Eastern Texts Relating to the Old Testament. Princeton: University Press.
1963 The Wife-Sister Motif in the Patriarchal Narratives. Pp. 15-28 in A. Altmann, ed., Biblical and Other Studies. Philip W. Lown Institute of Advanced Judaic Studies. Studies and Texts: Volume I. Cambridge, MA: Harvard University Press.
1964 Genesis. Introduction, Translation, and Notes. Anchor Bible 1. Garden City, New York: Doubleday.

Stamm, J. J.
1939 Die Akkadische Namengebung. Mitteilungen der vorderasiatisch-ägyptischen Gesellschaft 44. Leipzig. Reprinted; Darmstadt: Wissenschaftliche Buchgesellschaft, 1968.
1967 Hebräische Frauennamen. Pp. 301-339 in H. Güterbock and T. Jacobsen, eds., Hebräische Wortforschung. Festschrift zum 80. Geburtstag von Walter Baumgartner. VTS 16. Leiden: E. J. Brill. Reprinted, pp. 97-135 in E. Jenni and M. A. Klopfenstein, eds., Johann Jakob Stamm. Beiträge zur Hebräischen und altorientalischen Namenkunde zu seinem 70. Geburtstag. Freiburg Schweiz: Universitätsverlag; Göttingen: Vandenhoeck & Ruprecht, 1980.
1980 Der Name Nabal. Pp. 205-213 in H. Güterbock and T. Jacobsen, eds., Hebräische Wortforschung. Festschrift zum 80. Geburtstag von Walter Baumgartner. VTS 16. Leiden: E. J. Brill.

Stark, J. K.
1971 Personal Names in Palmyrene Inscriptions. Oxford: Clarendon Press.

Strus, A.
1978 Nomen-Omen. Analecta Biblica 80. Rome: Biblical Institute Press.

Stuart, D. K.
1976 Studies in Early Hebrew Meter. Harvard Semitic Monograph Series 13. Missoula, Montana: Scholars Press.

Superanskaja, A. V.
1973 Obščaia teori'ia imeni substvennogo. Moscow.

Tallqvist, K.
1906 Neubabylonisches Namenbuch. Acta Societatis Scientiarum Fennicae 32. 2. Helsingfors.
1914 Assyrian Personal Names. Acta Societatis Scientiarum Fennicae. Tom. 43. 1. Helsingfors. Reprinted, Hildesheim: Georg Olms, 1966.

Thompson, T. L.
1974 The Historicity of the Patriarchal Narratives. The Quest for the Historical Abraham. BZAW 133. Berlin and New York: Walter de Gruyter.
1987 The Origin Tradition of Ancient Israel. I. The Literary Formation of Genesis and Exodus 1-23. JSOT Supplement Series 55. Sheffield: JSOT Press.

Thureau-Dangin, F.
1937 Trois contrats de Ras Shamra. Syria 18: 245-255.

Tigay, J. H.
1986 You Shall Have No Other Gods. Israelite Religion in the Light of Hebrew Inscriptions. HSS 31. Atlanta: Scholars Press.
1987 Israelite Religion: The Onomastic and Epigraphic Evidence. Pp. 157-194 in P. D. Miller, Jr., P. D. Hanson, and S. D. McBride, eds., Ancient Israelite Religion: Essays in Honor of Frank Moore Cross. Philadelphia: Fortress.

Tomback, R. S.
1978 A Comparative Semitic Lexicon of the Phoenician and Punic Languages. SBL Dissertation Series 32. Missoula, Montana: Scholars Press.

Tsevat, M.
1954a The Canaanite God ŠALAḪ. VT 4: 41-49.
1954b Additional Remarks to 'The canaanite God Šalaḥ'. VT 4:322.

Ullendorff, E.
1956 The Contribution of South Semitics to Hebrew Lexicography. VT 6: 190-198.

van Beek, G.
1962 Abel. P. 4 in vol. 1 of IDB.

VanderKam, J. C.
1984 Enoch and the Growth of an Apocalyptic Tradition. CBQ Monograph Series 16. Washington, D. C.: Catholic Biblical Association of America.

van der Toorn, K., and van der Horst, P. W.
1990 Nimrod before and after the Bible. Harvard Theological Review 83: 1-29.

Van Langendonck, W.
1982 Socio-Onomastic Properties of By-Names. Onoma 26: 55-62.

Van Seters, J.
1992 Prologue to History: The Yahwist as Historian in Genesis. Louisville, KY: Westminster/John Knox.

Vattioni, F.
1969 I sigilli ebraici. Bib 50: 357-388.
1971 I sigilli, le monete e gli avori aramaici. Augustinianum 11: 47-87.
1978 Sigilli Ebraici III. Annali dell' Istituto Universitario Orientale di Napoli 38 NS 28: 227-254.
1979 Antroponimi fenicio-punici nell'epigrafia Greca e Latina del Nordafrica. Annali de Seminario di studi del mondo classico. Istituto Universitario Orientale. Sezione di archeologia e storia antica 1: 153-190.
1981 I sigilli fenici. Annali dell'istituto orientali Napoli 41: 177-193.

Vermeylen, J.
1991 La descendance de Caïn et la descendance d'Abel (Gen 4,17-26 + 5,28b-29). ZAW 103: 175-193.

Vinnikov, I. N.
1958-65 A Dictionary of Aramaic Inscriptions. Palestinsky Sbornik 3 (1958) 171-216; 4 (1959) 196-240; 7 (1962) 192-237; 9 (1962) 141-160; 11 (1964)189-234; 13 (1965) 217-262. Russian.

Virolleaud, Ch.
1951 Six textes de Ras Shamra provenant de la XIVe campagne (1950). Syria 28: 163-179.

Vollers, K.
1895 Review of C. Reinhardt and K. Dragoman, Ein arabisher Dialekt, gesprochen in ʿOmān und Zanzibar, nach praktischen Gesichtspunkten für das Seminar für Orientalische Sprachen in Berlin. Stuttgart and Berlin: W. Spemann, 1894, in Zeitschrift der Deutschen Morgenländischen Gesellschaft 49: 484-515.

Walker, N.
1962 "Adam" and "Eve" and "Adon." ZAW 74: 66-68.

Wallace, H. N.
1985 The Eden Narrative. Harvard Semitic Monographs 32. Atlanta: Scholars Press.
1990 The Toledot of Adam. Pp. 17-33 in J. A. Emerton, ed., Studies in the Pentateuch. VTS 41. Leiden: E. J. Brill.
1992 Adam (Person). Pp. 62-64 in vol. 1 of ABD.

Wallis, G.

1966 Die Stadt in den Überlieferungen der Genesis. ZAW 78: 133-148.

Waltke, B. K.

1986 Cain and His Offering. WTJ 48: 363-372.

Waterman, L.

1916 Business Documents of the Hammurapi Period from the British Museum. London: Luzac.

Wenham, G. J.

1980 The Religion of the Patriarchs. Pp. 157-188 in A. R. Millard and D. J. Wiseman, eds., Essays on the Patriarchal Narratives. Leicester: Inter-Varsity.

1987 Genesis 1-15. Word Biblical Commentary 1. Waco, Texas: Word.

Westermann, C.

1974 Genesis. I. Teilband. Genesis 1-11. BKAT I/1. Neukirchen-Vluyn: Neukirchener.

Whybray, N.

1987 The Making of the Pentateuch: A Methodological Study. JSOT Supplement 53. Sheffield: JSOT Press.

Williams, A. J.

1977 The Relationship of Genesis 3: 20 to the Serpent. ZAW 89: 357-374.

Wilson, R. R.

1977 Genealogy and History in the Biblical World. Yale Near Eastern Researches 7. New Haven and London: Yale University Press.

Winnett, F. V.

1970 The Arabian Genealogies in the Book of Genesis. Pp. 171-196 in H. T. Frank and W. L. Reed, eds., Translating & Understanding the Old Testament. Essays in Honor of Herbert Gordon May. Nashville and New York: Abingdon.

Wiseman, D. J.

1953 The Alalakh Tablets. Occasional Publications of the British Institute at Ankara 2. London: British Institute of Archaeology at Ankara.

1955 Genesis 10: Some Archaeological Considerations. Journal of the Transactions of the Victoria Institute 87: 14-24.

1959 Ration Lists from Alalakh VII. JCS 13: 19-33.

Wiseman, P. J.

1979 Clues to Creation in Genesis. London: Marshall, Morgan & Scott.

Wuthnow, H.

1930 Die semitischen Menschennamen in griechischen Inschriften und Papyri des vorderen Orients. Studien zur Epigraphik und Papyruskunde, Band 1/4. Leipzig: Dieterich.

Wyatt, N.
1981 Interpreting the Creation and Fall Story in Genesis 2-3. ZAW 93: 1-21.
Xella, P.
1973 L' "inganno" di Ea nel mito di Adapa. OA 12: 257-266.
Yamauchi, E.
1982 Foes from the Northern Frontier. Invading Hordes from the Russian Steppes. Baker Studies in Biblical Archaeology. Grand Rapids: Baker.
Zabeeh, F.
1978 What is in a Name? An Inquiry into the Semantics and Pragmatics of Proper Names. The Hague, Martinus Nijhoff.
Zadok, R.
1977a On Some Egyptians in First-Millennium Mesopotamia. Göttinger Miszellen 26: 63-68.
1977b On West Semites in Babylonia during the Chaldean and Achaemenian Periods. Jerusalem: H. J. & Z. Wanaarta and Tel-Aviv Universty.
1978a On West Semites in Babylonia during the Chaldean and Achaemenian Periods. An Onomastic Study. Revised edition. Jerusalem: H. J. & Z. Wanaarta and Tel-Aviv University.
1978b West Semitic Toponyms in Assyrian and Babylonian Sources. Pp. 163-179 in vol. 1 of Y. Avishur and J. Blau, eds., Studies in Bible and Ancient Near East: Presented to Samuel E. Loewenstamm on His Seventieth Birthday. 2 volumes. Jerusalem: E. Rubinstein.
1979 The Jews in Babylonia during the Chaldean and Achaemenian Periods according to the Babylonian Sources. Studies in the History of the Jewish People and the Land of Israel Monograph Series 3. Haifa: University Press.
1980 Sources for the History of the Jews in Babylonia during the Chaldean and Achaemenian Periods. With an Appendix on West Semitic Names in 1st-Millennium Mesopotamia. Jerusalem: H. J. & Z. Wanaarta and Tel-Aviv University.
1980-81 Notes on the Biblical and Extra-Biblical Onomasticon. JQR NS 71:107-117.
1981 Arabians in Mesopotamia during the Late-Assyrian, Chaldean, Achaemenian and Hellenistic Periods Chiefly According to the Cuneiform Sources. ZDMG 131: 42-84.
1982 Notes on the Early History of the Israelites and Judeans in Mesopotamia. Or NS 51: 391-93.
1984a On the Historical Background of the Sefire Treaty. Annali dell'istituto orientali di Napoli 44: 529-38.

1984b Assyro-Babylonian Lexical and Onomastic Notes. Bibliotheca orientalis 41: 33-46.

1985 Répertoire Géographie des Textes Cunéiformes Band 8 Geographical Names According to New- and Late-Babylonian Texts. Beihefte zum Tübinger Atlas des vorderen Orients B7. Wiesbaden: Ludwig Reichert.

1988 The Pre-Hellenistic Israelite Anthroponymy and Prosopography. Orientalia Lovaniensia Analecta 28. Leuven: Peeters.

Zakovitch, Y.

1980a A Study of Precise and Partial Derivations in Biblical Etymology. JSOT 15: 31-50.

1980b Explicit and Implicit Name-Derivations. HAR 4: 167-181.

Zimmermann, F.

1966 Folk Etymology of Biblical Names. Pp. 311-326 in Volume du Congrès Genéve 1965. VTS 15. Leiden: E. J. Brill.

Zimmern, H.

1924 Die altbabylonischen vor- (und nach-) sintflutlichen Könige nach neuen Quellen. ZDMG 78: 19-35.

INDICES

A. Text Citations

1. Bible

Gen 2:11 5
Gen 2:15 116
Gen 3:20 5, 22
Gen 5:29 116-118
Gen 6:6-7 116-117
Gen 8:21 116-117
Gen 9:27 31
Gen 14:14 39
Gen 25:2-3 145
Gen 36:15 5
Num 24:21-22 37

2. Ugaritic

KTU 1.100 21
KTU 1.107 21

3. Cuneiform Literature

Taanach 6, 6-8 39

4. Northwest Semitic Epigraphy

CIS 2/1 274 28
KAI 89, 1 24
KAI 222A:30-31 21

B. Lexicography

1. Common Semitic

ʾl 42-43
hll 68-69
hr 92
ḥyh 42
ybl 50
mḥʾ 42
mt 44, 70
nʿm 54-55
skh 90
ʿbr 81
ʿrd 40
ṣll 49
qṭn 75
rʿh 83-84
šmš/špš 64
š/śyt 65-66

2. Hebrew

ʾdm 15-16
ḥwh 22-24
ḥyh 20
ḥām 30
ḥanîkîm 39
yĕbûl 50
ybl 52
yôbēl 126
yānōaḥ 28
yrd 69
yrḥ 88
mlk[h] 90-91
mqneh 126
mrd 74
nwḥ 28
nhr 86
nsk 90
nʿm 54
ʿădî 47
plg 81-82, 152-153
pth 31
ṣēl 48
ṣll 48
qyn 37-38
śrg 86
šʾl 43-44

3. Northwest Semitic Epigraphy

ʾdm 16
ḥwh 21
ḥwt 24

4. Ugaritic

ʾdm 16
ḥwy 23
ḥwt 22-23

5. Akkadian

abālu 50-51
adam- 17
aplu 27
ardu 69
ḫa-wa/ya- 23
lumakku 46
maḫḫu 41
mutu 44
naḫraru 87
nērāru 87
palgu 82
re'û 84

6. Arabic

ʾdm 17
ḥawwah 20-21
habala 27
ylmk 46

7. Epigraphic South Arabic

ʾdm 17
nwḥ 28
qyn 25-26

8. Ethiopic

ʾadama 17

9. Hurrian

arip 77
qà-ti-nu-ma? 75
tb 51
ta-ba-li-iš 26, 53
tuppal 51

10. Egyptian

ḥm 30

11. Sumerian

á-dam 19
eme 20
ti 20
unug 39

C. Divine Names

1. Hebrew

lḥ 70
šʾl 45
šlḥ 70-71

2. Northwest Semitic Epigraphy

rbt ḥwt ʾlt 24

3. Ugaritic

trḫ 89

4. Akkadian

a-da-ma 59-60, 62

5. Epigraphic South Arabic

qynn 68

6. Hurrian

Ḥebat 19-20
dna-aḫ-ma-zu-le-el 29

7. Greek

Iapetos 31

Ugarit-Verlag Münster

Ricarda-Huch-Straße 6, D-48161 Münster

Abhandlungen zur Literatur Alt-Syrien-Palästinas (ALASP)

Herausgeber: Manfried DIETRICH - Oswald LORETZ

Bd. 1 Manfried DIETRICH -Oswald LORETZ, *Die Keilalphabete. Die phönizisch-kanaanäischen und altarabischen Alphabete in Ugarit.* 1988 (ISBN 3-927120-00-6), 376 S., DM 89,--.

Bd. 2 Josef TROPPER, *Der ugaritische Kausativstamm und die Kausativbildungen des Semitischen. Eine morphologisch-semantische Untersuchung zum Š-Stamm und zu den umstrittenen nichtsibilantischen Kausativstämmen des Ugaritischen.* 1990 (ISBN 3-927120-06-5), 252 S., DM 68,--.

Bd. 3 Manfried DIETRICH - Oswald LORETZ, *Mantik in Ugarit. Keilalphabetische Texte der Opferschau - Omensammlungen - Nekromantie.* Mit Beiträgen von Hilmar W. Duerbeck - Jan-Waalke Meyer - Waltraut C. Seitter. 1990 (ISBN 3-927120-05-7), 320 S., DM 94,--.

Bd. 4 Manfried DIETRICH - Oswald LORETZ, *König Idrimi von Alalaḫ.* Mit Beiträgen von Ruth Mayer-Opificius und Horst Klengel (im Druck).

Bd. 5 Fred RENFROE, *Arabic-Ugaritic Lexical Studies.* 1992 (ISBN 3-927120-09-X). 212 S., DM 74,--.

Bd. 6 Josef TROPPER, *Die Inschriften von Zincirli. Neue Edition und vergleichende Grammatik des phönizischen, samʾalischen und aramäischen Textkorpus.* 1993 (ISBN 3-927120-14-6). XII + 364 Seiten (im Druck).

Bd. 7 *UGARIT - ein ostmediterranes Kulturzentrum im Alten Orient. Ergebnisse und Perspektiven der Forschung.* Vorträge gehalten während des Europäischen Kolloquiums am 11.-12. Februar 1993, hrsg. von Manfried DIETRICH und Oswald LORETZ (im Druck).

Ugaritisch-Biblische Literatur (UBL)

Herausgeber: Oswald LORETZ

Bd. 1 Oswald LORETZ, *Der Prolog des Jesaja-Buches (1,1-2,5). Ugaritologische und kolometrische Studien zum Jesaja-Buch* I. 1984 (ISBN 3-88733-054-4), 171 S., DM 49,80.

Bd. 2 Oswald LORETZ, *Psalm 29. Kanaanäische El- und Baaltraditionen in jüdischer Sicht.* 1984 (ISBN 3-88733-055-2), 168 S., DM 49,80 - Neuauflage UBL 7.

Bd. 3 Oswald LORETZ, *Leberschau, Sündenbock, Asasel in Ugarit und Israel. Leberschau und Jahwestatue in Psalm 27, Psalm 74.* 1985 (ISBN 3-88733-061-7), 136 S., DM 44,80.

Bd. 4 Oswald LORETZ, *Regenritual und Jahwetag im Joelbuch. Kanaanäischer Hintergrund, Kolometrie, Aufbau und Symbolik eines Prophetenbuches.* 1986 (ISBN 3-88733-068-4), 189 S., DM 59,80.

Bd. 5 Oswald LORETZ - Ingo KOTTSIEPER, *Colometry in Ugaritic and Biblical Poetry. Introduction, Illustrations and Topical Bibliography.* 1987 (ISBN 3-88733-074-9), 166 pp., DM 49,80.